Text, photographs & artwork copyright 2012 & 2014   SCSTyrrell

First published 2012; paperbound reprint 2014

Set in Century Schoolbook 11 on 12.5

Published by Pasticcio Ltd. Registered in England No 5125728

01326 340153   www.pasticcio.co.uk

ISBN 978-0-9555511-9-2

Pasticcio

Trewinnard
A Cornish History

Introduction by
Sir John Nott

In memory of your visit

John Nott
July 2014

'Then [we] passed through the village of St Erth and came to Trewinnard, the oldest seat of the Hawkins family, where Sir Christoper had engaged to meet us at dinner, which he accordingly did.

I liked this place much better than Trewithen. It is situated in a better part of the country...there is an air of antiquity and cultivation about it. The house is indeed a collection of strange rooms huddled together with a number of inconvenient passages and narrow staircases.'

James Boswell's 'Journey through Cornwall', 1792

Contents

Trewinnard Manor
The drawing, dated 1835, is thought to be by Mary Esther Hawkins 1778-1861,
mother of John Heywood Hawkins and CHT Hawkins.

Introduction

by

Sir John Nott, KCB, PC.

Trewinnard has been our family home since 1967. In earlier times it was renowned for its association with three important families, the Trewinnards, the Mohuns and the Hawkins.

The site of an early farmstead or hamlet, Trewinnard was once a small harbour on a great trading route which goes back thousand of years into the Bronze and Iron Ages.

Originally a medieval courtyard house with hall and chapel, it was re-built as a charming country house at the end of the 17th century. Nowadays it is perhaps best known for giving its name to the terrific state coach in the museum in Truro.

Throughout its history, Trewinnard has always been a favourite home, even for those with business and interests well away from their much loved spot in Cornwall.

I was privileged to represent this far-flung peninsular for 17 years, as the Member of Parliament for St Ives. It is good, therefore, to feel that for the last forty years, Trewinnard has remained for us the same sort of house that it has been for successive families for nearly one thousand years. I hope to keep it so.

This book owes its origins to the excellent research of Stephen Tyrrell who has explored the history of the house, farm and gardens, and most importantly the story of a fascinating but long forgotten part of the United Kingdom.

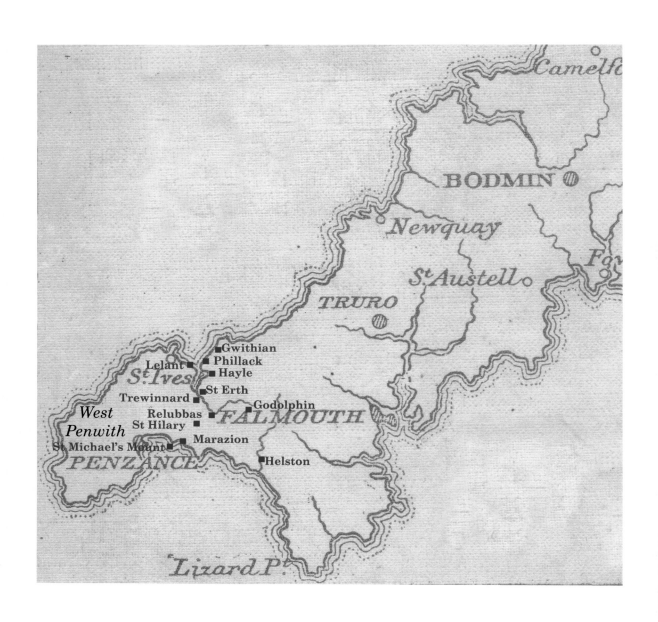

Trewinnard,
an Historic Site

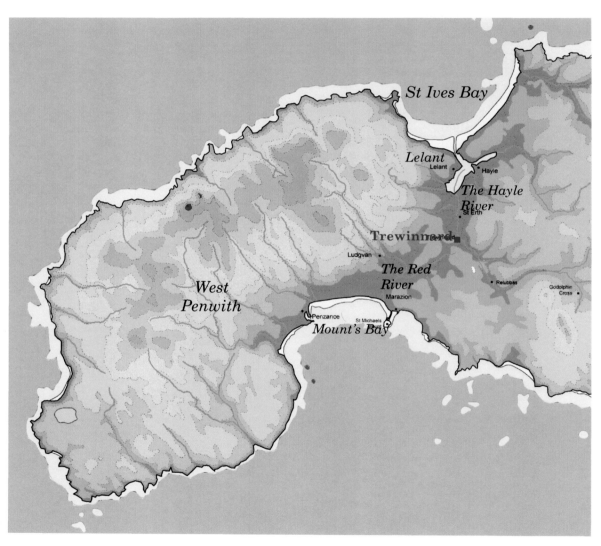

The geography of the Penwith peninsula and the Hayle estuary, today.

Chapter 1
Early History and Setting

Trewinnard Manor was built near the top of a hill on the west bank of the Hayle river, a once navigable estuary. Behind the house, a ridgeway provided routes to St Hilary, Lelant and St Michael's Mount. From here are views to Godolphin Hill, The Mount and across the valleys to Trencrom and West Penwith.

The farm is built on a Mylor slate formation, with some basic igneus rock insertions, in a band that runs north east and south west across the estuary and, unlike the harsher earth found over granite, provides very good farmland. The house is on land with gently sloping fields. For the last 700 years, it has been the site not just of a farm, but of a mansion whose owners' influence went far beyond the boundaries of the place.

Trewinnard owes its importance to its site and position on the river. Not only was it the highest tidal landing place on the Hayle estuary, but Trewinnard controlled the short-cut to the Red River at Mounts Bay, a trade route which avoided the long boat trip round Land's End. In addition, the river Hayle provided a natural physical and therefore political boundary, with Trewinnard in its centre.

The history of Trewinnard is not, therefore, the history of a few hundred years only, but of a few thousand.

Since records began, the south west of England has been a place of mystery and romance. Nowadays, Cornwall is a popular holiday destination. Many come not just for the sea and countryside, but because of the varied landscapes, which include cliffs, moorlands and small hamlets. Megalithic stone monuments and the remnants of an early Christianity hint at little known civilisations. For three centuries, Cornwall has been known as a land of mysterious rocks and peoples and of the tales accumulated around them. The megaliths and stone monuments of the South West accentuated the stories of an ancient and unknown people.

Far from the centres of population and activity in England, Cornwall was remote, a land of mystery and legend. Little visited by the rulers of England from the 12thC to the 20thC (only some three visits by the Crown are recorded in that time), a small ignored population retained the identity of earlier occupiers and acquired a sense of difference which remains today. Of the relatively few peoples' rebellions against the English Crown, two have involved the distant Cornish. This sense of difference continues in modern efforts to resuscitate the Cornish language, despite its disuse for some three hundred years.

Cornwall is all coast, long, narrow and with its interior split by rivers in steep valleys. Travel was always difficult. It is still a county with a relatively small population for its area when compared with the rest of England. In the 11thC, the population has been estimated to have been a mere 27,000 in the whole county. The Victorian interest in chivalry, romance and tales of forgotten peoples contributed to the rebirth of Arthurian romance and to the concept of Cornwall as a distant misty land of cliffs and moors, peopled by an ancient sort quite different from the English. For the Cornish, their traditions of seafaring and mining accentuated that difference.

Cornwall was also a turning point for seafaring traffic. It was a county with close connections with Brittany and Europe and a first port of call for invasion from the south and west. The relationship with Brittany has ebbed and flowed over the millennia, but continuing close contact ensured the importance of the sites at Mounts Bay. A relatively poor economy and agricultural base ensured that from the medieval period onwards the Cornish depended on and were renowned for their skill with boats.

The history of the south west peninsula, when not obscured by the fantasies of some Celtic writers, is genuinely exciting and interesting. West of the Hayle valley, Penwith remains a country obviously different from lands further east, and was perhaps the last refuge of those pushed steadily south west by traders, the Irish and by Saxon and English.

Trewinnard was therefore at the centre of an important trade route and of a natural land division which remained a political barrier for centuries.

St Erth Bridge and
the canalised water meadows

A deep lane worn into the countryside,
near Trewinnard

The Bronze Age

In Cornwall, the Bronze age, roughly 2500 BC to 600 BC, has been re-assessed as a period of greater culture, metal-smith skill and trade than had been recognised. Bronze and gold survive in the ground, but it is not just the survival, but the quantity of such finds, combined with evidence of craftsmanship and of trade, that is impressive. It has been suggested that 'by the later bronze age Cornwall was in the mainstream of British metal working and trade, with close continental links'.

The four Lunulae, crescent shaped gold necklaces found in Cornwall, are of cornish gold but Irish workmanship. Not only was there trade with Ireland but trade passed through and on to the continent. This trade was combined with trade meetings or gatherings at sites renowned for that purpose, such as Geer in the Lizard or at Trevone Head west of Padstow. Trade routes through Cornwall from the Mediterranean and from Germany appear to have been well used. Any traffic to Ireland, Wales, the Severn Estuary or to the Midlands would take a sea route and would pass through the Hayle Estuary as being shorter, quicker and safer than a voyage round the rocky coast of the Lands End peninsula.

The trade was not just in valuables but would have included such items as hides, tin, pottery, even wine but the trade is most easily recognised by the bronze and gold items abandoned along the way. Such finds demonstrate that the workers of metal were not crude but extremely skilled craftsmen. Discoveries of metalworkers' caches, like the one recalled by Leland in 1540 of copper axe heads, war axes and other copper items or like that found at St Michael's Mount in 2011, are outside markers for a considerable number of finds, caches or items which have turned up along the route taken by these traders.

A map of finds shows a concentration along the edges of the Hayle estuary and at the mouth of the Red River where it joins Mounts Bay. A trade route necessarily used the Hayle and Red Rivers. The tide could take a boat up the Hayle to Relubbus, where there was a ford and the river turned east. However it was not necessary to travel that far, since there was a large pool and good landing place at Trewinnard. From here a short portage to the top of the Red River would allow a boat to float down with the tide to Mounts Bay.

At Mounts Bay, sediment and changes in the coastline mask what may have been the early landing places. The original settlement of Marazion may have been some 500 yards further west, where a chapel was lost to the sea. The marshes and sands at Marazion have

A bronze axe from the St Erth Hoard. This hoard was discovered in 2002-3 and probably dates from the 8th to 9th century BC.
Probably a metalworkers stock, it included:
2 gold ornament fragments, 5 sword pieces, 3 socketed axe pieces, 1 socketed gouge piece, a knife fragment, a plate fragment, 16 lumps of bronze, 1 winged axe, a plate like fragment and 15 other fragments.

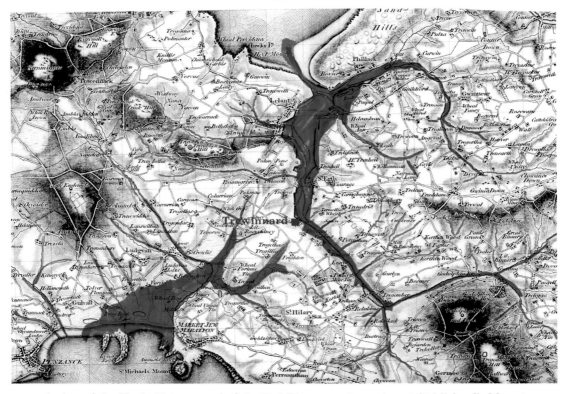

A plan of the Hayle Estuary and of the Red River running out past St Michael's Mount
shows the possible extent of tidal waters in the last millennia BC. (Map based on 1813 Ordnance Survey)

provided a number of finds, of which the earliest include
the bronze vessels and tin smelting items found in 1849
and the Roman coins found in 1845.

The width of the estuary at Trewinnard and the
pool with a landing at the bottom of a track straight up
to the ridgeway, meant that Trewinnard was a landing
place of importance. As late as 1540, Leland wrote of the
Red River from Marazion, that *between the head of the
river and the nearest part of the Heyle that cometh in to
the sea at Lenant is not a myle'*. This is inaccurate, but
reflects the view of the time that the sea route from Hayle to Marazion was relatively straightforward. Although
they did not mark all such river outlets, the earliest car-
tographers noted the Red River, presumably because of
its remembered importance.

Bronze Age boats have recently received considerable attention, not just because further discoveries are being added to such well documented examples
as the Dover Boat, but because replicas have provided
a better understanding of their capacity and use. The
boats used by Bronze Age traders were bigger than
might have been expected, with 60ft being typical. Flat
bottomed, and with sewn planks, they were capable of

carrying a considerable weight and, with cargo, might have weighed some 11.5 tons. Carrying a crew of paddlers, they were of shallow draft and could slip up a muddy estuary with relative ease.

One boat of this type could be that discovery made around 1946 in Trewinnard Pool, when the river was diverted in order to dredge and pump for tin. The river pool at Trewinnard was very deep and it was some 60 to 80 feet to the bedrock. At the bottom of the mud of the pool was found a 'large wooden barge about 60 ft long'. In the hull were some black coal like lumps and a wooden pump made from a hollowed tree trunk. Near the boat were two mooring posts. Too big to pass under St Erth Bridge it is probable that the boat must therefore predate 1340, the date of the bridge.

The description of the find, although not properly recorded, suggests this 'barge' could have been of Bronze Age type. Although site, mud and description of the boat support the theory, we can never know whether this was indeed an old boat.

The existence of such a boat would support the view that Trewinnard was a 'port', a place whose pool was therefore a way-station on continental trade routes during the period from the Bronze Age until AD 1000. Trewinnard Pool may well have been the factor that gave Trewinnard early importance.

A half size replica of the Ferriby Bronze Age planked boat.

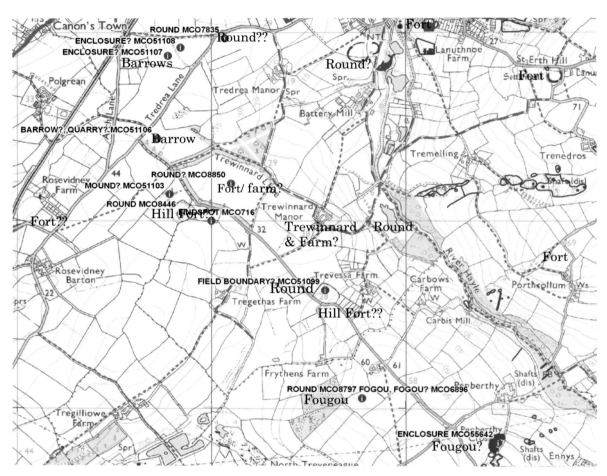

A selection of prehistoric sites adjoining Trewinnard

Reproduced by permission of Cornwall and Scilly Historic Environment Record, Cornwall County Council and annotated.

The Iron Age

The Bronze Age gave way around 800 BC to the Iron Age, a time of new materials and changing agriculture, possibly brought about by a deteriorating climate. Although usually defined as ending in AD43, Iron Age practices and culture continued through the Roman period and after. The most dramatic of hill top castles, of cliff forts and many stone monuments are associated with this period. One of the most magnificent was Chun Castle, built with stone faced banks between the 3rd and 1st century BC, evidence either of tribal warfare or of controlling high status.

The Historic Environment map records a number of Iron Age sites around Trewinnard. Above the modern farm, the ridgeway runs past forts and rounds, and across the Hayle valley were others. A *round* was a farm, better called a banked enclosure, since not all were round or necessarily intended for defence. Some ten rounds have been identified on each side of the river in the area of St Erth parish alone.

Near Trewinnard, in a field called Parc Gear, is the site of an Iron Age farm. The lower settlement enclosure of Trewinnard appears to be another later farm enclosure. A further site south east of the house may have had round huts and then become the *lan* associated with

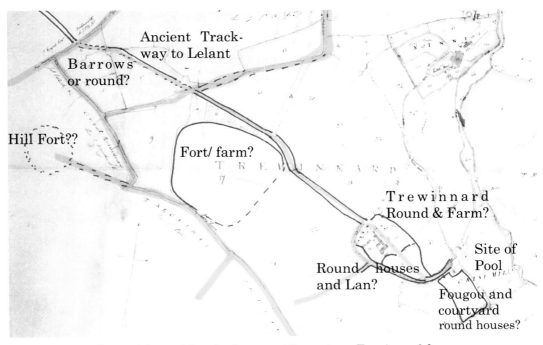

Some of the prehistoric sites or settlements on Trewinnard farm
Marked on 1821 plan of farm

the early chapel serving the hill areas of Lelant parish.

Another culture of the Iron Age lasted to around AD 300 and had villages of courtyard houses. The most famous is at Chysauster, in Penwith; surviving courtyard house sites are restricted to the south west since changing agricultural practices further east ensured their destruction.

Associated with a courtyard house hamlet was the stone roofed underground complex known as a fougou, possibly intended for ritual purposes. The identification of a fougou therefore implies the existence of a courtyard house hamlet. Two fougous have been identified off the ridgeway above Trewinnard. Trewinnard itself has a field known as Parc Foge, suggesting that here there was a fougou and its associated hamlet.

A preliminary geophysical survey carried out at Trewinnard in the spring of 2012, in poor weather conditions, suggested that archaeological investigation would be worthwhile, despite the later landscaping of the terrain around the house. Only excavation can help with answers, but that there were Iron Age settlements which included farm enclosures, round huts, courtyard houses and a *lan,* fits with what we know of Trewinnard and the monuments around it.

A fougou is a rock slab roofed excavation of underground chambers, possibly for ritual use, and is associated with late Iron Age courtyard houses. This picture shows part of a fougou at Trelowarren. There is some evidence that there may have been a fougou at Trewinnard.

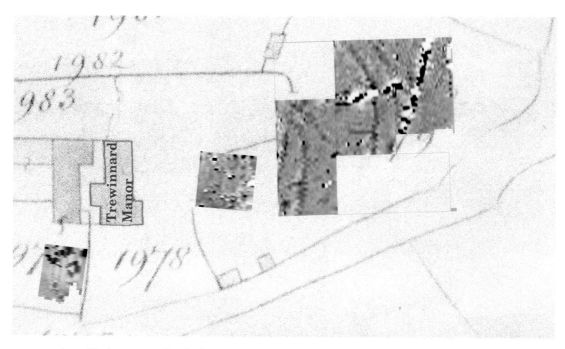

A preliminary geophysical survey showed activity in the so-called cemetary field.
Geophysical survey by Tamarside Archaeology, Les Dodd and Peter Nicholls. Plan reproduced with permission.

The Roman and Romano-British Period

It is usually suggested that the Romans never bothered with Cornwall. On-going studies are changing this view.

There is some truth in the statement that the county was never of great interest. With tin available in Iberia, Cornish tin was not a priority until problems in Iberia in the 3rdC and 4thC made tin more interesting. Grain was a different matter. It is possible that apart from the need for a politically useful triumph, the invasion of Britain was intended to consolidate control over a trading border country with which Rome had dealt for nearly 100 years and also to improve supplies of grain. Grain was the gold that kept Rome alive.

However, grain could be harvested up the centre of England but not in Cornwall. Even today, Cornish farmers find grain difficult to grow well on poor soils, with restricted field areas in damp conditions.

Once in control, Rome was successful because it integrated different races and because it operated administrations that gave local people power. Rome backed away from direct control, if, as with Cornwall, it simply did not seem worth while.

Cornwall (including Devon west of Exeter) is a good example. With a tiny population, with poor ground and little topsoil, with impossible communications in a long county of deep valleys to each side and with moors along the central spine, it seems little wonder that the Romans felt other places would be a better investment.

Since Roman territory was also peopled by towns of retired service men, retirement being possible once one was about 35 years of age, *Colonia* were an important method of colonisation and administration. It seems unlikely that ex-soldiers would want to retire to distant, uncultured, empty Cornwall. Although one probable Romano-British villa has been found at Camborne, there is little evidence of towns or villas.

Once pacified or controlled, it was not worth administering Cornwall on a day to day basis. Britain already required three legions on permanent duty, which was a heavy commitment for Rome when compared with larger territories which had only one legion. The interior of Cornwall was therefore managed through client leaders. Rome was good at operating with local people, offering them the opportunity to become citizens and supporting their administrations. They had probably been dealing and trading with client kingdoms for some time before the Claudius invasion.

Such client control continues to give archaeologists difficulty in distinguishing artefacts and sites

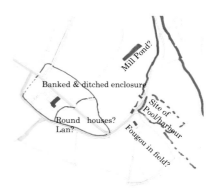

A plan of Trewinnard showing the surviving bank and ditch boundaries to an early settlement farm enclosure, based on 1821 plan.

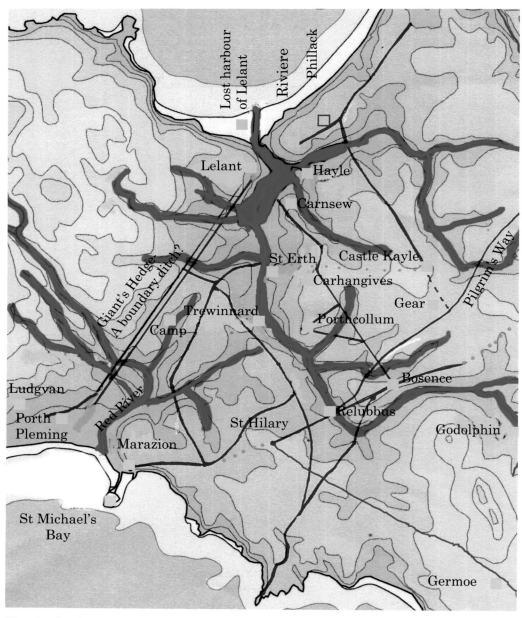

The plan has been marked to show ancient trackways and Roman tracks built to connect signal stations or marching camps. Roman camps may have been at St Hilary, Bosence, Porthcollum, Carhangives, Cockwells, Germoe and Carnsew. *Sites and roads are representational only.*

between the Roman, proto-Roman or Romano-British groups. Much of the surviving evidence in Cornwall may be proto-Roman rather than Roman.

However, this does not mean that the Romans never instituted controls over their territory. From around AD 70 and until demands on legionnaires and budget cuts reduced available forces, units appear to have been kept in Cornwall, even if they were on a limited basis. Paved roads may have not passed Exeter, but that does not mean that unpaved Roman roads were not built in Cornwall.

Although it was long said that Nanstallon was the only camp found in Cornwall, camps have now been found at Restormel, Calstock and recorded at many other sites for forts, marching camps and signal stations. Investigation of the sandy creeks and harbours used by boats at that time, show that a number of camps were built close to them, with straight line trackways joining ports and camps. One such trackway runs straight from Maen Porth, a port for the Falmouth region, past four camps and ends at legionnaire encampments at Helston and Looe Estuary. Such tracks used fords. The later building of bridges has disrupted the line wherever the route passes a stream.

Signal stations were also operated around the coast, and control of trade and activity in a barren hinterland was possible with control of shipping. There is much greater evidence of Rome in Cornwall than has hitherto been admitted.

Evidence of Roman occupation is found in the milestone or memorial standing stones common among army staff, or imitated by local rulers, like those found at Breague and St Hilary, thought to have been a Roman encampment. Numerous finds of Roman coin hordes from coins issued for soldiers pay are mostly around the landing and trading sites of the coast. In the Hayle area, finds include coins at Marazion, a horde at St Erth, coins at Carnsew and finds at Bosence, including an item with a Roman inscription.

After an initial drive to control the country with marching camps, there was a period of some 200 years when control of ports and signals meant that small camps were maintained, probably by smaller units under control of the Civitas Dumnoniorum centred on Exeter, and with contact by sea rather than land. This was an occupying administration in charge of trade.

Field walking suggests that the Hayle river was a Roman system for boundary control. There is no evidence of Roman activity west of the Lelant-Penzance line, but there are a number of camps, all within contact distance of each other along the east side of the Hayle river. Most have stunning views and fine positions, and are connected by dead straight roads, which have been engineered rather than evolved. Sites and traceable roads run from St Hilary, which controlled Mounts Bay, across to Bosence, to Porthcullom, (a word that may mean 'hidden creek') on to Carhangives and down to the estuary at Carnsew.

Although this could not be described as a defensive wall for the south west, the line probably served a similar purpose to Hadrian's boundary in providing control, observation, security of ports and the possibility of tax on trade.

To the west of Trewinnard are two more 'security lines'. The western one is just east of that A30 boundary entrenchment which may have been a territorial boundary and the other runs straight to St Hilary from Lelant, which at the time had a port since lost to the sea, and where an inscribed stone was found underneath the church foundation in 1856 with the inscription *Clotualus Mogratti*.

The sites of the roads and forts and their definition as roman or romano-cornish deserves and is receiving much further research, outdating past and current views. For Trewinnard, it confirms its place in the centre of a border area, which with its 'port', must have been a site of importance.

Post-Roman Celtic Rule

The departure of the Romans may not have made an immediate difference to Cornwall, since the Romans had instituted an administration based on local chiefs and area units, possibly dividing areas into units called *pagi*. The traditions of Rome persisted in areas which became kingdoms. An example of continuing Roman traditions in the post Roman period may be those inscribed stones, of which over 79 have been found in Cornwall and Devon, with nearly all being in Cornwall.

Trade too, continued down the important Hayle/Red River route, and finds such as the four ingots of tin found at Praa sands, Breage, probably dating from AD600 AD to AD790, support that supposition.

However tribal differences, a multiplication of chieftains, the growth of small kingdoms, 'kings', overlords and a confused story for a region which stretched into Devon, suggest that the area was gradually broken into segments. In Cornwall there is evidence of independent tribal areas in defining banks and ditches, such as the Giant's Ditch at Lerryn, which cuts off a great swathe of land based on a peninsula. Another such bank

The inscription is thought to read:
Flavio Julio Constantino Pio Caesari Dvci Constantii Pii Augusti Filio.
This can be translated as:
To Flavius Julius Constantinus, pious Caesar, the commander son of Constantine, the pious and august.
Emperor Flavius Julius Constantine died in 317 AD

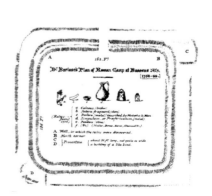

A plan of the supposed Roman camp at Bosence, prepared by Dr Borlase in 1758
Noted in RIC Journal Vol 10 of 1890-1

and boundary appears to run alongside the current route of the A30 and can be traced almost from Lelant through to Long Rock, where the last section of bank, known as the Giants Grave, is west of the modern road. To the west, the country had a number of hill forts controlling their neighbourhood. The line of the bank and ditch of the A30 appears to be a boundary between two types of civilisation, between the retreating south western peoples in the west of Penwith and to the east, the new types of farming and occupation which started around the sixth century AD. East of the Hayle, the fields are bigger and the system of administration appears to have become different. The line of the A30, if it does indeed follow this banked ditch, may therefore be a boundary which those east of the Hayle might have considered the frontier beyond which civilisation ceased. Trewinnard is only a mile or so inside that boundary; even there the field pattern is different to that further west.

The lane network west of the Hayle is based around the road from Lelant to Marazion. This runs along the ridges parallel to the A30, with links to Trewinnard. The river was a barrier with few fords and which only ferries could cross. Although there may have been a crossing by St Erth church, the first practical ford was some miles inland at Relubbus.

The history of the network of ancient kings, kingdoms and invading local chieftains who controlled much of Cornwall after the Roman departure is uncertain.

There were numerous invasions from Wessex, with power passing back and forth between the invaders and Cornish, but ultimately away from the Cornish leaders. In 682 Centwine 'drove the British to the sea', making the Ottery/Tamar line the boundary. In 710, further warfare took the boundary west to the Lynher, with counter offences and further battles in 752 by Cuthred of Wessex and in 815 by Cynewulfin. Egbert from Wessex harried the Cornish further and by around 800 the kingdom of Dumnonia had collapsed. In 838, the Cornish lost further land. By this time there was already a settlement pattern which took the invaders to the Lynher, pushing the indigenous peoples further west.

However, the great conqueror of Cornwall and Devon was Athelstan, who between 924 and 939 spent time on campaigns to the far west. He instituted a system of administration and control with areas known as hundreds, each hundred having, recent research has suggested, 100 'Tre' settlements. These areas may have been based on a network of late Iron Age farming rounds, which may themselves have been survivals from the roman system of *pagi*. Each such 'Tre' might have a couple of small farms and was more like a farming hamlet. This separation of the country into farming hamlets survived through to modern times. Whereas elsewhere in England dwellings were clustered in a village by the church, in Cornwall separated hamlets spread quite far from the church, which, despite being known as *churchtown*, had few houses save those of the priest.

To better control the country and church, Athelstan organised a parochial system and set up two church centres for the county, one at St Buryan in October 843 and the other at St Germans with a bishopric centred on St Germans. The country also had imposed upon it a patchwork of ecclesiastical and royal estates. Parish boundaries may have followwed those from earlier estates or chieftains. It is possible that the annual 'beating the bounds' recorded in many parishes, may have had origin in the defining of personal territory.

Despite reorganisation, Cornwall remained an area with a paucity of population and a dearth of income, wealth and rent, which may be why the dioceses of both Cornwall and Devon were held by one man from 1027 and and then, in 1046, formally amalgamated, an amalgamation which lasted until 1876.

By the time of the Norman Conquest, Cornwall was one county but one that was already divided in two along the line of the Lynher by immigration.

Irish Invasions

No history of the Hayle estuary can fail to mention the invasion of the saints who have given their names to Cornish churches and religious sites. Their names are, by and large, unknown elsewhere in England. Late medieval hagiographies provided detailed biographies, and related how saints had travelled to Cornwall from Wales, Ireland or Brittany, the importance of the Brittany connection being one that is sometimes overlooked.

Whilst we do not have to accept that several hundred saints arrived simultaneously in St Ives Bay, there is evidence of settlement from Ireland and evidence that they brought their own brand of Christianity with them. However, these saints were not missionaries, but probably emigrants building on trade links and arriving after defeat or famine in their home country. Nor was their arrival welcomed. There are records of their defeat at Riviere, a strong point just west of Phillack, and a loss and win with a massacre of inhabitants at Gwithian.

Nevertheless, based at Lelant and Phillack, two religious administrations based on monastic centres, one each side of the Hayle river, took control of a large area. These areas had their own strongholds. Castle Kayle seems to have been particularly important to the Phillack territory. One of the earliest Christian burials was at Carnsew, Hayle. Although, like the chicken and the egg, it is uncertain which comes first, the secular administrative areas appear to have shared the two monastic boundaries. West of the Hayle, the area south of Lelant became one great Saxon manor. To the east, Connerton became one of the largest manors of Cornwall, although following encroachment of the sea, it lost three chapels from Gwithian and the whole town of Winnianton.

Lelant, like other celtic churches, had a number of subsidiary cells such as those at St Ives and Towednack. It is thought that Trewinnard was an 'up-country' cell or chapel serving part of the area controlled by Lelant. An early trackway can be traced straight from Lelant to Trewinnard. The provision of an 'upcountry' chapel for distant parts of a parish is found elsewhere in Cornwall and a local example in the considerable area of Lelant parish was recognized when St Ives' petition for a chapel in 1409, because St Ives was so far from Lelant, was approved by a papal bull of 1410.

The Medieval Period.

Until the 13thC, the Hayle estuary continued to be the short-cut route for trade around the coast and between the continent, Ireland, Wales and Bristol. This included wine, salt, fish. hides, leather and tin.

A map of around 1550, when silting and coast changes had already made the Red River more difficult, shows a two-arched bridge over the estuary of the Red River. West of the Red River, there was once a port be-

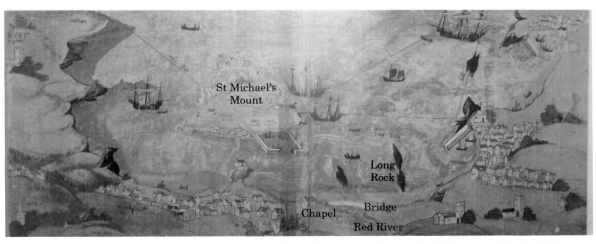

A plan of Mounts Bay and St Michaels Mount from about 1550 shows the bridge over the Red River.
British Library Cotton MS Augustus 1i.34

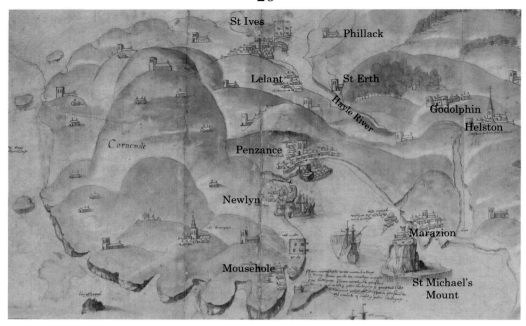

The Lands End Peninsula with the Hayle river and St Michaels Mount from the Henrician defence map of 1539. *British Museum: Cotton MS Augustus 1 i, f 35 (c315-72).*

hind Long Rock called Port Pleming and its name could mean 'harbour of the stones'. The port was still viable in the 13thC but already paying reduced rates to the king. The Black Death dealt it a further blow and in 1349-50 no fees were paid to the king because of the pestilence. By 1428, it was said that the port was blocked by sand. Pleming, now remembered in a farm name, is some way inland from the modern coastline.

These are indications that the Red River Valley was no longer viable as a tidal route for boats to its head waters. The river passage was made more difficult by the mining that started each side of those head waters, sending spoil down the estuary.

In the Hayle estuary, early mining also blocked the estuary with silt. Sand destroyed the town and port of Lelant and then a bridge was built at St Erth at the beginning of the 14thC. It is probable that the trade route from Hayle to Mounts Bay had fallen out of use by 1300. Perhaps the medieval Hayle village researched by Exeter University disappeared at that time.

When the Cornish Doomsday Book was written, Cornwall was a land of relative poverty and few people. The prosperous sections were all in the far north and east and to the east of the Lynher. In a population estimated at 27,000, over 20%, a high proportion, were serfs. This implies a backward economic culture with little trade or movement between population centres.

Following the Norman conquest, Robert of Mortain became one of the greatest of overlords. He held over 1000 English Manors, and had 277 estates in Cornwall. Robert of Mortain kept for himself the best 22 estates, those which produced a great proportion of the income.

Richard Fitz Turold, one of the more important of his followers, held 29 estates mainly in the west of Cornwall from Robert of Mortain. He set up his administration at Bodmin, in the middle of a small gap between the Camel and Fowey rivers, and built a castle at Cardinham.

In the west, Richard's power centre was set just across the river from Trewinnard at Carhangives, now called *Carnabeggas* (watchman, or shepherd's hill?), where, as Leland said, *'to the court hereof belonging many knightes and gentilmens services'*. It is suggested that this site was on the boundary of his controlled area. It remained within the manor of Cardinham until 1866, long after other lands had been sold.

Trewinnard and the Hayle estuary, from the south.

The mouth of the Hayle estuary today gives some idea of the meandering waterways that once ran some miles inland and of the shifting sands that have altered the coastline.

For much of the early medieval period, Cornwall seems to have been viewed as an uninteresting area whose profitable areas were in the far east, centred on Launceston.

Cornwall continued to be administered as land divided into 'hundreds' and by manorial courts, an administration complicated not only by the church courts but also by the peculiarly separate Cornish Stannery Courts. The crown also retained manors, interests, and rights. The Duchy of Cornwall was established in 1337 , perhaps based on boundaries inherited from the earlier kings. All Duchy manors, with the exception of Helston, were in the far east.

At this time farming, not fishing, was the mainstay of the country. Farming still reflected Celtic farming fields and usage. The Black Death of 1349 decimated the population and is said to have reduced tin production by 80%. This population reduction forced great changes. Fishing and shipping became more important and there was an increase in the number of boats based in Cornwall and in the number of Cornish working those boats. The streams of Cornwall were suitable to run mills and there were increasing numbers of tucking or fulling mills to add to trade in tin, slate, and goods.

Sand and Silt

Trewinnard is on an estuary which has been much changed over the last three thousand years. Some of these changes were as dramatic as the better known alterations and lost towns of the Suffolk coast. On the Hayle, Lelant lost its town and port and, as noted in a 1679 terrier, a second church. Three hundred years of sand invasion and coastal movement were only reduced by the introduction of elephant grasses. At Gwithian, a town, three chapels and farms have gone. The estuary at Hayle has changed its shape and position and not only has the bridge at St Erth altered the appearance and use of the river, but mining waste has changed the landscape. The same has happened to the Red River at Marazion where a lost village lies off the mouth and Porth Plement is now inland.

It seems appropriate to close an introduction to Trewinnard, with a picture of the sea and sand.

Sand at the mouth of the Hayle has shifted through the centuries.
The invasive sand has altered the entrance and covers lost towns.

Chapter 2
The Parish and Church of St Erth

The Early Church

The earliest Christian remains that survive in Cornwall are memorial stones from around AD 500. It is notable that the oldest of these came from Carnsew, Hayle, recognising the importance of this estuary in the history of the southwest. The first Christian immigrants were probably from northern France and arrived in the country at St Michael's Bay. Other Christian invaders from Wales and Ireland arrived at the north end of the estuary. Both immigrations therefore recognise the importance of the passage across the peninsula at Hayle.

The raiders from the west, usually described as groups of saints, travelled in families or floated across the sea on leaves or lumps of granite. One group of seven hundred and seventy seven saints arrived together at the Hayle river.

Rather than committed saints, these missionary invaders may, of course, have been tribes displaced by tribal warfare in their own country, rather than the saints reported by medieval hagiography. Theories of a contemplative priesthood count for little against the implications of an Irish law of 804 that first permitted the monastic community of Ireland *not* to bear arms, a date some 300 years after the early landings in Cornwall.

One Irish invasion at Phillack on the north bank of the Hayle arrived in the 6thC, where they were at first defeated by a chief, Teuder, or Theodore, who had a base at Riviere, just west of Phillack. This site can still be identified on the rising ground at the west end of Phillack, where there has also been found a stone cross. Eventually the raiders succeeded, displaced the existing tribes and enforced their Christian faith, although there is some evidence that the residents were then already Christian.

The structure of the early Celtic church was one of monastic communities with cells, rather than one of parishes grouped under a bishop. For some years the administrative manors may have defined the curtileges of ecclesiastical units which were grouped under a principle church in each area, the others being subsidiary chapels. The Lizard seems to have been under single control, and known as the Meneage, or monk's land. Breague managed the churches of Gunwalloe and Cury as dependants as late as the 14thC. The monastic centre at Constantine covered or controlled the area east of the Helford river. There are numerous examples of this grouping throughout the county.

The influence of 'monastic' centres was used in the new administration that seems to have taken place from around AD 800. The power of the church was supported by the change to rulers from beyond Devon, which became an assured part of west England, or Wessex, in the 7thC. This then permitted raids into Cornwall from Devon. In 813 Egbert ravaged Cornwall from one end of the county to the other. Cornwall was probably conquered by about 838. In 870 a Cornish Bishop, (Kenstec) appears to have recognised political reality and submitted to the Archbishop of Canterbury. In 926, Athelstan defeated the Cornish in battle and having subdued the county set up a system of administration which included two superior churches at St Buryan and St Germans.

By the time of the conquest, only a third of monastic early chapels and monasteries had been adapted to form the organised parish system under saxon administrators. The three monastic settlements around the St Erth area at Lelant, Phillack and St Hillary, remained in loose control of an area where no parochial system had yet been imposed.

Lelant and Phillack

The earliest churches for public worship were probably built as buildings separate from monastic or religious centres in the tenth century. Monastic centres were used as a method of state or regal control and were often associated with royal estates or areas where there might have been control issues.

It is thought that the section of the modern St. Erth parish which is on the west of the Hayle river was taken into the new parish of St Erth from the parish of Lelant, where there was a substantial religious centre or monastery on the west banks of the Hayle. This section on the uplands around Trewinnard was a considerable distance from Lelant and it seems possible that the settlement around Trewinnard would have had its own

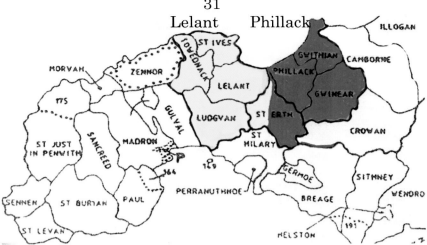

Lelant   Phillack

The plan shows parish boundaries. St Erth was established from parts of Lelant and Phillack, whose approximate areas are coloured yellow and green.

upland chapel, originally attached to or forming part of the religious foundation at the mouth of the river. Another example of an inland chapel, now a church, was Mabe, which, subsidiary to and 'a good four miles' from Mylor, petitioned the Bishop in 1308 for its own consecrated cemetery.

The area east of the Hayle river was under the control of the monastic centre at Phillack, which seems to have been an important ecclesiastical centre. Excavation has identified activity in the 5thC & 6thC. The Phillack church building includes rare early Norman stonework, the original cemetary was greater than the present boundary suggests, and it remained, during part of the middle ages, the mother church of Gwithian. Gwithian also had daughter churches and chapels and was probably the administrative centre of the lost manor of Connerton. East of the Hayle Estuary, about 1000 metres north east of St Erth Praze is Castle Kayle, an early earthwork, where Henderson recorded the existence of a chapel subsidiary to Phillack. Kayle seems to have been a place of such importance in the area east of the Hayle, formerly associated with the lost Connerton, that, in the time of Henry VIII, *Castle Cayle* was still a name given to the hamlet of Phillack. A cross from the way between Castle Kayle and Phillack is now in the churchyard at Phillack, next door to a 7thC inscribed stone. A further chapel or centre probably stood at Lanuthnoe, on the hill above St Erth.

The east portion of the parish of St Erth was taken from the larger parish of Phillack, which also had its 'up country' subsidiary chapel at Kayle, possibly with a further chapel at Lanuthnoe, just as Lelant had an up-country daughter chapel at Trewinnard.

A four holed cross and Christ at Phillack Church

Establishing a Parish

While most parishes in Cornwall can claim a history that dates from before 1050, St Erth is unusual in appearing to have sprung into existence in the 12thC. It is suggested that this was because the Bishop of Exeter decided to create a new parish, so that he might benefit from control of trade, from control of the river crossing and from control of the port below Trewinnard.

The nature of the parish and of its boundaries was unusual because, although centred on the ferry crossing, not many parishes appear to have been set up on 'new' territories where there had been no village, market centre, great house or older ecclesiastical centre. St Erth seems to have been established 'de nova' by the river crossing, some way downhill of the traditional controlling site. The establishment of the parish in the mid-12thC with the Bishop of Exeter as patron was also unusual, although typical of church efforts to control people and their markets.

The boundaries of St Erth are also unlike other Cornish parish boundaries which traditionally follow watercourses. St. Erth is unique in that the parish is divided by the river Hayle, at that time a much wider tidal estuary. St Erth is a parish whose boundaries, unlike almost every other Cornish parish, were not defined by rivers and watersheds, but were to be found on both sides of an unbridged estuary.

Before becoming narrowed and silted with spoil from the works at Godolphin, the Hayle river was a very considerable trade centre. Trewinnard had a natural harbour which may have been a considerable trading port. This might suggest why a Bishop would want to control both sides of the river and want to set up a parish on the crossing place at St. Erth. It may also explain why the portion of the parish west of the estuary follows the ancient boundaries of Trewinnard, the holding that was of commercial interest to him.

Twelfth century bishops regarded the encouragement of trade and markets as a natural way to finance their bishopric. Bishops formed part of an european brotherhood and their efforts to control and benefit trade are best seen in the surviving *bastides* of west and south west France but were also established in England and Wales. *Bastides,* new fortified towns with market places, became a way not only to control an area and that area's population, but also to control and tax trade. *Bastides* were established not only by the political leaders of factions but also by the church. In Cornwall, the Bishop of Exeter established and laid out new towns with burgess plots, markets and fairs to benefit from the taxes and trade which would then fill his coffers and to help control the church in an area.

Examples include the two new towns of St Germans where, together with rights given to town occupiers, the bishop also tried to establish a new port. Penryn, another 13thC establishment, was set up with the same purpose by the Bishop of Exeter, who laid out a town along a narrow ridge overlooking the main port in the area. This was not on the site of the earlier centre, or even near the parish church. At Penryn, he also established a college for the church at Glasney, although it is remarkable that this was established on the worst and wettest, but presumably cheapest, of land.

It is therefore possible that the bishop, with an eye to trade, wished to control the St Erth river crossing, the chapels that may have stood on each side and the pilgrim route that crossed to St Michael's Mount. He may also have hoped to make money from trade in the Hayle corridor and the harbour below Trewinnard, which the new parish boundary neatly enclosed.

In October 1272, Bishop Bronscombe acquired the church of Lelant from the prior and convent there, allowing a parish reorganisation. The establishment of St Erth parish was confirmed by the Bishop in 1180 and in 1199, when the parish was noted as under the direct control and ownership of the bishop, itself a step aside from the 'normal'. The bishop gained funds from the parish in 1233 and it was not until 1237 that St Erth was given to the Dean and chapter of Exeter.

The suggestion that St Erth was a 'new' enclosure is supported by the records of a parish boundary dispute which was taken to Rome and on which decision was reached there in 1237.

The monastic settlements at Lelant and Phillack therefore predated the parochial system and it was with lands taken from those monastic territories that the parish of St Erth was established.

Wayside Crosses

Stone crosses not only marked devotional sites, such as the chapel that may have stood where is now St Erth church, but were also boundary or way markers, and were common beside fords and ferries.

The main road past the church now ends at the river, but until the bridge was built, this road continued on the other side and can still be traced. East of the river, the path was probably marked by the four holed cross with a figure of Christ on its face and a long panel of early interlaced decoration, which was found built into the walls of the church and has now been re-erected

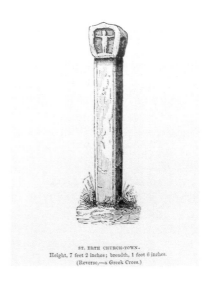

ST. ERTH CHURCH-TOWN.
Height, 7 feet 2 inches; breadth, 1 foot 6 inches.
(Reverse,—a Greek Cross.)

TREVAN, ST. ERTH.
Height, 4 feet 4 inches; breadth, 1 foot 9 inches.

ST. ERTH CHURCHYARD.
Height, 2 feet 2 inches; breadth, 2 feet 3 inches.

Drawings of the crosses at St Erth Churchtown, Trewan and St Erth Churchyard. Drawn and engraved by J T Blight and published 1856.

in the west end, *(Langdon West Cross no 37)*. West of the river crossing on the track towards St Michael's Mount another cross was found at Battery Mill in 1860. This also has a figure of Christ in relief and now stands in the churchyard over the grave of Mr Gilbart, an owner of Battery Mill.

St Erth has a further three surviving crosses. One is a fourholed cross which Langdon has suggested is a churchyard cross similar to others in pre-conquest Penwith. Another cross, a late medieval lantern cross, stands at the crossroads of the main street of St Erth, where it may have been a 'market' cross. Finally, in 2011, a cross was found in the north of the parish on the old way north.

It is probable that the bridge at St Erth also had a wayside cross when first built. The bridge was already in position by 1338, when a document refers to the hamlet of *'Penenpons'* (or bridge end) at St Erth. A century later, in 1447, a vicar left 12d towards the upkeep of this bridge. Leland, writing around 1540, suggested that the bridge was then 200 years old.

Finally, another cross, the 'Trevean Cross', is now at St Michael's Mount. Trevean is north of Trewinnard and west of the ferry crossing. It is possible that this cross, notable for also having human figures carved on the side 'ears' of the cross, once marked the top of the hill on the road west from the ferry by the church.

The Patron Saint of St Erth

Although the patron saint is now St Erth, the first saint was probably *not* called Erth but was a man associated with the earlier celtic cell up the hill. The early name of the settlement was not St Erth but *Lanuthnow*, a name which survives in the farm and banked enclosure on the hill between St Erth and St Erth Praze. The word *Lanuthnow* suggests an early religious site since the word Lan is accepted as recording an early cemetary or church site. Around a quarter of all Cornish parish churches are said to have names which included Lan *(Padel)*. The considerable number of early written references with the Lan spelling support the view that this was the church site and one of some historic importance. *Lannuthenoe 1223, Lanhoutenou 1235, Lanhuthenou 1235, Lanideno 1237, Lanuthno 1269, Lanuthno 1269, Lanuthenowe 1284, Lanuthnow 1342.*

One early record suggests that *Lanhudna* was the site of the church since a dispute in 1150 about the tithes at Gunhen, near Treloweth, St Erth, involved Master Valentine who was rector of both Lelant and of *Lanhudna* (St Erth).

A mutilated cross found in 2011 near the north of St Erth Parish. It may have marked either one end of the parish or the way between Trelissick and Churchtown.
Photo: Courtesy Andrew Langdon
The cross head is on private property and not accessible.

A four holed cross-head with inscribed Christ, by steps SE of the church. *(Cross number 36 in Langdon).*

Lanuthenow was the area name given to this holding of Turstin, Sheriff of Exeter. He held 23 manors at the time of Domesday which were in time inherited by the Dinhams. The Dinhams died out by 1428, but the small site with a tradition of importance still remained within the distant manor of Cardinham so late as 1866.

The second two syllables in the name, *Uthnoe*, are found elsewhere in Cornwall as a personal name. This supports the possibility that the site was the 'Lann of Uthenoe'. The first 'saint' of St Erth was therefore probably *not* St Erth but that 'Uthinock' who founded the *Lan* or monastic cell at Lanuthnow on the hill above the river crossing.

However, St Ercus is the saint associated with the early chapel and new church by the river crossing below Lanuthnoe. St Ercus was said to be one of the band of Irish saints who arrived to colonise and convert the country in the 6thC, 7thC and perhaps 8thC. The story of the Irish saint is quite detailed – but probably imaginery. Modern guides tell the history of an Irish bishop who arrived in Cornwall around AD 500. The histories attached to these saints are best taken with a good dose of salt since such details appear to be the invention of those 13thC and later hagiographers of which Nicholas Roscarrock's Lives of the Saints is representative. Writing between 1610 and 1620, Nicholas was firm in his statement that *St Earth* was born in Ireland and *'is noted to come from thence...miraculously into Cornwaille'*. He provides less detail than later authors, and was not even certain of the saint's sex.

Early references to the church at St Erth did not always record it as 'of St Erth' and the name of its saint was said to be either Erc or Uthinoch. These are not similar words and look more like confusion between river side and hill top sites.

It is therefore possible that the saint St Erth is a late addition. The earliest reference to the name is *Sanctus Ercius* in about 1270. In the taxation of 1291, the parish was still not called St Erth, but rather *Ecclesia de Lantrudnow*, (Lanuthnoe) after the older site up the hill east of St Erth. The parish is not found in the inquisition in *'decanatus de Penwid'* of 1294 but was called *Sanctus Ercus* in 1327. The earliest surviving name of a vicar is that of Henry, who served between 1310-1319. It was later still before the church was routinely referred to as of St Erth. In 1521 it was referred to as *St Erghe* or *Yrghe.* In 1564 it was referred to as *'ad ecclesiam de Ergh'.*

Common use of the name St Erth may therefore date from the 14thC. This is supported by Nicholas

Orme's suggestion that, unlike other saints of Cornwall, the name Erth was not in common use, nor used for the baptism of children.

Whether or not there was a Saint Erth will always remain a matter for conjecture. Unfortunately for sainthood, it is possible that the word *Erth* was *not* the name of a person at all, but rather a word derived from an early word for 'holy place' or, as suggested by Pryce in 1790, from the word *Earth* or *Arth* meaning 'high, or above', perhaps referring to the higher site at Lanuthnoe. The name St Erth has no other connection with Lanuthnoe, nor with a clearly identified saint.

It may be that if any saint were to be connected with the church, it should be that man *Uthinoe* or *Uthinoc* who gave his name to the Lan on the hill above.

The Church at St Erth

That there has been a church on this site since the 12thC is certain, but the extent of the building is unknown. When the chancel floor collapsed in 1991, excavation showed that the church was on the site of an earlier building and that the present 15thC arcades stood on the site of earlier walls.

Modern descriptions can be prosaic. They would record that the building itself is largely 15thC in date, the period when most of the Cornish churches were rebuilt or significantly altered and that much rebuilding has continued since the mid 18thC. Such bald narrative can not compare with the purple prose written by a mid-Victorian journalist in a report to an un-illustrated newspaper:

The whole structure of the church, although so simple in motive and so limited in its range of effects is worthy of study not only as a specimen of Cornish work, but for its own sake. Its effects, though seemingly so artless, are, in truth, full of art...It would puzzle the modern British Architect to scheme a church...so full of design and of imaginative effects as is produced here....It is art that did this and art that obtained the proportion of length by the sub division of arcades of six bays. It was art that gained so much richness of effect out of the narrowness of the lights of the window and it was scientific appreciation of the strength of the granite employed in the moulded shafts of the arcades that suggested their slight sectional area.....How simple must be the range of art when trifles [the upper string course and figures]...

So the prose runs on. It is more likely that the church was designed in accord with current fashions in church building, combined with available materials and a wish to build well for the glory of God.

The exterior, from the south west, and the interior of St Erth Church in drawings by T Raffles Davison, circa 1886.

The tower and west end of St Erth Church, across the reeded water ways of the Hayle, close to the early crossing point.

The church has a chancel, nave, north and south aisles, south porch and tower.

The 14thC tower, some 54 feet high, is battlemented and has three string courses but, unusually for Cornwall, is built without corner buttresses. Magnificent gargoyles were once on each string course corner and are unique in this part of Cornwall. Four gargoyles remain on the second string course. An earlier pinnacle than the four now on the tower stands on the ground outside the north east corner of the porch. At the parapet's four corners are carvings of the four evangelists. Above the west window of the tower is a window which may be that original east window removed in 1874.

The church has, like most others, undergone a number of rebuilds or alterations to reflect changing beliefs and custom. It has also had enthusiastic and involved vicars. In 1742 the chancel wall was rebuilt. Five years later, in 1747, Vicar Collins made *'zealous and extensive repairs'*, which included removing *'sentences painted on the walls and stained glass from the windows'*. He also re-plastered the walls, probably removing the last remnants of the medieval scheme of decoration.

In 1873-4, there was a considerable restoration to the designs of J R Sedding, who did fine drawings of the church. Until that date the floor had risen gradually in steps from the west end. That level was so close to that of the river that it had a history of flooding and so a new higher floor was provided, which covered the plinths of the pillars.

One of the early carved ribs
and bosses of the roof.

A 'green man' boss: north aisle

One of a number of bosses from
1912 in the south aisle

Pew ends, panelling and carving
in the Trewinnard Aisle

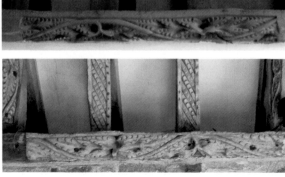

Details of wood carving to the cornice below the barrel roof: above, the south aisle and, below, the porch.

With the support of the 'Incorporated Society for the Building of Churches', new seating replaced the high box pews of the previous century and seats were provided for a further 51 persons.

During the 1870s the chancel was repaired, the south chancel wall rebuilt; the east wall, with a new east window, was moved some six feet further east, therebye obscuring the view of the Hawkins tomb; a new organ was supplied; a new doorway was built in the porch. Unusually for Cornwall, two dormer windows were installed on the north side of the nave and south aisle, each of which has a pair of angels carved in wood at the corners. The font, which has a bowl 15.5 inches deep, was discovered under the floor and re-erected with a marble and stone stand and surround.

The early font on the base added in 1874.

In 1912-13, the wealthy widow Mrs Hawkins, who contributed much to the funding of the cathedral, cathedral school, the school in St Erth and to other charities, refurbished the Lady chapel – or Trewinnard Aisle. Although no longer living at Trewinnard, she was proud of her family's association and the roof, walls, pews and furniture were all replaced. The fine carvings to the chapel were done by Miss Violet Pinwill. A new rood screen (including escutcheons with the date 1912 and the letters T, H and StE) was carved, based on a small piece of the original screen from the church which had been traced to Dorset and recovered. The earlier rood screen had been so famous that it was mentioned as the purpose of a pilgrim visit to St Erth in 1520.

Decoration to a nave capital.

The carved and painted woodwork is worth inspecting. It includes pew ends and other carvings to reflect the history of the Hawkins family, and also includes small sections of tapestry that once hung in Trewinnard. A window in the south wall has, in three panels of glass, St Conan, the bishop of St Germans in 930, to the left of St Erth. On the right Benson, the First Bishop of Truro, later Archbishop of Canterbury, holds a model of the Cathedral at Truro.

Despite alteration, this is still a church of 15thC date with much to look at. The Rood screen stair can still be seen. The roof timbers of the south aisle have carved wood bosses. These have mainly floral designs as well as one or two faces and a *green man*- that centuries old figure whose importance in a church is still uncertain. The church has many monuments including a memorial to Davies Gilbert of Tredrea in St Erth, one of those few whose reputations have survived since the 18thC. He was a supporter of mining enterprise, member of the Royal Society and the writer of a parochial history of Cornwall in 1820. Another note remembers the VC won

The Coat of Arms of George I, including the arms of Hanover, hangs in the church. The thanks written on wood and sent by King Charles 1 to many Cornish Churches hang on the wall to the east of these arms.

The carved screed and vault of the Trewinnard chapel.

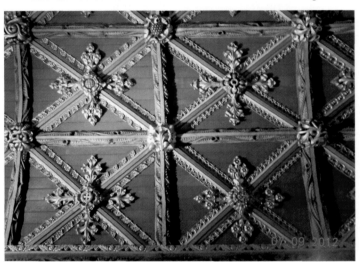

A section of the roof of the Trewinnard chapel at St Erth.

The roof of the Trewinnard chapel
with one of the carved dormer windows.

Two of the grotesque gargoyles on the tower. Of these two examples, that on the left is double headed.

The blocked north door.

The buttressed porch with the sundial of 1826 above the door, has the original barrel roof to the interior.

The lych gate to the north west, given in 1926 by the Misses Vivian.

A 19thC drawing of St Erth, from the south east.

by Major Carter of St Erth, whose widow later erected the war memorial.

Finally, it is notable that the church has a rare full peel of bells, some recast, but re-assembled in 1999, after many years of fund raising and donation under the chairmanship of Sir John Nott.

The Vicars

Parish and parochial histories record the progress of vicars - a progress that reflects political change and fashions over the years. Records may therefore note a vicar's disagreement with a bishop, removals, absences, vacant parishes and pluralism, (that is vicars who hold positions in several parishes). More unusual records include the theft report of 1331, when thieves entered through the windows and stole the chalice, books and wax, or the time in 1350 when the Vicar was accused of beating and wounding a parishioner in Trelissick and then doing the same again in 1357 at Bosworgey.

The priest or vicar had lived in a small house on the east side of the churchyard, but it was from this house that Mr Whiteinge the Vicar was turned out in 1644, leaving an ignorant incumbent for whom the squire had to keep the register. By the time the Vicar returned after the Restoration in 1660, the house was in ruins. After that, a new site was chosen to the northeast of the Village, some way from the church, and a new considerable rectory built there.

During the 19thC and early 20thC several vicars made substantial contributions to the church and are there remembered.

However, nowadays few churches can retain a vicar working only in one parish. Like many others, St Erth was amalgamated in 1995 as one of a 'team' parish which included the five churches of Gwithian, Gwinear, St Elwyns, St Erth and Phillack.

Over the last twelve hundred years, the wheel has come full circle, since the area now covered by that team parish is similar to the area that was first established for administration under Phillack in the 8thC.

Chapter 3
The Name *Trewinnard*
& the Trewinnard Coat of Arms

Although it was claimed that Trewinnard was listed in Domesday Book as *Treuiunadoi* or *Trewinedoi*, it is now believed this was Trenderway, Pelynt, in east Cornwall and did not refer to Trewinnard. In any event, the west of the parish of St Erth may, in the 11thC, have been included as part of Lelant, for which there are no Domesday entries, perhaps because it was considered church land. The earliest records we have of Trewinnard are therefore manuscripts of the 14thC.

The First Syllable

A Cornish name starting with the letters *Tre* was once the site of an estate or farming hamlet. The division of Cornwall into districts, or 'hundreds', (a division which continues to the present day), probably started around AD800. Each 'hundred' was then further divided into a hundred hamlets or farm centres, for control, administration, justice and defence. Such farm centres weres then recognized by having *Tre* at the beginning of the name. Certainly the use of *Tre* has long been recognised as defining a place that was not just a single farm but a farming hamlet, often called a 'town', a word which lives on in the word 'town place' as describing the small area, often with a well, between two farms.

The site at Trewinnard had had earlier Bronze and Iron Age settlements and was of some importance for centuries before the Norman Conquest. The first syllable suggests that this has been a farming hamlet for some 1200 years.

Early Academics

Although we can not assume that a meaning will necessarily be found for every place name, early definitions included that of the unreliable Hals, who wrote in the early 18thC, when some knowledge of Cornish was available. He translated the word either as 'high haughty beloved town', a phrase that does not obviously fit the site at Trewinnard or as *Trewinar*, referring to the large estuary pool just down the hill, and interpreted as dwelling by the 'beloved lake or river of water.'

Tonkin, another writer of the early 18thC, believed the word Trewinnard to mean a 'town or dwelling on a marsh', a name which could suit the site.

Around 1707, Lhydd had researched the Cornish language. This and other 18thC sources were gathered in the Cornish grammar, vocabulary and place name identification book published by William Pryce, in 1790. This work was further analysed and added to in Jago's dictionary of Cornish published in 1887.

Pryce translated the words *Tre-win* as 'the dwelling on the marsh'. This, if combined with *ard* would give a meaning for Trewinnard as 'the dwelling before, facing or beside the marsh' or as 'the dwelling-marsh-high'. Tonkin's suggestion that the word *Trewinnard* can be translated as 'the dwelling on the marsh' therefore gains some support from William Pryce,

The Second Syllable

Early academic sources suggested that the word *Trewinnard* could have a second syllable of different origins, depending on whether the vowel was an *e* or an *i*. One option for this second syllable, if that syllable has an 'e', was that it represented *Wen* or *Wyn* meaning *fair*, as in *Trewen*, (fair town).

Alternatively, if the vowel was an 'i', it suggested *winn* or *winnick,* which was the word for a 'marsh, fenny or moorish place'. Examples of this last were said to be Trewinnow, in Creed (the dwelling on the moors), Trewinny and Trewinnick in Mevagissey, (the boggy town), Trewin, (the dwelling on the marsh), Penwinnick in St Agnes, (the dwelling at the head of the marsh) and Arwennack of Falmouth (upon the marsh).

Another option, arising from the 'y' used for *'Trewynnard'* in early documents, which suggests a longer second vowel, would change the second syllable to a long 'y' sound, with uncertain meaning.

Finally, and perhaps more simply, the second syllable could by *yn,* which is said to indicate 'in the...'.

The Third Syllable

In the 1610 map of Cornwall by John Speede the word Trewinnard is written as *'Trewnard',* which is presumably his written interpretation of how the word was pronounced. This suggests that the name was spoken as a harsher word with the second syllable almost ignored, and the accent on *'ard'*, perhaps the most important defining adjective.

This third syllable could be *Ar,* which is said to be 'upon, above, or before' as in Arwennack of Falmouth, but is more likely to be *ard,* which means high.

Modern Place Name Research

Modern research suggests that nothing can be so definite as the earlier suggestions. Dr. Oliver Padel has written that Trewinnard is a three syllable compound. He suggests meanings for the syllables to be 'place-white-height', *Tre* being place, *gwyn* being white or fair, and *arth* or *ard* being height. He also suggests that the word may have as yet unexplained compounds, and that the use of *ard* at the end of a word could be a diminutive, or have some other as yet uncertain implication.

The Place of the Thrush

Some had thought that the name Trewinnard included the word 'winnard', which is the Cornish word for a redwing or fieldfare, a small bird of the thrush family. In the later Cornish dialect, the winnard was a woe-begone miserable little bird rummaging in the bottom of hedgerows for food and giving a startled call when alarmed. Although such a bird is an unlikely object for admiration, it was on the basis of this interpretation that several writers, including Henderson, stated that Trewinnard was 'the place of the thrush'.

Although this translation is *not* now accepted, it gained credence through the grant of arms claimed by the Trewinnard family.

Three Birds suggested for Trewinnard:
Top: Fieldfare or Redwing.
Centre: Daw or Jack daw.
Bottom: Cornish Chough.

The Trewinnard Name and Coat of Arms

Some early references to the family describe them as 'de Trewinnard' since, as was customary, they were described by the place at which they lived. This habit, which extended to changing a surname when moving to a different site, continued through to the end of the 17thC, after when the use of a portable surname became common through greater literacy and increased population movement.

The 14thC custom of saying that the Trewinnard family was of, or from, Trewinnard demonstrates that the place name existed long before the family name.

The spread of coat armour from the 14thC onwards and the liking of families and heralds for punning blazons meant that a high proportion of blazons used puns on the name of the family. The Trewinnards were no different. It was said that their earliest blazon was

Trewinnard

On a field argent, a chevron azure between three Cornish Daws proper.

of three 'winnards' on a silver shield, with a blue bar or chevron across the centre. Although this suggests that the origin of the word Trewinnard had some connection with the winnard or redwing, it is more likely that this is just a heraldic pun and that the design was subseqent to the origin of the name.

Curiously, the birds and design of the Trewinnard shield have differed over time. Perhaps because the direct male line of the Trewinnards died out after the 1580s, the family do not feature in the Visitations made to check the heraldry of the county, so no defining record seems to have survived.

The earliest records refer to 'daws', or jackdaws rather than winnards. Hals, writing about 1720, liked his heraldry and may have known Trewinnard well. He recorded the pre-1600 arms in the glass of the windows at Trewinnard as 'on a field argent, a fess azure between three Cornish Daws proper'. A daw was a bird of the crow family, usually a Jackdaw, so this identifies the three birds as Jackdaws, since it is also clear that each Jackdaw stood normally in their 'proper' black colour.

By 1814, the arms had changed, since the crow had now become a Cornish Chough. Daniel and Samuel Lyson's book of 1814 described the Trewinnard arms as *Argent, a fesse (a bar, not a chevron) Azure, between three Cornish choughs, two in chief pecking, and one in base rising, proper*. The three choughs were also differenced because the top two are shown pecking and the one at the bottom rising to fly.

A picture in CS Gilbert's Survey of 1820 adds confusion by illustrating the arms with a central chevron, rather than bar, or fesse, and by showing the three birds as standing jackdaws. It is this that is likely to be correct, since it agrees with the Trewinnard arms used by Elizabeth Killigrew,(born a Trewinnard) on the brass for her husband which recorded his death in 1567.

Like the change from chevron to fesse, it seems that the changes in bird and bird posture were deviations. It is likely therefore that the Trewinnard arms had a silver background with a central blue chevron, between three identical Jackdaws which were nothing to do with the origin of the place name.

The Dwelling above the Marsh

Although it is contrary to modern linguistic research, the most satisfactory translation of *Trewinnard* may be the 'dwelling above, (or by) the marsh', if only because it so well fits the site and setting.

The right hand side shows the chevron and three daws of Elizabeth Trewinnard as shown on the brass to her husband, who died in 1567.

The Families of Trewinnard

Trewinnard
On a field argent, a chevron azure between three Cornish Daws proper

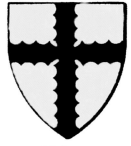

Mohun
Or, a cross engrailed, sable

Hawkins
Argent, a saltaire sable bearing five fleur de lis, or
Motto: Servare modum- 'to serve the utmost'.

Nott
Argent, on a bend engrailed or, between three leopards faces one and two or, three martlets gules

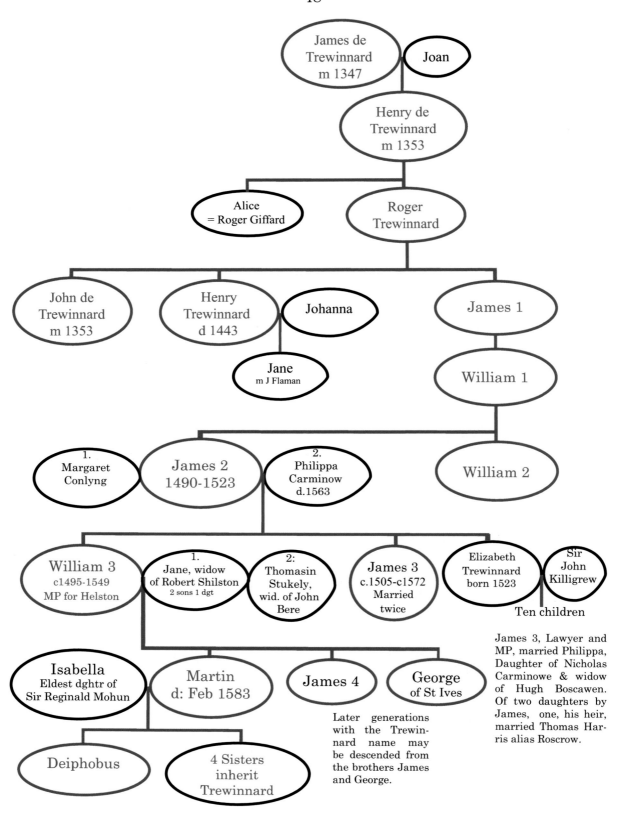

James de Trewinnard m 1347

Joan

Henry de Trewinnard m 1353

Alice = Roger Giffard

Roger Trewinnard

John de Trewinnard m 1353

Henry Trewinnard d 1443

Johanna

Jane m J Flaman

James 1

William 1

1. Margaret Conlyng

James 2 1490-1523

2. Philippa Carminow d.1563

William 2

William 3 c1495-1549 MP for Helston

1. Jane, widow of Robert Shilston 2 sons 1 dgt

2: Thomasin Stukely, wid. of John Bere

James 3 c.1505-c1572 Married twice

Elizabeth Trewinnard born 1523

Sir John Killigrew

Ten children

Isabella Eldest dghtr of Sir Reginald Mohun

Martin d: Feb 1583

James 4

George of St Ives

Deiphobus

4 Sisters inherit Trewinnard

Later generations with the Trewinnard name may be descended from the brothers James and George.

James 3, Lawyer and MP, married Philippa, Daughter of Nicholas Carminowe & widow of Hugh Boscawen. Of two daughters by James, one, his heir, married Thomas Harris alias Roscrow.

Chapter 4
The Trewinnard Family

If our understanding that Trewinnard was a place of some importance during the 11thC is correct, then the owners of Trewinnard must also have been of some importance.

The farm at Trewinnard appears, since the earliest records, to have been rather larger than the standard Cornish farm unit. Such a farm would, in modern acres, have had about thirty ploughable acres, some fifteen or so of pasture and about thirty or forty acres of moor and furse for wood and fuel. The total acreage for a typical gentry farm of the 16thC was therefore about 90 modern acres, a size that continued until greater amalgamation took place in the 20thC. Trewinnard may have been of between 130 and 180 acres, implying the existence of both a farm and separate gentry house with its own land. We may therefore assume that a gentry house, separate from the operational farm, existed from the earliest times. It was in this house that the Trewinnard family are thought to have been for some centuries before the first written records of their occupation, at the end of the 13thC.

Records for the next three hundred years occupation are mainly found in reports of court cases, disputes, taxes or famous crimes. However, such papers can only give a limited idea of centuries of activity and only a restricted impression of a family, particularly as those few surviving court records also record 'fines' which were really a form of stamp duty on land transactions. Courts were also used to record the transfer of lands under, for example, a marriage contract. A 'donor' would sue the proposed recipient of land and then fail to appear in court, thereby granting the land to the defendant.

Although the number of records supports a view of the Trewinnard family as wealthy and with influence, one has to be cautious about the inferences to be drawn

Trewinnard
On a field argent, a chevron azure between three Cornish Daws proper

A schedule of records for the Trewinnard family is at the end of this chapter.

from court cases alone. Because there is so little surviving paperwork, five court transactions over 50 years may now appear evidence of continual wrongdoing. However a mere five such entries are really few in a generation or more. They may merely record a family's relative importance and wealth. In two hundred years time, the only record of existence for a landlord of today might be a VAT claim, the mortgage on a property, or the parking ticket acquired during a delayed business meeting. This can only give an inaccurate idea of life and person.

The history of England records many families that have come and gone. The survival of the Trewinnard family for some 300 years from 1300 to 1600 was, therefore, a considerable achievement, although their fall from wealth and power and the loss of their family home may remain an enigma.

Tracing the family is made more difficult through their apparent absence from the Herald's Visitations that record descent, pedigree and marriages and were carried out in 1530, 1573 and revised in 1620. It is thought that the death of the last surviving heir before 1600 meant that the Trewinnards were not included in the revision of 1620.

A further difficulty with many families of these times was the continuance of the same Christian name through the generations. The Trewinnards favoured the names James and William, so that the frequent listing of James or William in a 50 year period and the use in documents of 'familiar' names as well as Christian names, ensure that confusion is all too easy. Fortunately, surviving records and the historian Charles Henderson's notes are sufficient to provide a glimpse of the family history.

The Trewinnards: 1300-1550

It seems that the Trewinnard family took an active part in the lawlessness that existed in the southwest between 1300 and 1600. Cornwall was far from the centre of authority, had a long coastline and a tradition of seafaring lawlessness. Its lands were run by the gentry of the time as personal fiefdoms rather than as districts under a centralised crown. It was also a land that was far from the central authority of the church as represented by the Bishop in Exeter.

Few references to the family at Trewinnard exist before 1300, when Stephen de Trewinnard and forty others raided a place near St Austell. This single record sets the tone for activities over the next 300 years, the period when the Trewinnards are wealthy, are Members of Parliament, land owning, and with influence, but perhaps always outside the margin of that success that takes a gentry family to greater positions in central government. They appear to have lived with a cheerful disregard of the law, although unlike other gentry, they were less succesful in getting away with it.

The license granted for their existing chapel at Trewinnard and at another of their houses in 1372, was a clear indication of their wealth and status in the relatively small gentry class.

Like others of the upper gentry, the Trewinnards had an apparently casual attitude for others' property. Although the odd Trewinnard became a priest or respected academic, and although some of the reports may be of lesser relations rather than the main line of the family, there appears to be a continuous Trewinnard tradition of helping oneself. From that first raid recorded in 1302, there are a number of instances of savage activity.

We can not understand the strange story of 1381, when a Trewinnard, with another, cut off a priest's head and took it on a pike to London. Although this may have been part of some church and state power struggle and although this was not the only story of a priest being attacked in Cornwall at that time, we have no details save that the Trewinnards survived even the issuing of Excommunication, probably by the payment of a large, perhaps crippling, fine.

It also seems possible that the Trewinnards were not good at getting on with their neighbours, even if, as in the legal disputes of 1393 about the manor of *Tolgollou,* they started from the avarice of others. The story that a Trewinnard had been imprisoned and forced to sign papers is thought to be true, and although the details of the outcome of the case are unknown, the Trewinnards kept the great tin-rich manor of Tolgollou. Even success in law cost much through the necessary absence and the costs of London hearings. The costs of land recovery or dispute were ruinous.

It was Charles Henderson who wrote that the Trewinnards were 'mixed up in riots of a most exciting and romantic character'. It is not every family of whom it is claimed that a mistress has been asked to murder a man's wife (1497). Although we seldom hear both sides of a story and although as late as 1568, Cornish tin miners were described as a *'rough and mutinous multitude',* it was a Trewinnard who proceeded, like the villain in a western, to take over a mine and force the miners from their diggings.

The time line of events associated with the family and set out at the end of this chapter, gives an idea of their activities. Some items suggest that the Trewin-

Tollgullow, the mining manor owned by the Trewinnards was at St Day, in the parish of Gwennap. This plan of 'Tollygellow' was surveyed in 1772 by Francis Welch and is reproduced by permission of the North Devon Record Office and photographer Mark Johnson, of St Day.

nards must have acquired considerable wealth. The taxes paid, the accumulation through marriage of bridal dowries, the control of the 'great manor' of Tolgollou, (which alone had some 2000 acres), interests in mining, in property management, their responsibility for collecting sums due to the king, the appointments to the Duchy or county (usually seen as money making opportunities), all confirm that the Trewinnards probably did live up to the claims made for them as having the enormous income of £3000 per year in the mid 16thC, a sum that probably represented 400 times the average wage of the time. From the 1350s, the Trewinnards were also reputed to have made a fortune in tin through mining management and ownership. Finally, they were related to many of the great names and families of Cornwall, every marriage bringing land and funds.

These dynastic marriages were a form of acceptance. Martin's marriage to Reginald Mohun's eldest daughter must have been a single great stroke which brought great wealth. We do not know how much this wealth might have been but can compare it with the wealth brought on the marriage of a younger Mohun daughter to the Nicholl family of Trewane. This marriage brought to the Nicholls a considerable dowry and a splendidly rebuilt house.

Such a background should have ensured that the Trewinnard family would survive most events save the loss of an heir, or choosing the wrong side in a national struggle. They survived the Cornish rebellion of 1497, although it appears it cost them a considerable sum.

However they seem to have become enmeshed in disputes, and it is not often clear to us what is really going on. Why had William not paid a debt of £75 and then stayed at Trewinnard, allegedly, 'upon his guard' for three years, in order to avoid his creditors? What had an MP done to result in him being forcibly taken from his home to prison in the east of the county?

William Trewinnard c1495-1549

It is thought that William's father was probably a dependant of the Arundells of Lanherne, one of the greatest families in Cornwall before the reign of Elizabeth. Their refusal to renounce catholicism was a big factor in the Arundel decline and perhaps that of their dependants. William made two good dynastic marriages, both to widows presumably of wealth and dower, and should have been set up for life. However, when William's father, James, died, most of his lands remained in the dowry of William's mother, and thus became the source of endless legal dispute. It is even possible that

William sought election as an MP to avoid the dispute with John Skewys who sued for recovery of a debt of £74 15s. This dispute became extremely complex and included a period in prison for William only ending when William paid £66 13s 4d. William Trewinnard's disputed incarceration became one of those cases of importance for constitutional law not just for deciding the relative importance and powers of different courts and officers, but also for defining the prerogatives of a member of Parliament.

It may also be that William owed far more – or had trod on the toes of someone rich and powerful. He was an active lawyer, but also a frequent litigant, like his father and other members of his family. During the last 20 years of his life, the actions brought against him by his relatives, neighbours, and business associates were usually for debt. Early in 1549 he was obliged to pawn plate and jewellery to meet creditors. However, even if beset by serious liabilities, William was still able to make an allowance to his son Martin of £20 a year at about the same time that he was being pursued for debt.

We are uncertain of his religous convictions, if any, or of what part William, or his son Martin, (MP for Launceston in 1547) played in the Cornish rebellions of 1548-49 or those of 1554. We do know that William's lands and goods were despoiled by rebels in the rising of 1549, and that as a result he fled to St Michael's Mount, where, when the place was attacked, he 'received a great hurt and mortal wound'. He died of this wound, and died intestate, which may have lost more money. His son Mathew (?) and his brother James 4 were made the executors, giving further opportunities for family discord.

James Trewinnard 3 c1505-c1572

James was William's brother and Martin's uncle. He too was probably a dependant of the Arundells and, aged 24, was returned to Parliament as the senior Member for Liskeard in 1529. He was also a lawyer since, in 1544, he was described as 'a man greatly studied in the laws of the realm'. He was later MP for Newport of Launceston and for Penryn, where he was also deputy captain of Fort Pendennis. He was later to survey St Michael's Mount. James, too, had married twice. His second wife, Philippa, was not just the Carminowe heiress, but also the widow of Hugh Boscawen of Tregothnan. With such good connections he spent time away from Cornwall, but, like others of his family also devoted his time to legal dispute, including disputes with his nephew Martin. Soon after his second marriage, when he

St Michael's Mount: A detail from the Henrician defence map of 1539.

British Museum: Cotton MS Augustus 1 i, f 35 (c315-72).

may have lived at Tregothnan, he became involved in a dispute with his stepson John Boscawen and the young man's guardian John Carminowe over some livestock. Matters came to a head in February 1560 when there was a skirmish in which Trewinnard was injured and his companion Carew Courtenay killed.

James' history is not always clear, save for our certainty that he shared the family love of dispute, and can not have been too helpful to his nephew, Martin.

Elizabeth Trewinnard c.1523 - d.post 1583

Elizabeth Trewinnard seems to have inherited the Trewinnard approach to property, an approach that, in the Killigrew family into which she married, has been called piracy. Elizabeth Trewinnard was the second daughter of James Trewinnard and Philippa Carminow, another old gentry family of Cornwall.

Elizabeth married John Killigrew who lived at Arwenack, before Falmouth was built. The Killigrews were notorious traders, merchants and ship despoilers. John was the first Captain of Pendennis Castle.

Elizabeth and John Killigrew had five sons and five daughters. The daughters married the great, good and wealthy; the sons had court appointments and positions in control of trade and tax.

It is said that by 1567, the year of John Killigrew's death, Arwennack had been renovated and fortified and was then used as a base for raids on ships and a store for stolen merchandise.

John and Elizabeth Killigrew (née Trewinnard) probably bribed the harbour master and other officials to look the other way during their raids on ships. Elizabeth was an active planner and supporter of these exploits, which continued after her husband's death. Described as a tough, unprincipled business woman, and known as 'Old Lady Killigrew', she continued the raids into her 60's, apparently burying the treasure she took from ships in her garden.

In 1582 she heard that a Hanseatic ship anchored in the harbour might have treasure. The raid resulted in Elizabeth's staff murdering a merchant. Elizabeth and her extended family were arrested and charged with piracy and with receiving and dealing in stolen goods. Elizabeth Trewinnard herself was put on trial and sentenced to death. Eventually, Queen Elizabeth I pardoned her from the death sentence, although her sons still had to pay 'enormous' bribes to get their elderly mother released from prison.

HEERE LYETH IOHN KILLIGREW ESQVIER, OF ARWENACK, AND LORD OF Ᵹ MANOR OF KILLIGREW IN CORNEWALL, AND ELIZABETH TREWINNARD HIS WIFE, HE WAS THE FIRST CAPTAINE OF PENDENNIS CASTLE, MADE BY KING HENRY THE EIGHT, & SO CONTINVED VNTILL THE NYNTH OF QVEENE ELIZABETH AT WHICH TIME GOD TOOKE HIM TO HIS MERCYE, BEING THE YEARE OF OVR LORD 1567.
Sᵗ IOHN KILLIGREW KNIGHT HIS SOÑE SVCCEEDED HIM IN Ᵹ SAME PLACE BY THE GIFT OF QVEENE ELIZABETH.

A fine brass in Budock Church records the death of John Killigrew in 1567 and of his wife Elizabeth Trewinnard, who died after 1583. *(Layout altererd for reproduction)*

Martin Trewinnard d.1583

It seems likely that William had wasted much money on the court cases in London, and lost other sums through his absence from or poor management at home. The existence of a bailiff or manager in 1557 suggests that he was an absentee, as does the family representation for different parliamentary boroughs through these years. It also seems that Trewinnard was mortgaged and tenanted in 1562, suggesting a shortage of cash.

One possibility is that Martin's two younger brothers, James and George, had both reduced the value of the estate through being given a share of the family wealth. However, despite the costs of law, or of residence in London, there should have been good opportunities for wealth. Martin had, for instance, married Isabella Mohun, the eldest daughter in this important family, which should have brought him a good dowry. His own connections included his aunt, Elizabeth Trewinnard, who had married Sir John Killigrew. Martin's brother had married a rich heiress of the Carminow family.

Early married life to a wealthy heiress, and his positions as collector, should have brought him money. However it may be that Martin, who as a young man had received that considerable sum of £20 per year from his father, was just a rather silly person. A picture of him as 'a merry Cornish gentleman', survives in a tale by Richard Carew of Antony. Even allowing for the different tastes of the time, the tale of Martin's practical jokes, of his scaring of the ladies and of his eventual 'come-uppance' was thought worth re-telling some fifty years later. *(The story is set out on the next page)*.

By the 1560s Martin was already in debt, as his father had been before him. Although the Steward of the Stanneries and, in 1570, given the lucrative post of Collector of the Subsidy, his financial position seems to have worsened, despite inheritance, land, mines and contacts. By now he seems to have been incapable of handling his difficulties and his life become mired in one problem after another. He mortgaged Trewinnard to Sir John Nance, who is then said to have foreclosed.

Sir John Nance, or Nans, (alias Trengove) was married to Margery, the daughter of Sir John Arundel of Trerice. Sir John Nance inherited four properties from the Arundels in 1580; it seems likely that a 1578 deed represented a property sort out among inter-related families. A family connection may also be why Sir Thomas Arundel of Tolverne is thought to have sold part of his 'interest' in Trewinnard to Sir Nicholas Hals, and why Arundel signed the 1578 deed. In 1605 it seems that Sir Nicholas Hals transferred 13/16 of the manor

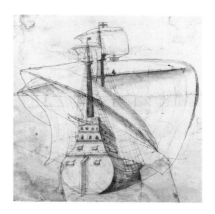

A ship off Lands End: A detail from the Henrician defence map of 1539.

British Museum: Cotton MS Augustus 1 i, f 35 (c315-72).

of Trewinnard to his daughter Mary, although this may have been a lease of the manor, not the house or farm.

After 1578, Trewinnard was lived in by Sir John Nance's second son, John, who was styled 'of Trewinnard'. He inherited no great estate and may have been a tenant. When he was the captain of the trained bands of Penwith in 1595, for raids expected by the Spanish, he used Trewinnard as his western headquarters. On his death, he is thought to have left an interest in Trewinnard to his own second son, another John.

Although the ownership of Trewinnard may have been confused and its unravelling remains uncertain, the end result was that the freehold of Trewinnard ended up in the hands of the Mohun family in the early years of the 17thC.

What was behind Martin's Ruin?

First, Martin seems to have fallen out with his two brothers, James and George. James had married well and to a rich heiress. George was based in St Ives with businesses and some wealth. The dispute with his brothers rumbled on for years, and George Trewinnard, at St Ives, continued the family tradition of getting and taking what was wanted. In one petition, Martin claimed he was being tormented by his relations.

Second, he seems to have fallen out with the Killigrews, the family of his aunt Elizabeth. This falling out grew to include further members of the Killigrew family. For instance, the powerful Killigrew sons of his aunt Elizabeth Trewinnard, included Henry Killigrew,

---

Martin Trewinnard and his Snake

This mention of snakes called to my remembrance how not long since a merry Cornish gentleman tried that old fable to be no fable, which showeth the dangerous entertaining of such a guest.

For he, having got one of that kind [a venomous snake] and broken out his teeth (wherein consisteth his venom) used to carry him about in his bosom, to set him to his mouth, to make him lick his spittle; and when he came among gentlewomen, would cast him suddenly out to put them in fear.

But in the end, their vain dread proved safer than his foolhardiness. For as he walked alone and was kissing this gentle playfellow, [then] the snake, in good earnest, with a stump either newly grown up or not fully pulled out, bit him fast by the tongue.

[The gentleman's tongue] therewith began so to rankle and swell, that by the time he had knocked this foul player on the head, and was come to his place of abode, his mouth was scarce able to contain it.

Fain was he therefore to show his mishap, and by gestures to crave aid in earnest of the gentlewomen whom he had aforetime often scared in sport.

The Survey of Cornwall: Richard Carew of Antony: 1602

MP for Truro, a senior politician doing genuinely secret missions for Queen Elizabeth, and William, who helped collect money for the Duchy and ended up years later as Chamberlain of the Exchequer. The Killigrews were seriously competent men with influence and power and not the people to have against you. In a petition of 1575, Martin Trewinnard complained that his brother-in-laws James and John Killigrew were *'A cruel worker of your orator's destruction who had longe tyme vexed him with law suits and unjust demands'* claiming that they had tried to lay hold of the *'tithe sheep'* which belonged by right to Martin. Although friends presumably secured him the position in 1570 of *Collector of the Subsidy*, his enemies were powerful.

Third, he seems so to have failed those to whom he owed money, that the last ten years of his life were spent in the Fleet prison.

Fourth, his long period in prison gave to his creditors, his enemies, his tenants and to opportunists, the chance to take advantage of his absence and to rob him of lands and goods. This included the great manor of Tolgollow which was 'taken' by John Calwadley when he threw out Martin's tenant with *'great cruelty and oppression'*, despite having no claim to the estate at all.

Fifth, the Black Death returned to Cornwall from around 1578. Burial records suggest that this savagely reduced the population and in turn the numbers of those available to work the land or mines or pay rents.

On his death in 1583, Martin Treweinnard left to his son Deiphobus, a terrible state of affairs.

The 1578 assignment by John Nans of Nans (alias Trengove) of 'all his manors at Trewinnarde' for the use and 'behoofe' of those who signed, until such time as Diophebus Trewenarde, son and heir of Martin Trewenarde shall attempt to recover the manors, with provision for that eventuality.

This document on vellum, c.13.5 inches x 21.25 inches, and dated 20 November 1578 bears the seals and signatures of Sir Richard Grenville, Richard Carew, Sir Richard Bassett, John Arundel of Trerice, Thomas Roscarrocke and others. The reasons for the document, the presumed underlying mortgages or history, the position of John Nans and the reason for inclusion of the various signatories are not certain. It is assumed that this was part of a programme of rearrangement, trusts, mortgages and land transfer. whose purpose and progress is not yet well understood. *Private collection: Sir John Nott.*

Deiphobus Trewinnard

Deiphobus Trewinnard had been christened after the greek hero Deiphobus, a son of King Priam and Queen Helen of Troy. In Homer's Iliad, Athene disguises herself as Deiphobus, who is then slain and mutilated during the siege of Troy. Deiphobus was not a common name, and the associations behind the choice of such a name are not now understood.

We know that Deiphobus seems to have taken over his father's estate before that man's death and at the same time entered into a string of complex deeds relating to his lands and title.

Despite the debts to pay and problems with neighbours left to his son by Martin Trewinard, the 1578 reorganisation of affairs by Deiphobus may have been forced upon him by events recorded by the historian Hals, writing in the early 18thC, who suggested that a murder by Deiphobus was behind the end of the Trewinnard family's connection with Trewinnard.

Deiphobus Trewinnard, [son of Martin Trewinnard, steward of the stanneries], ..in his rage or anger killed an innocent man and buried him secretly in Trewinard Chapel, [which] was of public use before the church of St Erth was erected.

However this fact was not so covertly carried, but the coroners of the shire had notice of it, who accordingly came to the place, opened the grave, took forth the body, and impanelled a jury thereon, who upon oath gave their verdict, that this party's death happened upon a wilful murder of Trewinnard's. Whereupon he was carried before a justice of the peace, and upon further examination of this matter, had his mittimus made, and was accordingly sent to Launceston gaol, where he remained till the next assizes.

In the mean time, foreseeing that this barbarous fact would tend both to the destruction of his life and estate, he applied to Sir Reginald Mohun, Knight, a favourite of the Queen Elizabeth's and proposed to him that he would make over and convey to him, his heirs and assigns for ever all his lands and tenements whatsoever, under this proviso or condition, that in case he were condemned for the murder aforesaid, that [Sir Reginald Mohun] should or would procure the Queen's pardon or reprieve for his life;

Which proposal being accepted by Sir Reginald Mohun, lease and release of his lands were made and executed upon a valuable consideration accordingly to [Sir Reginald], bearing date the day before this tragical fact [the murder] was committed. Whereupon Sir Reginald Mohun forthwith became seised of this barton and

manor of Trewinnard....At the next assizes held for this
county, Mr Trewinnard being indicted for this murder,
was found guilty by the grand and petty juries and ac-
cordingly condemned to be hanged to death.

At [this] instance, Sir Reginald Mohun, having
gotten the Queen's reprieve or pardon for Mr Trewin-
nard, put it into the sheriff's hands, wherebye his execu-
tion was stopped and himself afterwards, on sureties for
his good behaviour, was set at liberty from the gaol. [He]
subsisted upon some small stipend allowed him by Sir
Reginald out of his lands during life.

Because Hals has had a poor reputation for reli-
ability, this report has been dismissed by all, including
Henderson, as unreliable or false. However, it bears further investigation.

First, the family home of Hals at Fentongollan,
was also the home of that Nicholas Hals, described as
both of Fentongollan and of Trewinnard, who had an interest in or was a tenant of Trewinnard at the end of the
16thC, 100 years before Hals was writing. The family
connection gives some credence to the story of Deiphobus, as does the legal language of the story, which suggests Hals had obtained the details from records.

Second, the division between the sisters of Deiphobus some time around 1600 has become confused
with a division between the sisters of Reginald Mohun
in the 1650s. Setting out events in diagrammatic form
shows there is logic to the story.

Third, further muddling was provided by similar
Christian names within the Mohun family. The Mohuns,
who arrived in England with William the Conqueror,
had used the name Reginald for almost every generation
from around 1180. Historians of the 18thC and 19thC
found each Reginald difficult to tell apart.

Fourth, Sir Reginald Mohun was not just any
great man, but a close relation of the Trewinnards. Martin Trewinnard had married Sir Reginald's eldest aunt,
so that Deiphobus was in fact Sir Reginald's first cousin.

Fifth, although surviving legal documents are
confusing, it is clear that Sir Reginald Mohun ended up
with possession of all four parts of the freehold, which
were transferred to him from the sisters of Deiphobus.

Deiphobus signed away Trewinnard and vanish-
es from the records. There are no records of his death,
nor whether he was married or had children. By 1580,
the house at Trewinnard was occupied by a Mr. Man-
waring who was married to one of the sisters of Deiphobus. Later, each of his sisters also signed away their interest in the property.

Since his father had been Steward of the Stanneries only some eight years before, the fall of the Trewinnards seems so swift that an unusual event, such as murder would seem the reason. It is likely that the story of the murder, backed by Hals with examples of other condemned gentry murderers, is true. It also seems likely that Deiphobus lived on with a small stipend from Sir Reginald and that the murder was the underlying reason for the transfer of the property to Sir Reginald Mohun.

Has the Trewinnard name survived?

Charles Henderson reported that he was able to trace the Trewinnard family from the early 16thC to the 20thC and that he found only one period of 23 years between 1600 and 1623 where descent from a father to a son, both called John could not be proven. Sadly his researched family tree has not survived save as unfinished notes, which listed three branches of the family.

One of these branches continued through Martin's brother George at St Ives, where the family tradition seems to have continued in independent and 'dodgy' actions. During the 1620s, there are disputes about the spoils from French prizes, about problems with the 'Turks', and activities at St Ives. These disputes resulted in John Trewinnard being arrested on the instructions of Whitehall, only to then re-emerge 'clean and clear'.

Records of the co-lateral branches of the Trewinnard family show they were also active in the parishes of Gwinear, Mawnan and Constantine and that several members held positions in the church, including multiple parish appointments in different parts of Cornwall. A father and son Trewinnard were respectively Vicars of two Cornish parishes, Breague and Mawgan, at the end of the 17thC. Joseph Trewinnard held Mawnan and St Week Mary, some sixty miles apart in the years to 1716.

By 1814, Lysons recorded that the head of the family in the direct line was a Mr Joshua Trewinnard, a watchmaker of Rotherhithe, near London.

In the early 20thC, Charles Henderson corresponded with a Mr. Trewinnard who requested that his family tree be traced. Although not all the papers to which Henderson refers seem to have survived, it was that man's descendant, Geoffrey Trewinnard, who in 1966 visited Trewinnard and left some pages at the house from the Charles Henderson research. In addition to that research, some notes have survived which were sent by Henderson to the Vicar of St Erth.

When in 1966, Trewinnard was visited by Geoffrey Trewinnard, he listed 12 members of generation younger than him, suggesting that the name Trewinnard would continue.

In the 21stC, a brief search of directories records a considerable number of people with the name Trewinnard, although few, if any, appear to have a Cornish connection.

Charles Henderson and the Trewinnards

The early history of the Trewinnards is notable for being researched by that most famous of Cornish Historians, Charles Henderson, who devoted his life to research and to carefully recording in his papers details from now lost archives. An early death cut short the writing of his Parochial History for Cornwall, but his papers, in the Courtney Library of the Royal Institute of Cornwall, remain the first source for research on the history of Cornwall, particularly since destruction during the second World War has meant that the Henderson papers are now the only record for many lost archives.

Charles Henderson's papers record how his first-ever professional research was carried out on the Trewinnard family for a Mr Trewinnard.

It is fascinating to read the lengthy letters written in November 1918 to persuade the client not only of what could be found out, but of Charles Henderson's own suitability for the task and then negotiating for payment. He refers to *the immense amount about Martin and James Trewinnard [in the 16thC] at the Public Record Office.... and that both are constantly mixed up in riots of a most exciting and romantic character'*.

In lengthy prose paragraphs and the style of a different age, Charles Henderson goes on to say *'If however, you feel inclined to materially assist my work in a pecuniary way, I could write out an essay on the Trewinnards...In asking a fee, I do not do so with the idea of any pecuniary gain but with the intention of assisting a very expensive and costly undertaking. ......I am therefore going to ask a fee of £2-2-0 [two guineas]...'* In another letter of 30 November, 1918, Charles Henderson declared that: *'This is the first occasion in which I have ever acted in a professional way"*.

For the enthusiast of Cornwall's history and for admirers of the great historian, the notes on Trewinnard are a delightful record of Henderson's earliest and first professional research.

Records of the Trewinnard Family

The following is a dated schedule of known records and references to the Trewinnard family.

AD1300

1302   Stephan de Trewinnard and 40 other horsemen follow Ralph Bloyon (a powerful West Cornwall baron) and Michael Bloyon to a house at Penstrado (Penstrasso near St Austell). They break in and rob the occupier of eleven shillings and sixpence before fleeing.

1302   Bartholomew de Trewinnard appears as surety in connection with a murder at Ludgvan near Trewinnard.

1308   Roland de Trewynnard was confirmed by Bishop Stapleton of Exeter.

1316   Richard de Trewinnard representing the Hundred of Penwith, was fined for failing to do Jury duty at the Launceston Assize.

1318   John de Trewynnard obtained a 'writ of Protection'.

1319   Henry de Trewynnard obtained a 'writ of Protection'.

1327   Richard de Trewinnard having got prominent backers, failed to turn up to support his action against Oger, son of Alan de Kerny.

1327   This was also the year when the 'subsidy' or tax paid by Richard de Trewinnard in St Erth parish was 3 shillings. Allegedly a tenth of his goods, this was a sum as high as that of the great nobles and six times greater than the average taxpayer or landowner.

1327   In this year, complaint was made that Rouland de Trewennard, Richard de Trewennard and others had broken into Thomas Marceley's house at the Lizard, insulted him and carried away his goods.

1329   Richard de Trewinnard was again a defaulting juryman.

1331   Roland de Trewynnard obtained a 'writ of Protection' in Bristol where it is assumed he was trading.

1334   Roland Trewinnard is, at the king's request, entered in the priory of St Michael's Mount with free accommodation and clothing for life.

1337   Henry de Trewynard was MP for Bodmin.

1347   James De Trewinnard and his wife Joan defended a suit about land in Ludgvan and when the plaintiff did not appear, remained in possession of the land (perhaps an example of land transfer through the courts).

1353   Another friendly suit saw Henry De Trewinnard gain 300 acres at Trewelesek and Carneny in St Erth, probably part of a marriage settlement from his grandfather, the plaintiff.

1353   Stephan de Trewynard witnessed a charter in relation to Bodmin.

1362   John de Trewynard had land in Bodmin

1363   Henry de Trewinnard witnesses a charter. His daughter Alice had married Roger Giffard of Lannowmure who died without issue in 1362.

1372   Henry Trewinnard and his wife were granted a License to celebrate divine service or to have it celebrated in their presence in their chapels at *Trewennarde and Trevyrvy* (Trevorva in Ludgvan). The grant was made by the Bishop of Exeter, who was staying at Marazion, and seems thereby to have recognised two pre-existing chapels.

1381   The same Bishop of Exeter, following an examination carried out by his archdeacons in 1380, excommunicated John Browdrer, a sergeant at arms. The accusation claimed that around 1375 at Trevarthyan in the Parish of St Hilary, Master William Sancre of Trevarthian, a priest of good report, who had committed no crime whatsoever, had had his 'vestments' publicly insulted by John and Roger Trewinnard. They had next tied the poor man's hands behind his back and then cut off his head with great violence. After this the head had been placed on a pike and taken to London City *as if the priest had been an abominable traitor, albeit common report described him as a man of good reputation and blameless life*.

Then in November 1380, the 'greater excommunication' was issued against Roger Trewinnard, since his complicity in the crime *'was so notorious that by no sort of subterfuge could it be concealed'*. The Bishop of Exeter issued orders to imprison the criminals, but we do not know what happened. This story of violence must have been resolved because Roger appears to have continued to live on in Cornwall. The reports remain puzzling and the truth or actions behind them unknown.

1388   Roger Trewynnard acts as a surety for a friend's good behaviour.

1393   This year saw a serious dispute about the great Trewinnard held manor of Talgollou, which included 100 houses, 400 acres of arable land, 100 acres of meadow, 100 acres of woodland and 1000 acres of moorland. This was an important estate of nearly 2000 acres, particularly rich and valuable because it was a great mining centre at that time. It was alleged that the Trewinnard title to Talgollau was only signed away by Roger Trewinnard in a deed of 1380 because Roger had been imprisoned at Lostwithiel and kept there until the deed was signed. The plaintiffs also claimed that the gift of the manor was in the right of Wynon Tyrell, one of those alleged to have imprisoned Roger Trewinnard. Since the manor continued in Trewinnard ownership, it seems the story of imprisonment and co-erced signing must have been believed.

AD1400

1401   This year saw another dispute about rights to that same manor of Talgullow.

1405   John Boscawen gained custody of Henry Trewinnard, brother and heir of John, who was himself son and heir of Roger Trewinnard. Custody was also given over Henry's younger brother James.

1443   A deed done at Trewinnard recorded that the trustees of the just died Henry Trewynard, together with his widow Johanna, gave a lease to their daughter Jane's husband,

J Flaman of *'Nesager'* and other lands.

1470   Michael Trewynnard, who had become a great churchman and man of importance, became provost of Glasney College in Penryn, (before dying in 1471) having earlier been a fellow of Exeter, Oxford from 1429-1438.

1497   The rebellion from Cornwall, led by Thomas Flammock and Michael Joseph against taxes levied to pay for a Scottish war, was defeated at Blackheath outside London in June 1497. In consequence, leading inhabitants from each parish became responsible for raising fines assessed by the King and then paying the necessary sum to royal officials. Although raising the money may have given some opportunity for profit, it may also have been a heavy burden. William Trewynnard was one of several who each took more than one parish in charge. William Trewynnard in person with Nicholas Enys paid the large sum of £30 for John Tresynny of Penryn. (John Tresynny seems not only to have played a considerable part in the rebellion, but also used the rebellion for robbery and personal benefit). William Trewinnard of St Erth also paid forty shillings on behalf of the inhabitants of St Erth and 10 marks for the Vicar of St Erth. His brother(?) John Trewinnard (with another) was charged with sums to be paid on behalf of Warlegan, St Neot, Lanteglos, Fowey and Goran.

1497   Star chamber proceedings suggest that James Trewynnard, had married Margaret, the daughter of Robert Conlyng, gent. However, there was no issue of the marriage. Then Margaret died in such suspicious circumstances that her relations openly accused James Trewynnard of arranging her murder by a Janett Vincent, who may have been James' mistress. Margaret's family then took back her inheritance by force, and 'great rioting ensued at Trewinnard, in which James Trewinnard was badly beaten.'

AD1500

1512   James Trewinnard and his brother William sued the parson of Ludgvan for a breach of trust.

Circa 1520   James Trewinnard was assessed at 10 marks in Land and £40 in goods in the Parish of St Erth.

1534   Parliament: James Trewinnard represented Liskeard among a group critical of the King.

1535   A complaint was made by 'poor tin miners' that James Trewinnard and 15 servants had broken into their tin mine, assaulted and wounded them and then taken the mines for himself.

Other cases involving James included:

- James Trewynnard v John Coulying & Robert... re forcible entry etc in *'Wonwyn'* (possibly Goonwin in Lelant) (Star Chamber: temp Henry VIII).
- James Trewynnard took legal action against John Carmynowe and John Boskawen over the estate of Hugh Boscawen deceased, and, in another case, against John Cowlying about land. (Star Chamber: temp HenryVIII)
- James Magar against James Trewinnard about tenements in Trevellean (Court of Requests)
- Another claim was made by John Thredrere, William Plemen & James William Thomas against James Trewinnard, William Foye and others about a *tinwarke in Tremellyn Moor*, across the stream from Trewinnard. This bill was addressed to Wolsey.
- Then there was the case by Hobkyn Jenkyn against Warren Trewennard, alias Warren John and others for assault. Although Warren may not have been of the family but named after the site, it was still unusual to take an assault case to court in London.
- During the reign of Queen Elizabeth, actions continued to the end of James' life, with him taking action against John Bosotwen and others for 'premises' (land).

1542   William Trewynnard (James' son) was the member for Helston. He was imprisoned for a debt of £75 first claimed in 1539 as owing to John Skeves, which was three years before William became an MP. Eventually, having been five times summoned, he surrendered to the Sheriff in November 1543 and was imprisoned at Lostwithiel until March 1544 when, having claimed parliamentary privilege, he was released by a different sheriff on a writ of privilege from the King. However, there was dispute about the timing, about whether the sheriffs took over responsibility for the debt and whether parliamentary privilege covered periods when Parliament was not sitting. Much further litigation followed about different points of law, including cases from Skews' executors against the Sheriff and from a Sheriff against Trewynnard. Appeals were made to the Star Chamber and higher courts. The Trewynnard case became a debate about constitutional law and the privilege of Parliament. A century later, the Trewinnard case was much referred to during debates about parliamentary privilege and freedom of speech under Charles 1 in the 1620s.

1544   Martin Trewinnard was given, by his father William, a yearly rent of £20 from Trewinnard funds.

1547   Martin   Trewinnard   represented Launceston in the House of Commons

1554   Martin Trewinnard represents Penryn in the House of Commons.

1557/8 It was recorded that the bailiff at Trewinnard was one Nicholas Mylle, whose listing may hint at the administration that must have been necessary for a great estate and perhaps a measure of disinterest on the part of the owner himself.

1562   13/16ths of Trewinnard is transferred from Nicholas Hals and his Wife Grace to

Thomas Walker, although it seems Martin Trewinnard retained the reversion.

1564   Further appeal in Trewinnard case about appeal from Stannary Courts.

1570   Martin Trewinnard is Steward of the Stanneries, and collector of the subsidy.

1574   From around this date Martin Trewinnard alleged to be imprisoned in the Fleet Prison London, for debt.

Other cases involving Martin included:
- Martin Trewennard v John Kyllyger the younger, John Marshall and Thomas Weston with an inquiry about a supposed riot at Trewennard.
- 1552 Martin Nansellyn of Peryn (Penryn) took action against Martin Trewynnard about dealings in tin.
- Martyn Trewinnard also took action in the Star Chamber against John Kyllegrewe, Philip Fitacke, John Roscarrock, William Gilbert and others about the seizure of cattle in Trewinard and Tregyllis.
- 1575 Petition from Martin Trewinnard against thefts by members of his family.
- 1578   An assignment is made by John Nans of Nans of 'all his manors at Trewenarde' to Richard Grenville (of *The Revenge*), Richard Carew, (author of the Survey of Cornwall), Sir Richard Bassett, John Arundel of Trerice, Thomas Roscarrocke and others, 'so that they may use them until such time as Deiphobus Trewenarde, son and heir of Martin Trewnarde shall attempt to recover the manors', with provision for that eventuality.
- Proceedings in Chancery were undertaken against John Nans otherwise Angove, to redeem mortgages of the Manor of Trewynarde with the appurtances and messuages and lands in the parish of Saint Earthe, mortgaged to the defendant by the plaintiff's father (Martin Trewinard)
- 1579   The mortgage(?) to Nicholas Hals is

thought to have been settled or amended by John Trengove (Sir John Nance q.v.).
- The property was surrendered to the co-heirs of Martin Trewinnard in 1600.

1580   Trewinnard is occupied by Deiphobus' sister and brother in law, Anne and Christopher Mainwaring, signalling the end of Trewinnard as the home of the heir.

1583   Martin Trewinnard dies in the Fleet Prison, in February.   Deiphobus takes over the Trewinnard estate.

AD1600

1600   Deiphobus appears to have died without issue, and the property is inherited by his sisters. The four sisters, and their husbands recover the manor of Trewinnard and then proceed to settle or dispose of their interests.

1606   Nicholas Hals 'of Trewinnard' is still active in property transactions and appears to be tenant of Trewinnard.

The early years of King James note further cases involving St Erth and Trewinnard, but one was by Thomas Mohun against his brother, Reginald Mohun, knight & JP, Dorothy his wife and Elizabeth Pollard her mother. This was about getting charges on land in St Erth made by the father William Mohun to his two sons, the plaintiff and defendant. Although probably a question of simple land transfers, this may not have referred to Trewinnard, because the Mohuns had long had other interests in the parish.

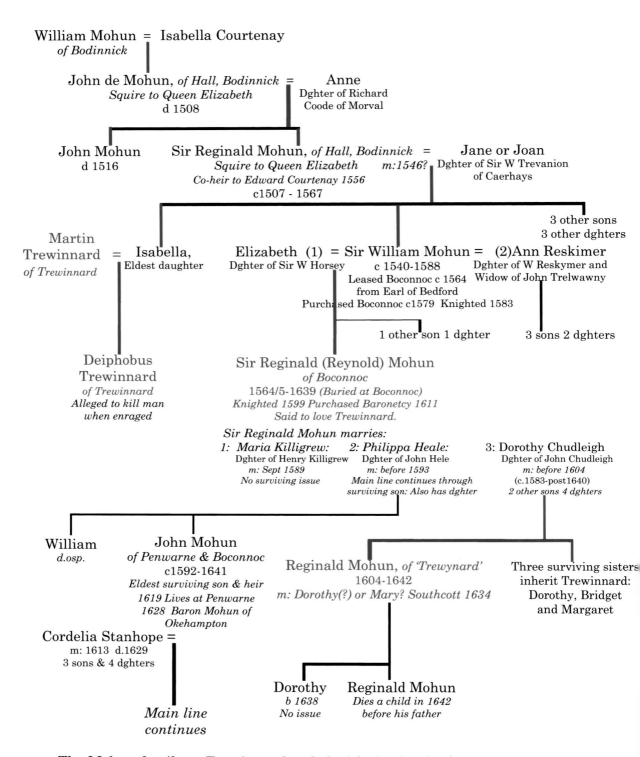

William Mohun = Isabella Courtenay
of Bodinnick

John de Mohun, *of Hall, Bodinnick* = Anne
Squire to Queen Elizabeth Dghter of Richard
d 1508 Coode of Morval

John Mohun
d 1516

Sir Reginald Mohun, *of Hall, Bodinnick* = Jane or Joan
Squire to Queen Elizabeth *m:1546?* Dghter of Sir W Trevanion
Co-heir to Edward Courtenay 1556 of Caerhays
c1507 - 1567

3 other sons
3 other dghters

Martin
Trewinnard = Isabella, Elizabeth (1) = Sir William Mohun = (2)Ann Reskimer
of Trewinnard Eldest daughter Dghter of Sir W Horsey c 1540-1588 Dghter of W Reskymer and
Leased Boconnoc c 1564 Widow of John Trelwawny
from Earl of Bedford
Purchased Boconnoc c1579 Knighted 1583

1 other son 1 dghter

3 sons 2 dghters

Deiphobus
Trewinnard
of Trewinnard
Alleged to kill man
when enraged

Sir Reginald (Reynold) Mohun
of Boconnoc
1564/5-1639 (Buried at Boconnoc)
Knighted 1599 Purchased Baronetcy 1611
Said to love Trewinnard.

Sir Reginald Mohun marries:
1: Maria Killigrew: *2: Philippa Heale:* 3: Dorothy Chudleigh
Dghter of Henry Killigrew Dghter of John Hele Dghter of John Chudleigh
m: Sept 1589 *m: before 1593* *m: before 1604*
No surviving issue *Main line continues through* *(c.1583-post1640)*
surviving son: Also has dghter *2 other sons 4 dghters*

William
d.osp.

John Mohun
of Penwarne & Boconnoc
c1592-1641
Eldest surviving son & heir
1619 Lives at Penwarne
1628 Baron Mohun of
Okehampton

Reginald Mohun, *of 'Trewynard'*
1604-1642
m: Dorothy(?) or Mary? Southcott 1634

Three surviving sisters
inherit Trewinnard:
Dorothy, Bridget
and Margaret

Cordelia Stanhope =
m: 1613 d.1629
3 sons & 4 dghters

Dorothy
b 1638
No issue

Reginald Mohun
Dies a child in 1642
before his father

Main line
continues

The Mohun family at Trewinnard ended with the death of Reginald in 1642.

This family tree has been simplifed and does not show all children, descendants or marriages.
Dates transcribed from original sources can differ through their varying methods in recording the calendar.

Chapter 5
The Mohuns

The Early Mohun Family

With five hundred years of family history behind them, the Mohuns became, during the 16thC & 17thC, one of the great families of Cornwall.

The family name, (pronounced Moon) had been prefaced by the Christian name William from the time of the Conquest until around 1250, when Reginald became the favoured name. Thereafter, the forename Reginald abounded, interspersed with William or John. This no doubt admirable family tradition has, however, produced a confusion of identity between the generations of Mohuns.

William Mohun arrived with William the Conqueror in 1066 and was made Earl of Somerset, responsible for security and administration over an area in the south west. The family later gained the title of Baron of Dunster. Two hundred years after the conquest, the direct line then died out. The family name survived through William Mohun, a fourth son who settled at Lanteglos, near Fowey around 1350, and through a cousin who settled at Tavistock.

Of William Mohun of Fowey we know little save that he is thought to have done well in shipping and that he married a Fitzwilliam heiress who brought him the house at Hall, Bodinnick. It was his son, William Mohun of Bodinnick who made the marriage that set the family up for the next two hundred years. William married Isabella, the Courtenay heiress, famous throughout England for her lands and wealth. Their son was known by the higher status name John de Mohun of Hall, Bodinnick. At his death in 1508, the family were well established in the great house of Hall, across the river from Fowey, one of the largest ports of 16thC England.

Mohun
Or, a cross engrailed, sable

Sir Reginald de Mohun of Hall (1507-1567)

By the time of John's grandson, Sir Reginald de Mohun of Hall, the family was established as a power in Tudor England. This Reginald, who inherited when still a child, attended the court of the Tudors, was twice sheriff of Cornwall and was knighted. He was also co-heir of Edward Courtenay, Earl of Devon. He married a sister of Hugh Trevanion of Caerhays, who was a man of influence, a courtier and friend of King Henry VIII. It was this Sir Reginald's eldest daughter, Isabella, who married Martin Trewinnard of Trewinnard, introduced the Mohuns to Trewinnard and added the Trefrys of Place and the Bellots of Bochym to the relations of Martin Trewinnard.

Hall was quite a place. Little now survives of the house, save the site of the bowling green, the long walk and a 14thC chapel, since the considerable Mohun complex was demolished during fighting in the Civil War.

In his Survey of Cornwall published in 1602, Richard Carew devoted nearly two pages to the delights of the gardens and views from Hall.

The same is appurtenanced with a walk....of diversified pleasings....cut into the side of a steep hill... evenly levelled to serve for bowling, floored with sand for soaking up the rain, closed with two shorn hedges and banked with sweet scenting flowers. It wideneth to a sufficient breadth for the march of five or six in front and extendeth to not much less than half a London mile....... and is converted on the foreside for the planting of ordinance [guns] and the walkers' sitting and on the back part into summer houses for their more private retreat and recreation. ....

Sir William Mohun of Boconnoc (c1540-1588)

Sir Reginald's son, Sir William, twice sheriff of Cornwall, married Elizabeth Horsey first and then secondly, Anna, a widow and daughter of the wealthy William Reskymer. Around 1564, Sir William Mohun leased the estate and mansion of Boconnoc from the Earl of Bedford. In 1579, he purchased this estate as his principal family seat. Boconnoc and its deer park was a few miles northeast of Fowey and was of considerable status and importance. Referred to as *The Tower of Boconnoc* in the mid 15thC by William of Worcester, this was a large courtyard house built round an early great hall.

Sir William started some rebuilding, probably adding a new east wing. In the early 17thC the house was noted for its interior and decorative plasterwork and was grand and large enough to be used for King

A detail and further tracing from the Henrician defence map show Boconnoc and its deer park around 1539.

British Museum C13517/74
Cotton Augustus11 Folio 38

Charles I and his court during the Civil War.

Having served twice as sheriff of Cornwall, Sir William died in 1588. Having married twice, he left another Sir Reginald Mohun as his heir, together with numerous children with connections to the leading families and wealth of the county.

It was for Sir William's widow that a dowager house was built at Trevego, just beyond the gates of Boconnoc deer park. This house still survives as a house rather bigger than many gentry houses of the time, with remnants of fine plasterwork and interiors.

Sir Reginald (Raynold) Mohun (1565-1639)

Sir Reginald, a nephew of Martin Trewinnard and first cousin to Deiphobus Trewinnard, was a power not only in Cornwall but in the country. He was also an important landowner in the parish of St Erth since Borlase reported that the Mohun coat of arms had decorated an early 16thC window in St Erth church. Knighted in 1599, he purchased a baronetcy in 1612. Sir Reginald married three times and spent around fifteen years in painful court cases about the settlement of his estates with his heir, John, the son of his second wife. Sir Reginald lived for seventy five years, dying only one year before his heir John and three years before his 'favorite' son, Reginald of Trewinnard.

Although John was left the family estate at Boconnoc, it was to his second son, Reginald that he left Trewinnard, which was said to be Sir Reginald's favourite house.

In trying to understand the appearance and gardens of the house at Trewinnard, we must consider the other houses that Sir Reginald owned and the monies he spent on both his and his family's homes.

One such is the still standing house at Trewane, in St Kew parish. This house belonged to the Nicholls family, and was extended and rebuilt to celebrate the marriage of Sir Reginald's daughter Brigett, to John Nicholls in 1635. The new house, in the latest large roomed style, had three storeys, decorative gables, and astonishing plasterwork.

It is important to the story of Trewinnard, therefore, that the Mohuns, owning a great house at Hall with walks and gardens, a rebuilt mansion at Boconnoc, who provided for relatives such fine buildings as Trewane for his daughter Bridget or the splendid Trevigo for his father's widow, yet delighted in the house and garden at Trewinnard, where lived Reginald's second son, his alleged favourite by his third, yet surviving, wife.

Sir Reginald Mohun & his
3rd wife, Lady Dorothy Mohun,
née Chudleigh,
painted c 1603 by an unknown English Artist

This fine memorial to Penelope Mohun is in Boconnoc Church. Penelope, buried in March 1637, was a daughter to 'Sir Raynold Mohun, knight and baronet'.
The punning verse notes that, as a young girl before marriage to William Drew, she was:
'a virgin starre, on earth, a while I shin'd with noted splendour, chiefly of the mind till my Will:Drew me to his nuptiall bed thence soone, by Gods high call to Heaven I fled
not without hope in Christ, to be a gemme set in the walles of New Jerusalem'.

Reginald Mohun (c.1604-1642)

Reginald Mohun described himself as 'of Trewinnard' during his adult life. Not much is known of this life. Although he married, his wife's name is uncertain, perhaps because she was christened by one name and known by another. He had a daughter baptised at Boconnoc but both his children, a girl and boy, died young, and his wife chose to have nothing to do with his affairs or estate after his death.

Reginald's interests and lands were therefore inherited by those three sisters who shared with him the same mother and father.

Although there may have been tenants right at the beginning of the 17thC, it seems that for forty years, two Reginald Mohuns, father and son, were at home at Trewinnard. This was a favourite house of Sir Reginald Mohun and the chief residence of his son, the second member of one of the great families in Cornwall.

To have been a Mohun house suggests that this lost house must have been quite a place. It would have retained the courtyard design of the early medieval mansion, although fitted out with extra buildings and fine gardens in the style of the time. We know that there was a garden with a series of terraces, culminating in a long bowling green.

We assume that the house was fitted with an astonishing collection of tapestries, which are described at page 169. We imagine that private quarters had been fitted out in the previous century with some magnificence and can assume that in those quarters, the favourite Mohun son would have emulated the plasterwork and internal decoration of which we have evidence at Boconnoc, Trewane and Trevego.   Trewinnard is likely to have been a magnificent courtyard house, with a great hall and suites of personal chambers, which would have included guest wings for the visits of father and mother.

Some of the fine plasterwork and fireplaces at Trewane, St Kew, which was rebuilt following the wedding of Brigett Mohun in 1635. The lavish renovation and decoration of this house for his daughter suggests that Trewinnard, the home of Sir Reginald's favorite son, must also have been as splendid.

What happened to the Mohuns?

The family supported the King during the Civil War and were at the heart of the fight-back by the King that started in Cornwall. The Sir Reginald who died in 1639 was succeeded by his forty year old son, John, who had been created the Baron of Okehampton in 1628, but who only lived a year longer than his father. He in turn was succeeded by the second Lord Mohun who died in 1665. Thereafter only two generations survived before the line died out with the death of the fourth Lord Mohun in a duel in 1712.

The last two Mohuns were notorious for living a dissolute, immoral life, spending time wenching, wasting their estates, murdering, and providing much fine 'newspaper copy' even by the more lax standards of that time. But that is another story and far from Trewinnard.

After the Mohuns.

We have little information as to what happened at Trewinnard between the death of Reginald Mohun in 1642 and 1650, when John Hawkins is thought to have taken a lease of part of the house. A freehold ownership divided between three families probably meant a lack of real interest from all three, particularly during the uncertainty of a civil war and Protectorate. It seems likely that the house was let and divided among opportunistic tenants and received little if any maintenance. Lack of maintenance in the fifty years before the purchase of a part interest by the Hawkins family, was probably one reason that the old building did not survive.

The Arrival of the Hawkins Family

Documents from Trewithen suggest that John Hawkins first took a lease of Trewinnard in 1650.

The Hearth Tax assessment of 1664-5 for St Erth parish does not give addresses for the properties for which each person was liable. The Mohun house at Trewinnard seems unlikely to have had less than 10 tax bearing hearths, so that although it is difficult to be certain who was paying tax for Trewinnard, it seems probable that the mansion house was in multiple occupation at the time of the Hearth Tax assessment.

This possibility is supported by an entry for *John Hawkinges* with six hearths 'examined' and another entry for *George Trenhale* with another six hearths. Since John Hawkins had married a Loveday Trenhayle of St Erth, we can imagine that George Trenhale was John Hawkin's father in law, and that Trewinnard was shared between the Trenhayles and the Hawkins. This would give a total of twelve taxable hearths for Trewinnard which is much more likely for a house of this status, although still rather fewer than might have been supposed for a great Mohun house.

Between 1642, when the property passed to the three sisters of Reginald Mohun, and 1685, when one third passed to the Hawkins family, the house can be supposed to have decayed during a period of multiple ownership and different tenants.

John Hawkins may have made this his principle

residence, but, like many a tenant, is unlikely to have spent money on repairing and improving someone else's house. The site was thus ripe for the addition of the modern extension added by the Hawkins family.

John Hawkins' family continued to live there until 1685, when Thomas Hawkins purchased the one third freehold interest in Trewinnard that gave him the incentive to rebuild the old house.

Ownership of the Freehold to Trewinnard.

One of the difficulties in sorting out who lived at Trewinnard has been the confusion between those having a part interest in the freehold of the property, those with a long lease, those who were tenants or sub-tenants, those who were stewards or trustees and those occupying different parts of the same property, such as the farm, mill or mansion.

Early records appear to have confused the inheritance of the sisters of Deiphobus with those of the sisters of Reginald Mohun some seventy five years later.

A further confusion is the Hals family, which was first connected by land, lease or mortgage with Trewinnard in 1562. Transactions or mortgages seem to have continued a relationship thereafter. In 1606 it was said that a Nicholas Hals 'of Trewinnard' was still living at the house. It has also been suggested that Sir Nicholas Hals of Fentongollan bought one third of the freehold interest from the Arundels and had a lease of the other two thirds and that his son, John Hals, sold his freehold interest to Thomas Hawkins. The involvement of the Arundel family is also not clear.

It is difficult to tie this information together. Events in 1685 have been confused with those a century earlier and there has been confusion between the different tenants at the mansion or farm, and between freeholder and lessee at Trewinnard.

The diagram on page 73 shows the line of ownership from the three sisters of Reginald Mohun as that is currently understood, although the diagram should, for the present, be accepted as a 'work in progress'.

Inheritance of the Freehold to Trewinnard

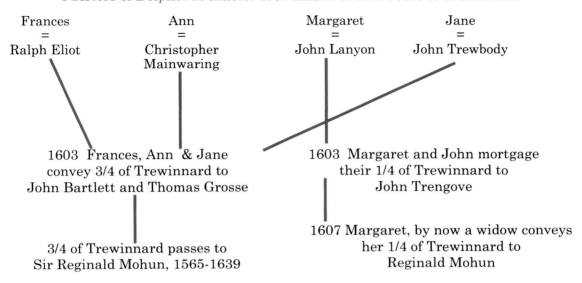

4 Sisters of Deiphobus inherit Trewinnard & hold 100% of Trewinnard

Frances
=
Ralph Eliot

Ann
=
Christopher
Mainwaring

Margaret
=
John Lanyon

Jane
=
John Trewbody

1603 Frances, Ann & Jane
convey 3/4 of Trewinnard to
John Bartlett and Thomas Grosse

1603 Margaret and John mortgage
their 1/4 of Trewinnard to
John Trengove

3/4 of Trewinnard passes to
Sir Reginald Mohun, 1565-1639

1607 Margaret, by now a widow conveys
her 1/4 of Trewinnard to
Reginald Mohun

4/4 of Trewinnard left to Reginald Mohun of **Trewynard** 1604-1642,
son of Sir Reginald Mohun. Reginald's son does not survive and so the estate passes
to the sisters of Reginald Mohun of Trewynard.

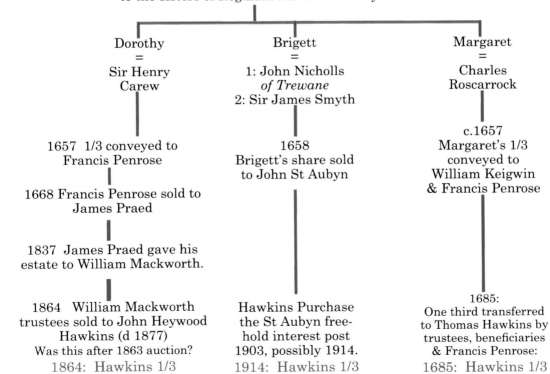

Dorothy
=
Sir Henry
Carew

Brigett
=
1: John Nicholls
of Trewane
2: Sir James Smyth

Margaret
=
Charles
Roscarrock

1657 1/3 conveyed to
Francis Penrose

1668 Francis Penrose sold to
James Praed

1837 James Praed gave his
estate to William Mackworth.

1864 William Mackworth
trustees sold to John Heywood
Hawkins (d 1877)
Was this after 1863 auction?
1864: Hawkins 1/3

1658
Brigett's share sold
to John St Aubyn

Hawkins Purchase
the St Aubyn free-
hold interest post
1903, possibly 1914.
1914: Hawkins 1/3

c.1657
Margaret's 1/3
conveyed to
William Keigwin
& Francis Penrose

1685:
One third transferred
to Thomas Hawkins by
trustees, beneficiaries
& Francis Penrose:
1685: Hawkins 1/3

Jane Ellen Hawkins sold Trewinnard House, farm and mill in February 1930.

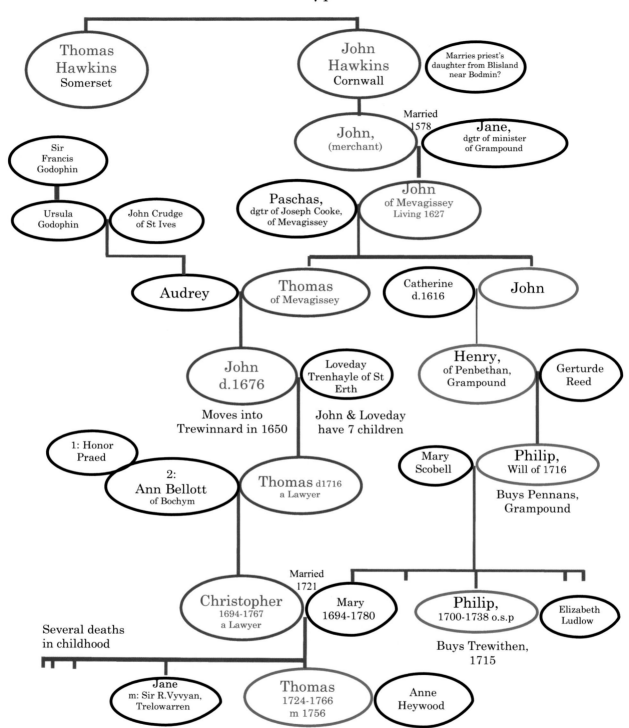

The Hawkins family of Trewinnard and of Trewithen:
Names in red follow the senior Trewinnard line; Names in blue follow the line for Trewithen.
The two branches intermarry with Christopher and Mary in 1721.
The surname 'Hawkins' is not noted on the chart.

Chapter 6
The Hawkins Family

The Hawkins Family of Kent and Devon

The Hawkins family tradition was that the Hawkins were respectable Kent gentry, originally from the village of Hawking, near Folkstone in Kent. They had served at the court of Henry VIII but then moved to Cornwall in 1554 to escape persecution, or civil disturbance in Kent. Although any connection with Kent is uncertain, both the Cornwall and Kent Hawkins families have similar coats of arms and also share this coat with the Hawkins seafaring family of Plymouth.

This coat of arms is said to have been given to the family following a successful siege of the town of Manconseil in France in 1338, during the reign of Edward III, by 300 men under the command of Rabigois of Derry, an Irishman, and two English esquires Franklyn and Hawkins. It is said that the origin of the coat of arms reflects the exploits of that siege, the scaling ladders being represented by the saltaire, and the captured standard of France by the fleur de lis.

It seems more likely that the Cornish branch were descended from the branch of the family that had moved from Kent to Plymouth during the 15thC, and are recorded as having land there before 1480, and in 1485. The Hawkins family produced three generations of famous seamen in the reigns from Henry VIII to Elizabeth I. They also became extremely wealthy. In 1545 William Hawkins represented Plymouth 'for the burgesses of Parliament' and was elected MP in 1553, dying in the same year. A deed from February 1554 says that:

'Henry Hawkins, clerk [that is, in clerical orders and believed to have held the living of Lamerton for some years] *recently of Plymouth, brother and heir of William Hawkins Merchant recently deceased, for a sum of money gives up land in Plymouth to William Hawkins son of Joan Trelawny'*.

The Hawkins coat of arms was shared by branches of the family, in Kent, Plymouth and Cornwall.

Argent, a saltaire sable bearing five fleur de lis, or.

This version appears to have been used by the early 17thC Cornish family, although the arms were later *'differenced'* for different branches and generations. Sir Christopher Hawkins' arms had differencing additions.

Two sons of William Hawkins became sea heroes of the Elizabethan reign. It seems probable that the Henry of the 1554 deed was the connection to Cornwall, particularly since the coincidence of the phrase ' recently of Plymouth' and the date 1554 accords with the Cornish Hawkins family tradition of arrival in that year.

The Hawkins Family of Mevagissey

Some fifty years later, the first recorded Cornish Hawkins was John, said to have married a priest's daughter, possibly from Blisland, around the beginning of the 17thC. Little is known of the family save that, after a couple of generations, the family were living in Mevagissey, as merchants.

Two brothers continued the family line. The elder brother was Thomas, the senior line that moved to Trewinnard. The younger brother, John had a son who moved to Grampound. His son, Philip, became a successful attorney and purchased Pennans, Grampound.

The older brother, Thomas, described as a gentleman, married Audrey, from the important family of Sir Francis Godolphin, in a marriage that suggested that the Hawkins were of recognisable wealth and status. Perhaps because of the Godolphin connections, Thomas moved to Helston. It was the son of Thomas and Audrey who moved into Trewinnard.

John Hawkins of Trewinnard (d.1676)

Thomas and Audrey's son, John, married Loveday, daughter of the Trenhayles of St Erth. In 1650, they moved into Trewinnard as a tenant. The Hearth Tax assessments of 1664/5 suggest that, as mentioned on page 71, the house was shared by *John Hawkines*, with six hearths, and *George Trenhale*, also with six hearths.

Some records survive of John's life in St Erth, such as when he paid poor rates of 12 shillings in 1653, 12 shillings again in 1658 and 6 shillings in 1664. Although the Hawkins were well established in Helston, where it is possible they already had a house, we know little of John and Loveday, save that they had several children, and that the heir was Thomas, who inherited on the death of his father in 1676.

Thomas Hawkins (d 1716)

Thomas Hawkins was a lawyer based in Helston. His first wife was a daughter of the Praed family who were rich in lands and influence in Lelant and St Ives, a family who in 1668 had acquired a third of the freehold

The 1683 marriage settlement for the marriage of *Thomas Hawkins of Helston gent and Anne, daughter of Christopher Bellott of Bochym, esquire.*

of Trewinnard. Thomas and Honor had one daughter but neither wife or daughter appear to have survived and Thomas was free to re-marry.

A deed of 1683 details the settlement made for the marriage of *Thomas Hawkins of Helston, gent and Anne, daughter of Christopher Bellott of Bochym, esquire.* This deed, signed and sealed by Ann Bellott, Christopher Hawkins, Christopher Bellott of Bochym and George Hawkins, was a complex arrangement. George Hawkins, presumed to be acting for Thomas' late father, gave to the Bellott family one third of Trewinnard, on the understanding that on marriage between Thomas, the son and Anne it should, together with the sum of £500, be brought back to Thomas as her dowry. Anne Bellot was not only a daughter with a dowry, but the co-heiress of a wealthy estate at Bochym.

Another curious survival is the document by which it appears Thomas was arranging to obtain the St Aubyn one third interest in Trewinnard Manor and Trewinnard Mills. The document states that Thomas Hawkins of Helston, gent. *"promises to pay the said Sir John [SeyntAubyn] 20 guineas when he shall marry and bring his lady (whoever she may be) home to Clowance".*

Nothing may have come of this, since in 1685 Thomas is said to have purchased the one third interest in Trewinnard that had been in the Penrose family. This purchase presumably gave him some security and enabled him to start building a new house at Trewinnard.

Thomas died in 1716 leaving his estate to his son Christopher, who was 22 years old. He also left him the stone built town house in Helston, already owned in

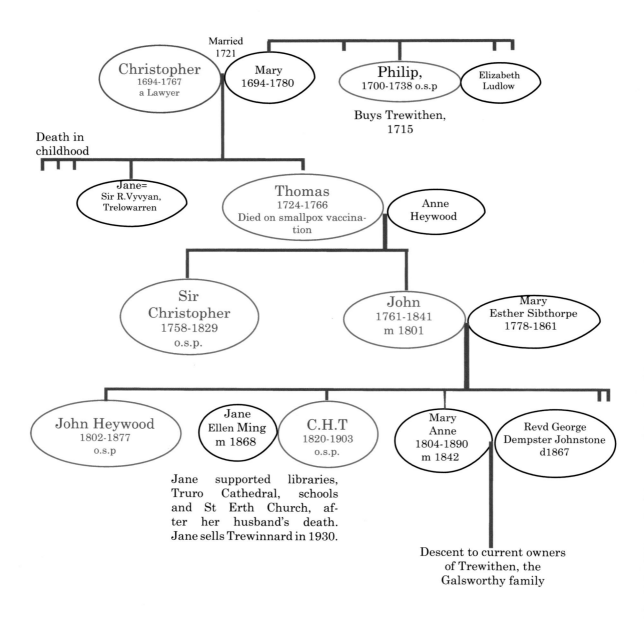

Married
1721

Christopher
1694-1767
a Lawyer

Mary
1694-1780

Philip,
1700-1738 o.s.p

Elizabeth
Ludlow

Buys Trewithen,
1715

Death in
childhood

Jane=
Sir R.Vyvyan,
Trelowarren

Thomas
1724-1766
Died on smallpox vaccina-
tion

Anne
Heywood

Sir
Christopher
1758-1829
o.s.p.

John
1761-1841
m 1801

Mary
Esther Sibthorpe
1778-1861

John Heywood
1802-1877
o.s.p

Jane
Ellen Ming
m 1868

C.H.T
1820-1903
o.s.p.

Mary
Anne
1804-1890
m 1842

Revd George
Dempster Johnstone
d1867

Jane supported libraries,
Truro Cathedral, schools
and St Erth Church, af-
ter her husband's death.
Jane sells Trewinnard in 1930.

Descent to current owners
of Trewithen, the
Galsworthy family

The Hawkins family of Trewinnard and of Trewithen:
Names in red follow the senior Trewinnard line; Names in blue follow the line for Trewithen.
The two branches intermarry with Christopher and Mary in 1721.
The surname 'Hawkins' is not noted on the chart.

1683 and which must have been of some consequence, since when visited by James Heywood years later, in 1757, he considered it

'a good house built of stone (which is the best I saw in the Town) where he resides for about two months of the winter season'.

Christopher Hawkins (1694-1767)

Christopher Hawkins inherited in 1716 and in 1721 married his cousin, Mary Hawkins from the Grampound branch of the family. They moved to London, where he was a successful lawyer, accumulated considerable wealth and the nickname *ironspurs*. He and Mary had several children. Although his son Thomas was then 26, it was said that it was because only two of several children survived childhood that they 'determined on removing to the country'. They left London for Trewinnard about 1750, taking with them the famous coach. However Christopher had kept in regular touch with affairs at Trewinnard, which had been left in the care of his steward, James Penrose who sent back to him monthly summaries of expenditure against income received. Christopher had also acted as trustee for his cousin Philip Hawkins who died young.

Christopher Hawkins
of Trewinnard (1694-1767).
This portrait by Alan Ramsey
shows Christopher's black eye.

Like other business men and attorneys of his time, Christopher had a wide variety of business interests and these included acting for estates, lending money and collecting money. One example is a deed that shows he had been appointed receiver of the very considerable Arundell and Harris estates of William Arundell of Trengwainton, which appear, in any event, to have been mortgaged to C. Hawkins of Trewinnard. Christopher also acted for John Prideaux, a minor, in managing the Bassett estates, giving rise to the Bassett conviction that Christopher had too greatly feathered his own nest. The accounts of his administration ended in 1756 but were disputed and not agreed until 1768. Christopher also acted for his relation Philip Hawkins in administering Trewithen, completing work on the new house at Trewithen, which had been left to Philip's sister, Mary (Christopher's wife) and her son. It was Christopher who, in 1739, paid Thomas Edwards, architect and clerk of works, for work at Trewithen.

Christopher's considerable fortune was invested in all manner of trade and activities. His papers include a receipt of 1720 for the purchase, at a cost of £600, of £1000 of stock in the Royal African Company. He invested some £700 in the famous South Sea Company. When lotteries were introduced, he, like other gentry, spent

Mary Hawkins, (1694-1780)
Christopher's wife was his cousin.
This 'formidable matriarch' was
painted by the famous John Opie.

considerable sums, such as first £23 and then the enormous amount of £97 9s 6d for tickets in 1762.

Christopher also lent money. Interest on loans and the mortgages, such as those he had on the Godolphin estate, provided him with a substantial income.

He made some monies from mineral rights, and from a variety of other ventures, such as cellars or his share in a pilchard seine at Pentewan, St Austell.

A curious light is shed on the legal practice of the time and perhaps on the way a lawyer accumulated wealth by the will of Mary Gryles of Trebartha in 1728. She was a widow who left specific bequests which included that to *'my servant maid, usually distinguished by the name of waiting-maid', £10*. She left a 'mourning ring' to four friends, but left all her lands in trust for the benefit of her kinsman Francis Rodd. However, this was only on condition that *'he is not already married to or shall not at any time take to wife Jane Parker, now living in Covent Garden'*. In the event that Francis married Jane Parker, all the property was to go to Chris. Hawkins of Trewinnard, who was possibly the attorney. We do not know whether Francis married Jane and suspect that Christopher kept the lands.

It was said that Christopher added to his inherited money, but that he was a man of prudence who saved and was careful with what he had. He does not seem to have been a man of excess or fancy, and neither at Trewithen or Trewinard is there any evidence of fashionable gothic decoration or even of architectural fancy. He died in April 1767, aged 73, only one year after the death from a failed small pox injection of his son Thomas. It was therefore Thomas' grandson, then a boy, also called Christopher, who inherited not only the assets at Trewinnard but also the assets of Trewithen.

The boy's grandmother was that Mary Hawkins who survives in story as a powerful woman. She controlled the destinies of Trewinnard and Trewithen from her husbands death in 1767 until her own in 1780. She continued to live at Trewinnard, although making regular visits to Trewithen. It was her famous coach that took her to church twice each Sunday, at St Erth.

The Hawkins Account Books

The ledgers cover a number of periods, particularly that from 1749 to 1767, and are a rare and fascinating account of household expenditure. The accounts record the expense of household and stable, payments to and the work of stewards, barber, gardeners and coachmen. They note supplies such as newspapers, books and

A receipt from 1720 for the purchase by Christopher Hawkins, at a cost of £600, of £1000 of stock in the Royal African Company.

Entries in 1729 include a doormat, gardeners' wages, horse-beans, apple trees, freight of sugar, nails, horsehair, a carrier from Falmouth, the glazier....

A summary of expenditure for the period May 1731-May 1732:

Stable	£68. 6. 6
Cellar	£36. 9. 6
Servants wages and Liveries	£32. 0. 0
Incidentals	£80.15.10
Cloth[e]s	£29. 0. 0
Housekeeping	£87. 5. 9
Total	£363.10s.10d.

There are other extracts from these accounts in chapters 11, (the house), 14, (the coach), and 16 (mills and waterways).

Cellar costs in 1727-8.
The considerable quantities include hogsheads of claret, hogsheads of red port, hogsheads of cyder, 10 gallons of Brandy, 10 gallons of rum, white wines in quantity, a lot more claret, and 'strong beer'.

Summary of expenses.
The year from May 1732 totals £319.2s.10d.
Photographs taken with the permission of the Royal Institute of Cornwall.

the post, and purchases made through Hawkins' own 'cellars', or warehouses. They record money spent on the parish roads, his own estate roads, on the bridge and causeways at St Erth, on the church and on the school where he contributed to and paid the master's wages.

There seems little of the 'inappropriate' spending that might justify the investigations of a modern newspaper, but the accounts are still a fascinating picture of every day life, even if some cryptic references are not understood. The expenses include the trivial, such as wigs, 'gouty shoes', knives and forks, a 'box of linen from Exeter' for a new bed and also larger amounts such as Lottery Tickets.

A considerable amount was spent most years on *liveries*, or servants and staff clothing, Entries include reference to a 'hop frock' for a male worker, since agricultural workers still wore frock dresses.

The amounts spent can be summarised and show that, for instance, a great deal was spent on the gardens in 1772-73. Between 1753 and 1757 the expenses of the house averaged about £400 per year, at a time when Thomas Pascoe, the farm manager, was paid £8 a year.

Jane, Lady Vyvyan, d.1776.
Daughter of Christopher Hawkins (d.1767) and aunt of Sir Christopher Hawkins (d.1829).

The Hawkins of Trewithen

Philip Hawkins senior was descended from the younger brother of the Mevagissey Hawkins family. This Philip Hawkins was, as reported by Tonkin, *'the wealthiest attorney this county ever produced'*. He lived in Grampound and renovated Pennans, adding, around 1720, an H shaped block. His daughter Mary married Christopher Hawkins of Trewinnard. In 1728, his second son, Philip, had, after university at Oxford and a

A design for Trewithen,
by Thomas Edwards, c.1735.
Trewithen, started much later than Trewidden, is larger and more ambitious than Trewinnard.

spell in London as an attorney, bought Trewithen from Courtney Williams for £2,700. Philip enjoyed life in London and a three month visit to Paris in 1722. In 1727 he became member of Parliament for the family controlled borough of Grampound and remained an MP until his death in 1738, spending much of his time in London rather than Cornwall.

Rather than demolishing the earlier house, Philip chose to improve it. By 1730, Thomas Tonkin wrote that Philip had 'new built a great part of the house'.

There are some sketches for improvements to Trewithen which appear to be from 1730. There are also unsigned and undated designs for rebuilding it as a Palladian villa, which are thought to have been drawn up by James Gibbs (1682-1754), of whose Book of Architecture, published in 1728, Philip had a copy. Work continued through the 1730s and, Thomas Edwards of Greenwich was commissioned to start work in 1735.

Philip died in 1738, only a couple of months after correspondence shows he was working on the additions and changes to the house at Trewithen. It is said that he had much loved his recently married wife but, although he provided for her a comfortable annuity, his will *'gave 'to my dear wife the liberty of remaining in Trewithen House three months after my decease and also the entire liberty of making use of the cellars and all sorts of provision which shall be in my house at the time of death'.*

Philip died childless, and the house, managed by his cousin Christopher Hawkins of Trewinnard as Trustee, passed to the family of Christopher's wife and Philip's sister Mary Hawkins.

Thomas Hawkins of Trewithen (1724-66)

Thomas was the son of Christopher and Mary Hawkins of Trewinnard, but inherited Trewithen through his mother, the sister of Philip Hawkins who had died without issue. Thomas Hawkins thereby combined the two branches of the Hawkins family. He had come of age in 1745, and joined the army, quickly achieving the rank of Colonel in the Guards. Since such positions were still obtained by purchase, this would not have been a reflection of ability, but rather of his considerable wealth. In 1747 he was elected MP for Grampound, which he represented for seven years.

He inherited Trewithen in 1738 when he was 14, but may not have visited or lived there until 1753, when he was 31, having been happy to let his father, mother and their agents run Trewithen. It was his father who finished works at the house and as trustee paid the bills.

This seal from an onion shaped bottle is the earliest dated fragment with a Cornish name. It bears *Trewithen 1695* below a helmet and crest. The date is prior to Hawkins ownership of Trewithen.
Private collection

A re-useable wine bottle from c1725 bears *Trewinnard* written over two lines. Until about 1720, onion shaped bottles were usual, but this is the rare half-size 'bladder' shape, that preceeded the more usual 'mallet' design. Following a treaty of 1705, Port became the principle available drink, so these bottles, now valuable items, were used to decant fortified wine.
Size: 7.5" high; Max. width: 5".
Private collection.

Thomas married Anne Heywood, the daughter of James Heywood, a wealthy London merchant. It is said that the interior designs at Trewithen by Thomas Edwards were down to Anne's 'metropolitan tastes'. Edwards seems to have left by 1761 and the interior designs were completed by Sir Robert Taylor.

Once Thomas and Anne were married, works continued at Trewithen. Records in the Royal Institute of Cornwall record the works, which have been admirably researched by Pam Dodds in her books on Thomas Edwards, the architect, and on 18thC building accounts. Much of Thomas' married life was spent at Trewithen, where he was an enthusiastic manager of his estate, interested in the wellbeing of his tenants.

Sadly, his enthusiasm for the new smallpox inoculations and a wish to set his tenants an example with this dangerous procedure, resulted in his death from smallpox at the young age of 42. His death took place a year before that of his father Christopher,

Thomas and Anne had five children, the eldest of whom drowned while boating at Eton. His second son, Christopher inherited the estates of both Trewinnard and Trewithen, which last, being the house in which he was brought up, thereby became the chief house of the family. A third son, Thomas *'died in consequence of eating an ice cream after dancing'*. The youngest brother, John, whose life-long interest was the sciences, lived to inherit from his brother, Sir Christopher.

Philip Hawkins (1700-1738)
Purchaser of Trewithen.

Thomas Hawkins
of Trewithen (1724-1766).

Sir Christopher 'Kit' Hawkins (1758-1829)

Christopher was only eight years old when his father died; his grandfather, Christopher Hawkins only lived another year. The young Christopher was therefore much influenced by his redoubtable grandmother, who is said to have made weekly visits to Trewithen and to have managed both Trewinnard and Trewithen with, so runs the legend, a rod of iron. Mary Hawkins lived on at Trewinnard until her death in 1780 at the age of 86, and was clearly a considerable character. When Kit died, it was in the family tomb at St Erth, with his grandmother, rather than with his father or mother, that Sir Christopher was interred.

Sir Christopher, known to all as 'Kit' Hawkins, was someone larger than life about whom stories accumulated. It is difficult to get a clear idea of what he was like. Now best known for the 'borough mongering' written up by S. Baring Gould, he owned and managed the appointment of several MPs in the so called rotten boroughs and his unwavering support for the government

Sir Christopher Hawkins.
(1758-1829)
This is said to be his only portrait.

or the importance of his parliamentary interest gained him his Baronetcy. It also brought him wealth, great notoriety, and in 1807 a criminal charge of corrupting a parliamentary election, a charge which apparently vanished when no witnesses turned up. Despite this he seems to have been respected in Parliament and was father of the House of Commons when he finally retired.

The 'Cornish Borough Monger' was recognised as a man of greedy business interests and an 'ambitious intriguer'. Richard Barwell, an opponent who lost an election to him at Tregony, wrote *'his unhappy affection for borough and parliamentary consequence appears to be as much under the stimulus of a blind God as is our vulgar and more common lusts.'* His competition with the Basset family for parliamentary influence ended in a feud, not only for political control and profits, but because there had long been claims that Kit's grandfather, Christopher Hawkins, had defrauded the Basset family while he was their trustee.

Another dispute resulted, on 28 March 1810, in a duel between Sir Christopher Hawkins and Lord de Dunstanville. It was said in a report in the Royal Cornwall Gazette that Hawkins was the challenger and that *'the boroughs were the cause'*. *'On Wednesday se'night a duel was fought near London…His Lordship was seconded by Sir Edward Buller and the baronet by Captain Temple. The parties exchanged two shots, neither of which took effect. The seconds then interfered and the parties retired from the field'.*

In 1792 James Boswell wrote of Sir Christopher Hawkins, *'The present representative goes on accumulating. He is said to be exceedingly rich, and he lives on a very economical plan, and very retired, though he has contrived to negotiate with Lord Falmouth for a seat in Parliament for the borough of St Michael, and thus has been made a baronet'.*

Sir Christopher Hawkins inherited great wealth and property, but continued to add to this property throughout his life. This included the purchase in 1813 of the manor of Connerton and the whole Hundred of Penwith. These lands had been in Arundel ownership since 1320 and this was the only Cornish hundred in private hands, giving rights over wide areas of land. When he died, the inventory of his property lists ran for page after page and to hun-

Trewithen, the seat of Sir Christopher Hawkins, Bart.
A hand coloured engraving from around 1820.

dreds of items. Given changes in value and purchasing power, it is difficult to relate this to values today, but it is sufficient to say that Sir Christopher Hawkins was an exceptionally wealthy man. This makes it the more surprising that he spent so little on domestic improvements at Trewithen or Trewinnard.

He did however spend money on business interests, which made him good returns. He opened tin and copper mines, invested in the new clay pits of St Austell, built a new harbour with a harbour railway at Pentewan and started a breakwater at St Ives, a town where he also had a wide range of interests.

A man of wide interests, he also enjoyed scholarly and scientific pursuits. Interested in the growing of apple trees, he had a new variety planted at Trewithen, a variety which is still there today. He was enthusiastic about improvements in agriculture, fertilizers, machinery and crops. Keen on new machines, he commissioned the worlds first steam threshing machine from Richard Trevithick, which was put to work for the first time at Trewithen in 1812.

Of Sir Christopher Hawkins, it was said, perhaps in an electioneering doggerel *A large deer park without deer, a large cellar without beer and a large house without cheer, Sir Christopher Hawkins lives there'*.

He seems to have been both mean or careful yet also generous and a convivial host. A man of energy who loved Cornwall, he also loved society life in London. We believe that he entertained well and at Trewinnard also, because a letter dated 1804 to him notes the delivery of *'5½ dozen claret being taken to Trewinnard'*.

James Boswell, the famous diarist, had met Sir Christopher in London and, when he visited Cornwall, used this connection to press for accommodation and food, as was, it must be said, customary for gentry travellers. Boswell was not altogether successful, complaining that Sir Christopher was difficult to pin down, *'which disconcerted my plan of quartering another night at Trewithen, which Sir Christopher by a letter to me... had endeavoured to evade. To Hawkins's evasive letter I had sent a verbal answer that we should be with him on Tuesday, so he was fixed by my resolute address and actually sent his chaise to Mr Gregors'*.

Boswell also mentions that on a very wet day in Penzance their party was joined by Sir Christopher who Boswell notes is *'a strange man to have a large fortune, for he rode without a greatcoat and was much wet'*. Boswell appears to contrast the Bassett family, who he describes as charming and entertaining, with that of the more austere bachelor Sir Christopher.

OBSERVATIONS

ON THE

Tin Trade of the Ancients

IN

CORNWALL,

AND ON THE

" ꙮctis "

OF

DIODORUS SICULUS.

BY SIR CHRISTOPHER HAWKINS, BART.
F.A.S.

WITH A VIEW OF THE MOUNT.

LONDON:
PRINTED FOR J. J. STOCKDALE,
41, PALL MALL.
1811.

Sir Christopher Hawkins published in 1811 an 80 page book on the ancient tin trade of Cornwall, principally aimed at showing the connections of the Phoenicians with that county.

An epitaph emphasised his charities, such as the free school for the poor of St Ives, and that he was a generous and benevolent landlord. He built on the wealth of his Trewinnard grandfather Christopher and so expanded the estate that it was his boast that he could *'ride from one side of Cornwall to another, without setting foot on another man's soil'.*

John Hawkins (1761-1841)

Sir Christopher had no children and so arranged that the Cornish estate should pass to his young nephew. However, the nephew, CHT Hawkins, was only nine years old on the death of Sir Christopher, so the estates went first to, and were administered by, Sir Christopher's brother, John, who had lived in Sussex most of his life, building the house at Bignor Park. A different sort of man to Sir Christopher, John was an academic, patron of the arts and founding member of the Royal Horticultural Society. John spent much time and money on the grounds at Trewithen but managed the estate for only 11 years before dying in 1841.

At Trewinnard, the only record of his work are the rebuilt farm barns, the two storey barn having a date stone of 1831.

John's eldest son was John Heywood Hawkins, (1802-1877), an MP for Newport, Isle of Wight. He inherited the Hawkins lands in Sussex, but died without issue in 1877 so that, on his death, his younger brother, Christopher Henry Hawkins, known as 'CHT', also inherited the Hawkins estates in Sussex.

CHT Hawkins (1820-1903)

The younger son, CHT, destined to inherit the Cornish estates from childhood, had no interest in Cornwall and there is no record of him ever visiting the county. Owner of an astonishing vast fortune he lived either at Bignor Park or in London, travelled much in Europe and concentrated on his collections of paintings, porcelain, stones, coins, ephemera and so on. After his death, the collection was sold for about £250,000 in a 16 day sale recorded with excitement in the newspapers.

He seems to have been an unusual and forbidding character, a dispiriting and retiring man, who at the relatively late age of 48, married Jane Ellen Ming. They are said to have met when she was running a pub in Dover. They had no children but after his death, she appears to have spent a fortune on charities, the Anglican church and Cornish causes.

The Hawkins vault lies immediately east of the Trewinnard chapel at St Erth. The chest tomb marks the burials of Jane Hawkins, 1776, Mary Hawkins, 1780, and her grandson Sir Christopher Hawkins 1829.
The coat of arms is cut in a decorative niche below the tomb.

Mrs Jane Ellen Hawkins

Despite her husband's lack of interest in Cornwall, Mrs Hawkins placed great store on the family connection with Trewinnard, rather than Trewithen, seeing Trewinnard as the original family seat. She spent a great deal of money in Cornwall, which included funding the west towers of Truro Cathedral, and the building of Trewinnard Court for the cathedral choir school, which opened in 1915. She also funded schools, including that at St Erth, where, in the parish church she also rebuilt and splendidly decorated the Trewinnard aisle. She reclaimed and had restored the Trewinnard tapestries and gave them to the Bishop and the Royal Institute of Cornwall.

After 1829, the Hawkins family had not much used Trewinnard Manor, which was tenanted and the mansion house became the farmhouse for the farm.

A deed of July 1914 may record the purchase of the final third of the freehold by Mrs Hawkins.

In February 1930, the freehold interest and 137 acres at Trewinnard was sold by Mrs Jane Ellen Hawkins to Mr Christopher Cardell Williams for £5,600, signalling the end of the Hawkins connection with Trewinnard.

Later Generations of the Hawkins Family

CHT Hawkins left no children and so the estate passed to the family of his sister, Mary Anne. She married the Revd. George Dempster Johnstone, so that Johnstone, therefore, replaced Hawkins as the family name. With the marriage of a daughter in a later generation, the family name changed again to Galsworthy, the name of the current incumbents at Trewithen.

Top: Outside the north gate of St Erth church is the school or church hall rebuilt by Mrs Hawkins.
Below: The inscription to a window in St Erth Church, where are also carvings commemorating the restoration by Mrs Hawkins and the connection with Trewinnard.

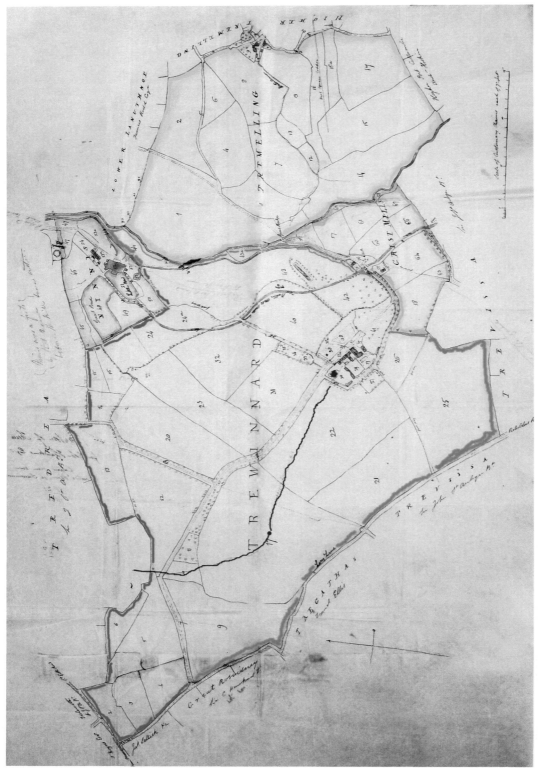

A plan of Trewinnard farm, copied around 1821 from one prepared for Sir Christopher Hawkins by Mr Proud, shows the extent of the farm, the separation of the two mill holdings and the farm and historic mining area of Tremelling, on the east of the estuary. *Photographed with permission of the Cornwall Record Office*

Chapter 7
Farming Tenants

Once Mary Hawkins had died in 1780, no member of the Hawkins family lived permanently at Trewinnard, Trewithen becoming the family home. Shortly after her death, the Trewinnard House and farm were advertised in the *Sherbourne Mercury* as for let with the description: *The genteel modern house has gardens, a pleasure ground and a few acres. Household goods and contents [which are] included in the letting, include a 'neat post chase' with horses.*

Whether it was let or not, Sir Christopher Hawkins appears to have kept the house available to him as a place to stay when on business in the area, his interests in St Ives, the mining areas, and in Penzance, being considerable. We know that James Boswell was able to stay at Trewinnard during his visit in 1792.

The main farm at Trewinnard had about 140 acres. A further 15 acres or so rested with the mill. Only a few acres were retained for the mansion.

The farm appears to have been one of the better farms in the parish. In 1658, of some 40 farms in the parish of St Erth been rated for taxes, 24 paid rates of under 4 shillings. Trewinnard on the other hand, was one of three (with Trelissick and Gurlyn) that paid 12 shillings, Trewinnard being the second highest rated farm in the parish. This suggests that Trewinnard was a farm on reasonable ground and one where a living could be made. Despite that, the Hawkins accounts of the 1750s show that the farm made a loss of over £96.00 between October 1757 and March 1759. although this loss may have included sums for mansion costs or for improvements charged against income.

Farming Tenants

During the 19thC, the farm was in the hands of the Goldsworthy family and would appear to have pro-

A 1788 newspaper cutting records a sad story which is one of few farm events from the 18thC to have been recorded.

... A *melancholy event at Trewinnard. On the preceeding evening, a lad, about fourteen years of age, came to a farmer's house to seek employ, but not getting any, desired to sleep that night in the barn, which was permitted. The next morning he came into the house and begged a bason of milk for his breakfast; but while a young woman, about eighteen years of age was setting it on the fire, he took up a gun and discharged it, by which the whole load of shot was thrown into the girl's neck, who languished four hours before she expired.*

On the coroner's inquest, the verdict was accidental death and the boy was suffered to depart. The innumerable accidents of this kind of which we have accounts from every quarter, shew that 'tis time for the legislature to enact some law, appointing a proper punishment for such persons as wantonly or at least carelessly plunge their fellow creatures into eternity by a sudden and immature death.

The dead serving girl was Miss Bethuel Bastard, the second name being a common one for children either found or illegitimate and supported on the parish.

---

vided an acceptable living for much of that time. In 1827, 2 shillings tax on Trewinnard mansion had been paid by Sir Christopher Hawkins with John Goldsworthy paying £1.10s.1/2d for the farm and John Gilbert paying just over 3 shillings for the mill. John Goldsworthy then moved into the mansion after Sir Christopher Hawkins' death. By 1835, John Goldsworthy was paying for both mansion and farm and John Gilbert for two other parts of the farm, presumably the mills. The size of these holdings was given in the 1839 Tithe Apportionment. John Goldsworth had farmhouse and mansion with 140 acres 1 rood and 9 perches. The value per acre in this apportionment placed Trewinnard farm in the middle of land worth for the parish.

The census of 1851 showed that John Goldsworthy of Trewinnard was a widower of 68 with two unmarried sons of 38 and 28 and two unmarried daughters of 36 and 34. He employed a live-in female servant and a live-in male farm servant with five labourers outside, employed on about 120 acres. He died in February 1865, two years after the auction in 1863 of one third of the freehold interest in the mansion, farmhouse buildings and land of 158 acres.

Mr Goldsworthy was of some importance in the area, and as a land commissioner, approved the enclosure for farming of 114 acres of common Towans at Phillack, *'there being no public highways or access across the land'*. He appears to have been succeeded by his son, since in August 1880, the Cornwall Times reported that Mr Goldsworthy had already cut the whole of his barley and that potato disease was particularly severe.

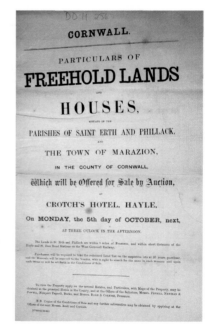

Advertisements for the auction in 1863 of Trewinnard and other freeholds.

In March 1918, James Hosking was recorded as having taken on the lease. Mr James Hosking must have been the farmer of a considerable enterprise, because a 1927 directory for the area notes his telephone number (Hayle 566), which was one of only seven telephones for the 63 people mentioned. These, save for a few gentry, were all commercial listings. James Hosking was still the tenant in 1930, when Jane Ellen Hawkins sold the freehold and 137 acres to Christopher Cardell Williams for £5,600.

It is thought that James Hosking continued as tenant of the farm during a number of changes in the freehold title. However he had left before October 1943, when the freehold and occupation of the farm and 137 acres was sold to Thomas Pascoe the Younger. Thomas Pascoe continued to run Trewinnard after the second World War, as a large mixed farm, bringing his family into the business as time went by. They also operated Trewinnard Manor for bed and breakfast with many

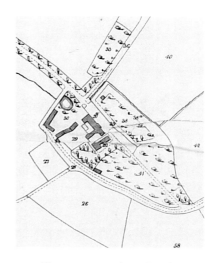

The 1863 auction plan for Trewinnard.

Note that a crease mars the house plan.

Details of the auction in 1863 of Trewinnard and other freeholds
and of land interests in St Erth and elsewhere.

bedrooms, but, it would seem, few bathrooms.

Popular and successful farmers, they sold the Manor House in 1967, and the farmland in 1970, to Sir John and Lady Nott.

The Title to Trewinnard

There had long been a difference between the owners of the freehold at Trewinnard and the occupiers of mansion and farm. The freehold had been divided amongst three families and although there had been changes in ownership of each third, the tithe roll of 1839 showed the freehold was still in the hands of three parties, namely the Revd John Molesworth St Aubyn, Mrs Sophia Praed (mother and guardian of William Blackwell Praed, a minor) and John Hawkins.

On 14 August 1863 an auction was advertised of a one third freehold interest in Trewinnard, thought to be the part belonging to the Praed family. When C.H.T . Hawkins took over from his brother in 1877, an abstract of title listed the Hawkins interest only in one third of the manor and barton of Trewinnard. By the time he died, in 1903, it was reported that his widow owned two thirds of the freehold, but that one third remained with the Reverend St Aubyn, a third which may finally have passed under a deed of July 1914. To complicate matters further, Hawkins seems to have had a lease or interest in the third controlled by St Aubyn possibly from an agreement in February 1760, when Christopher Hawkins had paid Sir John St Aubyn £90 for the reversionary interest on the barton for 'one life after two'.

In February 1930, all three parts of that freehold, the last Hawkins connection with Trewinnard, were sold by Mrs Jane Ellen Hawkins to Mr Christopher Cardell Williams for £5,600.

On 30 September 1931, Mr C.C.Williams advertised the manor house and farm for sale by auction 'at an early date', but eventually sold his freehold interest, in April 1934, to Councillor A E Ellis, a local business man from Penzance, for £8,500, thereby gaining a 30% profit. This was the last deal of a busy life for Albert Ernest Ellis. He offered Trewinnard to Penzance Council as an airfield, but did not long survive the purchase, dying a few months later in October 1934.

The freehold then passed first to Mr Ellis' widow, then to Frank Ernest Ellis a 'colonial solicitor', then to his wife, and was finally sold in October 1943 for the sum of £12,000, an increase that probably reflected the absence of a sitting tenant.

Trewinnard was owned by the Pascoe family from 1943, until sold to Sir John Nott.

Farming Life

Most farmers were for centuries the tenants of a landowning estate. This relationship had driven farming practice for centuries. Although farmers were often accused of being behind with rent, owners too found themselves in financial difficulty. Although it was common for tenancies to last several generations, as occurred at Trewinnard, the business relationship of landlord and tenant affected and often soured any approach to new ideas for farming, for capital improvements and farm planning. At Trewinnard, the landlord funded new farm buildings in 1831, but there is little evidence of other investment.

Day to day, a farmer's life continued to revolve around harvests and success when good weather made this possible. The 19thC had some particularly bad periods in the 1840s, in 1877-1879 and in 1883. The prolonged agricultural depression of 1887 became worse by 1893, one of many periods so bad that farmers wondered whether they would survive. Occasionally, political debates such as that on the Corn Laws would affect a farmer directly, but they were by and large immune to all but the events and trade of their immediate neighbourhood.

Between 1875 and 1896 rents fell by a half, a decline which gives some idea of how difficult farming was in that period. Periods of financial hardship were balanced by good years between 1850 and 1875, a period which also saw the rebuilding of many of the farmhouses around Cornwall.

The date 1831 records the rebuilding of a two storey barn and other farm outbuildings.

Water

Modern water systems have meant that we forget the difficulties and worries of previous generations about water supplies. Despite being in a river valley, water seems to have been a problem at Trewinnard, particularly in the quantities required by a 19thC house and by modern farming. The original wells and springs of the earliest farm have not been located.

An early improvement was the provision in the 17thC or 18thC of a leat or canalised water supply which ran from Trembethow Valley for about two and a half miles around the contours to Trewinnard. Fed by water from Trencrom Hill, it supplied a pond in the farmyard and pipes to the gardens and surrounding fields. This considerable feat appears to have been funded by the earliest owners of Trewinnard and the right to its use enshrined in the deeds. The leat from Trencrom hill is shown on the 1842 tithe map, but it is not certain when

A steam boiler re-used as a tank and placed on the wide hedge at the top of the farm.

it fell out of use. Although long disconnected, deeds still give to the owner of Trewinnard rights in respect of 'water from the Trembethow valley'.

Around Trewinnard, there is still evidence of attempts to improve water supply and storage. For instance, between the back door of the house and the farm cottage has been found a part brick lined cistern, probably for water storage rather than part of a sewage system. Although this may have been the site of the earliest well, the storage tank appears to be 19thC.

Another tank is under the north west corner of the house, where a large water cistern was built, as was not uncommon around 1820, under the floor of the raised ground floor.

Early in the 20thC there were tanks and pumps in the higher part of the garden. The top hedge, probably first built in the 18thC, was widened to a substantial bank so that a row of water tanks could be put on top, at the highest point of the farm. Old tanks were brought into use including a large steam boiler, itelf an interesting artefact. Pumps and a borehole were added to improve water supply to the house and farm.

Surprisingly, there is as yet no evidence of the hydraulic rams, pump systems or slate tanks common in late 19thC farming.

A Century of Changes

At the beginning of the 19thC, children tended to follow their fathers into farming. By the end of the century other opportunities meant that children could work and travel away. Farming, of course, was only one of the three activities for which Cornwall was famous and the other two, fishing and mining, were in decline.

Emigration from Cornwall, the object of much research and interest, resulted in changes in population and working habits. Following the failure of the mining industry in the 1860/70s, emigration overseas is famous for the part it played in changing the population of Cornwall; less well known is the emigration that took place 'up country' to England, not just for work in different industries but to where it was thought there were better farming opportunities.

Journeys remained difficult, although easier than in the previous century. During the 18thC it was unlikely that many farm workers would travel beyond immediate parish boundaries. It is difficult for us to imagine how little a man based or living on a farm near Trewinnard would have travelled. Improved roads and railways changed both attitudes and practice. Travel

Every farm made cider, and the granite troughs and crushes often survive as ornaments, as they do here at Trewinnard. This pile has pieces from two different crushes. The top piece, half rounded, should stand at right angles in the outer bowl of the lower piece. The middle piece of granite, with the spout, is not part of this crush, but part of a diffferent process.

brought new outlooks to a population who had very seldom moved far from the parish in which they were born. Farmers are recorded as having visited London to see the Great Exhibition of 1851, although until then they had never left their parish.

The arrival of train services allowed not only people but also goods to be shipped up country. Until milk could be stored and transported it could only be sold as butter, an example of how farm trade was restricted by poor transport. Travel improvements changed farms from being self sufficient in all things to providing trading opportunity to ship off the surplus produce. The improvement of roads meant that dung, manure and lime could more easily be obtained and the earliest machinery made the manual labour of endless forking of dung, field and so on, unnecessary.

Mechanisation was the most obvious of changes to a farmer's life. There had been some improvements at the end of the previous century, and machinery of increasing complexity was introduced through the 19thC, culminating in the steam threshing machines available from around 1900. These had a dramatic effect on the needs for labour and therefore on farming practice.

The labour required to work farms declined over the years and life for many farmers was, therefore, much easier. The women too did not have to work so hard in the fields or in cutting turves for the fire, or to cook and arrange for harvest suppers with large numbers of men assembled from other farms for harvest. The children of farmers could benefit from work at mills, and contribute funds to the central family farm fund.

Mechanisation meant a drop in labour but there were other changes as well. Railways and transport allowed the development of the early vegetable or flower markets. Even eggs were shipped up country, despite complaints that railway charges swallowed the profits so that some farmers arranged for shipment by steamer.

Farmers could now accumulate money reserves, unknown in early generations, although this also exposed them to other disasters such as losses through poor investment or from bank failures such as that at Helston and a later one at Penzance in 1896.

Although the Parish remained the focus for activity and social connection, wheeled traffic allowed greater connection between farms, villages and towns.

Religion had been of absorbing interest for most farmers. The rise of Methodism and of disparate independent churches had resulted in as many as three or four competing chapels being found in each parish, a process which only slowed with the appointment of a

Top: The main front in the 1930s, before landscape alterations of the 1950s.
Bottom: The stable yard. The early, re-used crested ridge tiles can just be seen on the stable roof.
From Reginald Tredinnick's manuscript History of St Erth, 1936.

Bishop to Cornwall at the end of the century. It was parish and chapel life which remained important until the First World War.

Despite the changing horizon of the Cornish farmer, the writings and diaries of such men demonstrate the continuing limits of their outlook and interests. Few events in London and even fewer events overseas were of interest or were considered relevant to their life on a farm.

Some political and administration changes did affect a farmer's life. These included the change in control of local rates, the start of the Poor Law Unions, and the arrival of paid rural police. In particular, the Education Act of 1875 provided more opportunities for a farming population.

The beginning of the 20thC continued to bring changes that would have been inconceivable in 1800. In 1902 a travelling myriorama, (a form of early cinema) visited the St Erth area and a motor bus started a local passenger service in 1903.

By 1910, the most apparent of the changes was in the farmer's living conditions, which had become more comfortable and spacious. In the farmhouse, likely to have been new-built within the previous forty years, cooking was no longer on an open hearth where turves or furze (gorse) were burnt, but on an iron range which transformed the labour of the housewife. Earth floors changed from being of beaten or limed earth to solid floors of timber or cement. Bedrooms acquired ceilings.

Outside in the fields, barbed wire and galvanised sheeting transformed life for the farmer. Fields and boundaries, animal control, shelters, even the storage and temporary waterproofing of ricks were dealt with differently.

Above any other element of change, the use of cement transformed farm and home. Cement floors to cattle and farm yards eliminated the deep mud and dung that had until then lain around the farmhouse.

A farmer of 1910, just before the First World War would have lived in a comfortable house with good floors, a parlour and bedrooms for the family, with a separate area for the servants. The days when all farm staff men slept in one room and women in another had gone.

Finally, The First World War not only changed the world and outlook of many, but also changed forever the old relationship between landlord and tenant. The previous century had seen more farmers becoming freeholders. Change in land ownership accelerated after 1918. It was this alone which made the greatest difference to farming life in the 20thC.

The Farmyard in 1967, before conversion of redundant barns as holiday cottages. Concrete hardstanding and pens show use for cattle. Buildings out of sight to the left were cart or implement sheds.

42 The Farmers Weekly, January 6, 1956
ADVERTISER'S ANNOUNCEMENT

THIS CORNISH MANOR HOUSE stands near the Hayle River and was once used by smugglers as a very convenient depot for their goods. There still remains part of a secret tunnel which is said to lead to St. Michael's Mount. Although the Manor was first mentioned in Doomsday Book, the present building is Georgian, dating from about 1740. It contains some valuable tapestries and panelling, and the grounds are noted for the fine box and yew hedges.

The Trewinnards lost their ancestral home hundreds of years ago after a family quarrel had led to the murder of a brother. The land then became Crown property until, years later, it was acquired by Sir Christopher Hawkins, High Sheriff of Cornwall.

The present owner of Trewinnard Farm is Mr. T. Pascoe, who breeds South Devon cattle and is a well-known show judge. He also has a large acreage planted with vegetables for the London markets.

Mr. Pascoe uses Shellspark vaporising oil in his tractor and Shell petrol in his lorries. All his vehicles are lubricated with Shell oils. The provision of top-quality fuels and lubricants is, of course, only one part of the Shell and BP Farm Service. The Service also provides technical advice on agricultural machinery, the storage of petroleum products, aids to poultry rearing and many other farming matters. From time to time, too, the Service organises the showing of films which have special appeal to farmers and countrymen.

A 1956 advertisment for Shell oils has a fine drawing by Roy Morgan. Although a tribute to Mr Pascoe and his farm, the history and the story of a tunnel are not accurate.

Sir John Nott stands before a
portrait of General Nott.

Miloska Nott and
grand daughter Siena.

The three children of Sir John and
Miloska Nott in March 2012:
L to R: William, Sasha and Julian.

Members of their family stand each side of Miloska and John Nott, in front of Trewinnard.

Chapter 8
The Notts, Farming and a Family Home

John and Miloska Nott bought Trewinnard in 1967 from the farming family, the Pascoes. The Pascoe family were respected for their fine herd of South Devon cattle, and for having built the imposing granite cattle yard with the proceeds from sales of winter cabbage during the Second World War. Although the land was high Grade I and II quality, the house and farm buildings were hard to maintain on a farming income. Jane Pascoe therefore took guests in the Manor House which had, at that time, 13 bedrooms. After the purchase John and Miloska reduced the size of the house to eight bedrooms and bathrooms. Over the years, the traditional farm buildings were converted into seven holiday cottages, supplementing the farm income from the 200 acres of good land. To this was added another 50 acres of ancient woodlands on the Devon/Cornwall border in the valley of the River Lynher, where the family own freehold fishing and shooting rights over around 500 acres.

Various Coats of Arms have been attributed to the Nott family over the years. This example is from the 16thC.

Nott Family Ancestors

The Nott family came from Hereford and Worcester to which counties it is possible that they arrived with Viking invaders of the 10thC. The origins of the name, *Nott*, appear to be Scandinavian. In the Dictionary of English Surnames, *Knott, Cnut, Knut, Canut* are all prominent. In Iceland, where there has been little further immigration since the time of the Vikings, the telephone book is full of Knuts and a few Notts. In England, the name Nott survives on the Herefordshire/Worcestershire border, the Devon/Cornwall border and in Yorkshire, all of which were once the border lands of the invaders. The Notts survived the depredations of the Norman invaders, but were reduced to local squires and yeoman farmers working good farmland on the

Welsh border.

It is from this stock that the Visitation of Worcester noted the armiferous and land-owning family of Nott which commenced with *John and Anselm Nott* in 1558.

At Shelsley Beauchamp in Worcestershire, the earliest names in the Parish Register include the Nott farming families who were parsons and who owned a watermill in 1613.

The Civil War raged fiercely in this corner of England and many parish registers and records did not survive. The Revd. Charles Nott, a parson of Shelsley Beauchamp, led the *Clubmen*, who were bands of local defence vigilantes. On March 5 1645, they drew up the Woodbury Declaration to protest at the *utter ruin by the outrages and violence of the soldier; threatening to fire our houses; endeavouring to ravish our wives and daughters, and menacing our persons.* Parliamentarian sources claimed the Clubmen had been stirred up *by malignant priests.*

The destruction of records during the 17thC has meant there is a gap in the family history until 'Burke's Landed Gentry' notes Charles Nott of Staunton-upon-Wye as baptised in 1695. Like many families of that time, few of his many children survived. His great grandson, a younger son and another Charles, left home to make his fortune.

Mr Nott of Carmarthen

Charles Nott had been a Herefordshire farmer, but in 1794, settled in Carmarthen in Wales where he became the owner of the first coaching inn on the road from the Irish ferry at Fishguard to London. He became wealthy as a large farmer and mail contractor. A traveller, 'Mr M' kept a diary of a visit to Carmarthen with his wife and son in 1801 at the time of the Napoleonic Wars. He describes Mr Nott's hostelry, the Ivybush Inn, as a very ancient built house,

...[with] good accommodation and civil people... Mr Nott, the master, appears to be far above the common rank of Inn-holders in Wales. The full entry from the diary of Mr M appears at the end of Chapter 14, a chapter which describes the difficulties of travel at that time.

General Sir William Nott (1782-1845)

William Nott, the great great grandfather of John Nott of Trewinnard, was the third son of Charles Nott of Carmarthen. As a boy of fourteen he joined the Carmarthen Fencibles and was one of the local militia hastily assembled by Lord Cawdor to march out and defeat a drunken French rabble which had landed at Fishguard as an invasion force in 1798, the last time invaders came to England. William's father, Charles Nott purchased a Bengal cadetship for William and commissions in the Royal Army for his elder brothers. Although William twice tried to retire from the Indian Army to manage his estate at Jobs Well outside Carmarthen, he lost all his savings when the Calcutta Bank went bankrupt. After this, he returned to India. A successful career saw him made a Sepoy General. He won a reputation as the hero of the First Afghan War and his statue stands in Nott Square, Carmarthen.

Or, a saltire gules between a medal proper, two eagles and a crown

The Twentieth Century

Although Nott cousins still farm in Herefordshire, John Nott's immediate family abandoned the land and became professional soldiers and colonial servants. John's grandfather joined General Allenby's advance into Palestine and became Governor of Gaza after 1917. His uncle Admiral Martin Nott DSO became the last Chief of Staff of the Royal Indian Navy. A distant cousin, Brigadier Donald Nott DSO OBE MC and bar, became Regimental Colonel of the Worcestershire Regiment. John's father broke the family's soldiering tradition and joined a family business in the City of London.

John's mother came from a Devon land-owning family called Francis. One of their ancestors, Sir William Francis, led the government's army when the Cornish laid siege to Exeter during the Prayer Book rebellion in 1549. Over a thousand Cornish rebels were slain at the Battle of Clyst St Mary. It was a disgraceful episode in West Country history and this unfortunate family connection was never mentioned by John when he became a Cornish MP. John's grandparents continued to live in Devon. John was 7 years old when he was evacuated to his mother's parents in Devon, at the outbreak of the Second World War.

John and Miloska Nott

After serving in the army with the 2nd Gurkha Rifles, John Nott went up to Cambridge and it was at Cambridge that he met his future wife Miloska. He went on to become a politician, and was Secretary of State for Defence during the Falklands conflict. A second career saw him accept jobs in Industry and as a bank chairman. Miloska too had an astonishing life in Nazi occupied and later communist Slovenia. Much more about their life is set out in the books of John Nott and, in particular, his autobiography *Here Today, Gone Tomorrow:*

Sir Thomas Nott, Knt.
'One of the Gentleman Ushers in ordinary of the Honorable Privy Chamber to his present Majesty, King Charles the Second'.
A 1794 print by Wm Richardson taken from a 1670 drawing 'from life' by R White.

The grave of Edward Nott, Governor of Virginia, who died in 1706. The inscription records that: *Under this marble lies his Excellency Edward Nott, late Governor of the Colony, who in his private life was a Good Christian and in his public life, a Good Governor....* Williamsburg, Virginia

Susan, daughter of Sir Thomas Nott, 1680
after Willem Wissing (1656-1687)

The Marquise de Sivrac and Her Son
(French great-great-grandmother to Sir John Nott)
By John Hoppner, RA 1758-1810

Captain Pleydell Nott, RN. 1780
After Benjamin West P.R.A. (1738-1820)

General Sir William Nott, G.C.B.
(1782-1845)

An earlier version of Nott arms, in a Herald's Visitation of Worcester, has as crest, a fox holding a fish in his mouth.

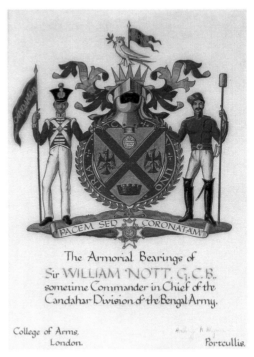

General Sir William Nott: The armorial bearings. The current arms of the Nott family are like those above, save that they are without supporters.

The Prime Minister, The Rt Hon Margaret Thatcher and the cabinet in December 1981.
Front Row: Peter Walker, Jim Prior, Keith Joseph, Peter Carrington, William Whitelaw, Margaret Thatcher, Quintin Hogg, Geoffrey Howe, Francis Pym, John Nott, Michael Heseltine

Recollections of an errant politician.

The Purchase of Trewinnard

With a love of the countryside and country life, the Notts needed a home where they could bring up their family. Not only that, but as a Member of Parliament for St Ives between 1966 and 1983, John Nott needed a house in his constituency.

It was by chance that John, alone in his cottage above the fishing port of Newlyn, saw an advertisement of a house for sale. A visit to the house with the cobbled courtyard, ancient stable block and panelled hall convinced him that this was the house to buy and love. His wife was persuaded to travel by sleeper from London to view it the following morning and the Pascoes, the vendors, accepted the offered asking price. The house, stable block and fifteen acres of land cost £18,500.

Three years later, having obtained a right of first refusal, the Notts bought the land and farm buildings from the Pascoe family for £40,000. Although this may seem a paltry sum for Grade I and II land today, the entire sum had to be financed. John Nott believes it was due to Miloska and her skill in running the farm that they survived.

Celebrating the General Election victory in 1966.

Inspection at Sandhurst as Secretary of State for Defence, 1982.

Miloska Nott picking daffodils at Trewinnard

Early Farming

The land at Trewinnard is warmed by the Gulf Stream. This, and mild weather, means that it is possible to double-crop the land, growing vegetables in winter and cereals in the summer. The farm is not far from that enchanted farmland in Cornwall known as "the golden triangle", because cash and vegetable crops can there provide a farmer with a good living. The West Country is gamblers' country because so much of horticulture there depends on weather. Spring greens, broccoli and early potatoes are very profitable when frosts in other horticultural areas mean that prices rise.

In the early days of living at Trewinnard, the Notts had no money for working capital or equipment, so the land was rented for growing daffodils. After four or five years spent watching others take the money, the Notts decided to develop the flower business for themselves and bought a ton of bulbs, enough for six rows of flowers. Since bulbs double in weight every two years, there were, by the time daffodil growing was given up, some twenty-five years later, nearly 75 acres of daffodils with thirty different varieties.

Miloska Nott was saddled with the responsibility of the farm because her husband was in London for much of the week. Raised during the war on a small farm in the hills of northern Slovenia, she was prepared to grow anything to meet the needs of the bank account. In the early days snowdrops, primroses, violets, pinks and anemones were all grown with Miloska sitting up half the night bunching flowers in the garage. As time went on, she had to manage up to 60 flower pickers and sell 300 boxes of flowers a day.

Stock Bull: *Merryhill Upstart*

On the land not needed for the bulb business, the Notts kept Hereford cattle, starting with four cows and a bull and building the herd up to number 100 Herefords in a suckler herd, the young bulls being sold to the local dairy farmers. Calving and chasing runaway animals kept them busy day and night, and ensured that the local MP was forced to keep close contact with the realities of life. However the land was too rich for the Herefords who were difficult to keep in condition. Even when established, the Hereford herd only just about broke even.

The Herefords were therefore replaced by sheep. These were at first Devon Longwool, which were then replaced by 300 Dorset ewes. Although their care involved long hours and much patience with an animal

A Dorset Ewe

Miloska, Lady Nott picking daffodils at Trewinnard with Trencrom hill in the background.

often described as motivated only for suicide, the sheep were profitable, despite the late nights involved with lambing. There was good business in the export of lambs to France. However, European Community rules, intended to subsidise hill farmers through profit claw-back, changed the operations and killed a perfectly viable business.

The flower business was profitable and it became the principal activity on the farm for many years. However this became a real burden. Caring for the bulbs involved nearly three months in the spring, after which the bulbs needed to be sprayed every week. In July, half the acreage was lifted and the bulbs graded. The surplus was then sold and the rest replanted during August and September.

Although the farm paid its way, it became apparent that, as had happened for several periods in the history of Trewinnard, the money that could be earned by John Nott when away from the farm, suggested that the daffodil business made little economic sense.

The concentration of purchasing power in the hands of large supermarket chains has killed the small farmers of West Cornwall. When Trewinnard was purchased, it was surrounded by dairy farmers who were the life and soul of the area. The greed and monopoly power of the leading supermarkets has destroyed every dairy farmer, and none exist there any more. The large supermarkets should have been broken up, but no government has dared to take them on.

Were it not for a farmers' love of the land, no one in their senses would engage in agriculture. John Nott believes that it is a love of farming and the land that has meant that the best experience of his life has been a return to farming after a family lapse of 200 years.

Maintenance and management of the land must continue whatever the economic environment, and just as has been the case for centuries, country activities continue at Trewinnard with the addition of a couple of days rough shooting a year.

The commitment of the Notts to such country pursuits resulted in their obtaining freehold fishing and shooting rights in East Cornwall, to which was added the freehold of some ancient woodlands. This has provided another element to the activities at Trewinnard, and another site to demonstrate a commitment to the preservation of the countryside.

Central to John Nott's love of Trewinnard was his early upbringing in the countryside of Devon and his interest not just in politics or business, but in farming or country pursuits. Trewinnard therefore remains a cen-

John Nott photographed during a ploughing competition.

Many pictures in this section are from originals painted by Ashley R Boon, in 1988.

Sir John Nott has always enjoyed country pursuits and the management of land for wild life.

tre of farming activities, and John and Miloska hope that their grandsons will feel as passionate about the countryside as do they.

Although it is no longer possible to earn a living in the world of mixed farming unless part of a large farming enterprise, there is still a niche for the part-time farmer who earns some of his living elsewhere but sustains his spirit with country interests.

This combination of earning activity remains the same as that required of the owners of Trewinnard since the 14th century.

Dogs at Trewinnard.
Photograph by Angela and John Hicks.

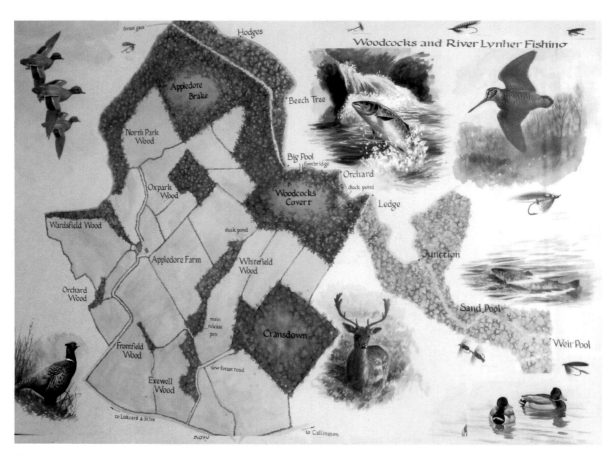

The Lynher valley, Cornwall: Fishing, shooting rights and ancient woodlands were bought to protect the countryside and animal life. *Painting by Ashley R Boom, in 1988.*

The farmyard and buildings before renovation.

The six holiday cottages after conversion.

The original farm house
renovated for holiday use.

A view of Trewinnard from the north east, with St Micha

From an oil, 135cm x 168

unt in the top left corner and St Ives Bay in the top right corner.
Marcus May: 2006.

Trewinnard from the south,
painted by Ashley R Boon, 1988.

Trewinnard Manor and farmbuildings in the 1980s.

The Development of House and Grounds

This building, which has an early central chimney stack and 55 degree roof pitch for thatch, is the oldest surviving building on site and probably the 16thC farm house. It is now a holiday house opposite the back door of Trewinnard Manor

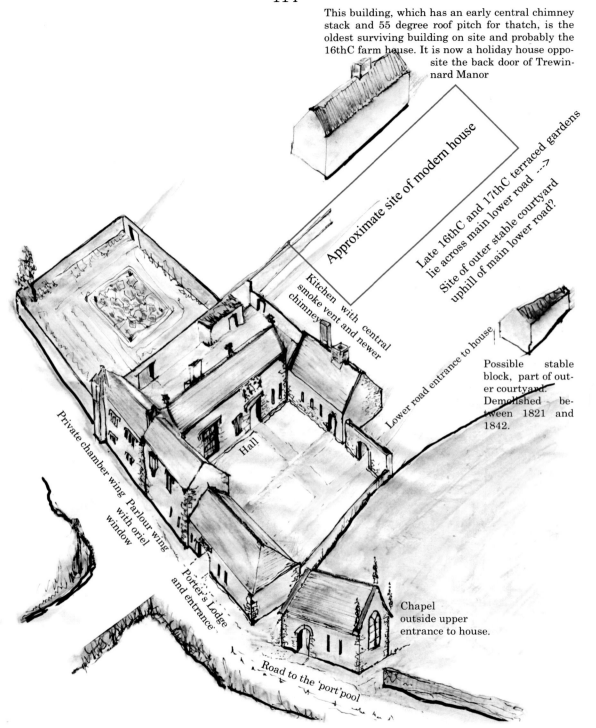

Approximate site of modern house

Late 16thC and 17thC terraced gardens lie across main lower road --->
Site of outer stable courtyard uphill of main lower road?

Lower road entrance to house

Kitchen with central smoke vent and newer chimney

Possible stable block, part of outer courtyard. Demolished between 1821 and 1842.

Hall

Private chamber wing
Parlour wing with oriel window

Porter's Lodge and entrance

Chapel outside upper entrance to house.

Road to the 'port' pool

A reconstruction of how Trewinnard might have looked some time around 1550, seen from the south.

The reconstruction is based on available evidence, but without archaeological examination is conjectural.

Chapter 9
The Early House

Trewinnard was the home of the Trewinnard family who, for three hundred years, were a leading family of the county from the 14thC to the middle of the 16thC. Although their earliest house may have been relatively small, the family were mentioned by Leland in the record of his tours between 1533 and 1550 and this Trewinnard house was the only one to be recorded near St Erth, suggesting that the house was of some importance. Comparison with other houses for gentry of similar status, power and influence suggests that the Trewinnard house must have been a considerable building. It is likely to have included a central hall, outbuildings, offices, a parlour, family wing, stables and stable yard and perhaps even a brewery.

The Site

It had long been thought that the current Trewinnard manor was built on the ruins of the medieval mansion. This cannot be so, since the first phase of the modern house was built as a new build. It is only the later phases of the current house which include materials from the demolished manor, implying therefore that the old manor was demolished in order to make materials available for the extensions to the modern building.

The site for the house has to be sought within the banked and ditched enclosure that bounded the earliest farm on the site. A number of sites both outside and within the original banked enclosure of Trewinnard have been suggested, and although archaeological excavation might provide certainty, we have other clues that suggest the site must be identified as lying to the northwest of the present manor house.

First, the road network associated with the earlier medieval farm above the harbour at Trewinnard suggests a logic for the house site. An early road entered the

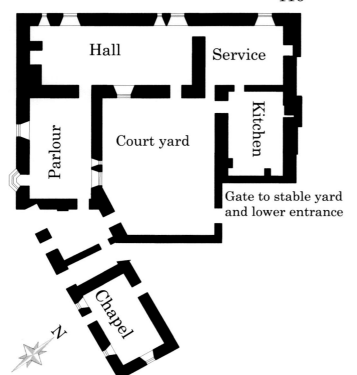

Hall

Service

Parlour

Court yard

Kitchen

Gate to stable yard
and lower entrance

Chapel

N

Trewinnard Mansion

A conjectural plan of the hall, courtyard and other buildings of the old house has the elements common to most courtyard houses of the time. It is based on Carminowe, a house for a family of similar status in the same area. However, the Trewinnard/Mohun house must have been larger than this with additional service yards and dwelling space, which are not shown.

In 1664, the house appears to have been occupied by two families and may have had 12 chimneys, suggesting additional accommodation wings.

Reconstructions are conjectural.

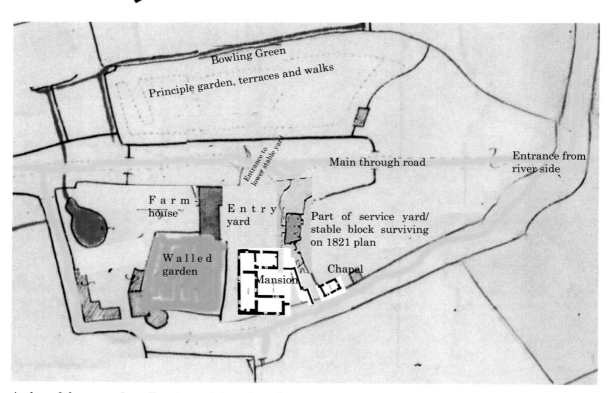

Bowling Green

Principle garden, terraces and walks

Entrance to lower stable yard

Main through road

Entrance from river side

Farm-house

Entry yard

Part of service yard/ stable block surviving on 1821 plan

Walled garden

Mansion

Chapel

A plan of the grounds at Trewinnard, based on the tithe map of 1842, shows the position of the early mansion block, chapel and stable yard. The walled garden is coloured green. The site stretches up the hill between two tracks. *Reconstructions are conjectural.*

south end of the fenced enclosure and ran straight across the middle, running out the other side along the line of the existing entrance drive. Another road ran outside the ditch on up the hill to a crossroads at the top where roads branched off to hamlets, farms, to trade routes and to St. Michael's Mount. This upper road curved around the early banked site. Close to the crossroads at the hill top may have been an upland chapel for the parish of Lelant, which later became the chapel to the manor.

Second, most house sites in Cornwall shared common factors. The earliest site was almost always a building platform made at right angles to the slope, with spoil dug from the upper end of the platform to level up the lower end. The bank at the higher end gave some shelter from the wind and weather. Such houses had the service end at the lower end so that any waste or liquid would, of course, run down hill. It is almost universal to find that early dwellings, whether moorland hovels, farm, hall or grand house, were built at right angles to the slope. These sites are usually about two thirds of the way up a hill, above stream level.

At Trewinnard, the original house would have been uphill of the lower road, stretching up to the higher road with a top entrance close to the chapel site. Access to the lower end of the house and to the farm below or to one side of it would have been from the lower road running straight through the site. There would have been no sense in first walking up hill, and then down again to get to the centre.

A site might have been considered to the north west of the enclosure, close to the existing holiday cottages. However, the earliest documents and maps all show a clear and consistent division of the enclosure between the mansion and farm elements. The Farm has always occupied that corner and so a site to the north west is unlikely given the historic division between mansion and farm.

Dwelling and status houses were usually uphill of farm activities, which would have been close to the lower through road. The principal entrance is likely to have been through a yard opening uphill of the central spine road. This siting of an outer stable yard is supported by the earliest maps of the site. Faint lines on the 1821 plan show a courtyard opposite the present front door with a building thought to be a stable block. These may be the remnants of an outer service court yard, demolished in the 18thC, because a new stable had been built that was not so inappropriately close to the new front door. Such a service courtyard would have been the normal entry point for a great house, since 'you sta-

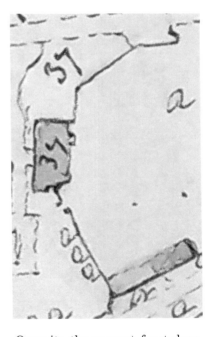

Opposite the present front door, the 1820 plan shows this building, which is thought to be from the earlier stable range. It has wide doors to the centre, a possible yard above it and below a gate to a field. It is on the line and position one could expect for a medieval entrance service yard.

bled your horse before you went into the house'.

The available evidence, the site, the earliest maps and the existing and historic road pattern all suggest that the site for Trewinnard Mansion was between the two roads, with the hall at the higher end, a site that fits available land study and practice in Cornwall.

The Term 'Mansion'

A further clue to the site of the early house is provided by the recorded separation in the earliest documents and plans between the mansion tenement and the home or barton farm. At Trewinnard there has always been a clear division between the mansion and pleasure gardens to the south east, separated from the farm to the north west. A mansion seems to have been defined as a house where the occupier did no land work, but merely received rents, dues or administered an estate.

Confusingly, a mansion would also have a smallholding acreage for domestic use. The principal farm had separate house, buildings, yards, farmer and staff. One indication of the early importance of the Trewinnard site is that the area of mansion and farm together was larger than the norm of some 80-90 modern acres common throughout much of Cornwall. An acreage of 140 acres is a factor supporting the existence of a mansion element of some importance. At Trewinnard, it is thought the earliest house must be sited within the area marked as for mansion and pleasure gardens.

The Early Hall House and Courtyard

A long single storey hall house built at right angles to the hill, would have become a hall of 1½ storeys, possibly raised by steps to allow secure storage below the hall. A courtyard would have grown round the hall. At the higher or up-hill end would have been added first a private room for the owners business, the 'Great Chamber' and then a parlour or family wing as changing times and status demanded more privacy for the family and a separation from communal living. The kitchen was usually separated from the living quarters to reduce the risk of fire, and so the main entry to the hall led in to a 'screens' passage built within the end of the hall. The timber partition to one side of the screens passage would then give on to the hall and in the solid wall on the other side would be two, perhaps three doors to provide access first to the drinks store, second to a food lobby area, third to a small court and thence to a separate building which was the kitchen. Kitchens, horses, animals and services would have been housed in wings or outbuild-

Open halls remain at Trerice, at Fulford in Devon, but are rare in Cornwall. This example from Cullacott, near Launceston, shows how the early hall at Trewinnard might have appeared.

ings around further courtyards.

Behind the hall, and near the private wings would have been a walled garden for family use, for herbs and for the women. This garden was seen as separate from the visitor's garden with more open walks and terraces for recreation or entertaining. At Trewinnard, this garden was below the through road. Their terraces can still be seen there today.

Throughout this period, basic defence against burglars, raiders or neighbours was necessary and the external walls of this courtyard and of the hall would have had relatively small windows. Trewinnard would have had a defendable gated entry capable of being barred and watched from a porters lodge. The hall, often at right angles to the entry would have been across the courtyard from the entrance. A courtyard house was capable of being defended against scavengers and the odd neighbour's raid. Records show that the Trewinnards were guilty of raiding other men's houses and that they also complained when such raids were made on them. The Trewinnards lived through 300 lawless years, and Cornwall was a long way from 'the King's writ'.

From about 1300, there was an increasing fashion for the licensing of chapels for family use. Such a chapel would normally have been available to tenants, visitors and travellers without need to enter the house area. Travel was considered a risky venture, and so, on arrival, one always gave thanks for the journey. A chapel would also be close to the house, and, as time progressed, sometimes provided with private access from the family apartments. At Trewinnard, the house was able to make use of the earlier chapel site, conveniently just outside the gates to the house. The site for the Trewinnard chapel has been identified as being on the upper road towards the top of the hill.

The roof for most houses of the time would have been at best of thatch, although reed, even gorse was used on occasion. Higher gentry houses had slate or stone roofs. The survival of medieval crested ridge tiles to the 1980s on the 1730s stable block, reused following demolition of the early house, suggests that the roof of that mansion was slated.

Although courtyard houses were the norm for gentry of the 15thC and 16thCs, few have survived in anything like their original condition. Courtyards can still be seen at smaller houses such as Roscarrock, (Port Isaac) or Pendeen, (St Just) and there are a number of houses where courtyards can be traced. One or two larger courtyard houses such as Penheale survive, although most of that court is missing, as it is also at Godolphin.

The small internal courtyard at Roscarrock has a courtyard typical of the 16thC.

The entrance to the courtyard at Pendeen, suggests how Trewinnard may have appeared.

Two or three strong doors built into the wall secured the screens passage. The door at Treguddick, South Petherwin, retains the early 16thC drawbar and slots.

Accommodation wings were only as wide as a single room with rooms leading one from the other. Early improvements were made by the addition of accommodation towers for visitors, towers which were fashionable for a brief period of the mid 16thC.

As further domestic accommodation was required, the size of courtyards changed to allow an inner court of smaller size, perhaps only 30-40 feet across, which provided domestic accommodation on all sides, although still with ranges of narrow width. There are examples of this late 16thC development at Menabilly and Caerhays. However, the courtyard house did not allow weather protected access from one room to another, so from the end of the 17thC onwards, almost all such courtyard houses were rebuilt and extended around the early hall. All other earlier buildings were usually demolished. The availability of longer pieces of imported timber in the 18thC also allowed larger spans and different designs for roofs.

The principle exception to the paucity of surviving courtyards in Cornwall is Cotehele on the Tamar. The building phases of this house have been much studied. The entrance gate seems first to have been to the west, adjacent to the chapel, with the hall at right angles across the court. A later southern entrance was then aggrandized around 1550, purely for display, to allow an entrance directly across from the hall. The often extended family quarters were at the higher end. The Trewinnards were not perhaps so mighty as the Edgcumbes, but, around 1500, as their marriages and connections show, would have been of similar status. It is not unreasonable to suppose that Cotehele suggests how the house at Trewinnard might have appeared.

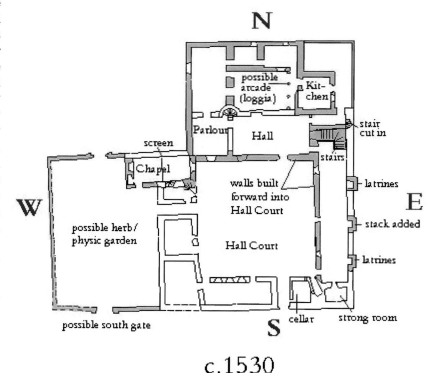

c.1530

A plan of Cotehele in the mid-16thC suggests how Trewinnard may have looked at the same time. *Picture courtesy CAU and the National Trust.*

Re-creating a plan for Trewinnard

Many houses of the 14thC to 16thC were buildings of similar style and size. We are fortunate that plans for the house at Carminowe, outside Helston, were drawn in 1860, when the little altered medieval house was demolished. Owned by what had been an important family, it had been of similar status to the house at Trewinnard, although unimproved in the 15thC or 16thC, when the family moved away. It is possible to use the plans for the building at Carminowe as a template for the Trewinnard mansion. If the plan for that building is superimposed onto a plan of Trewinnard, an astonishingly accurate and neat fit for the supposed site is provided. The plan also has the merit that the chapel is outside the entrance of a great gate and that the smallish courtyard has a hall with private chambers uphill of it and kitchen buildings behind it.

A Renovation in 1550?

The Trewinnard family appeared relatively well off during the first half of the 16thC, at a time when many in Cornwall were improving or adding to their houses in the latest style, benefiting from the rush of money brought to the country by the dissolution of the monastries and by the benefits that peace and trade brought to many families. Piers Edgcombe built a magnificent hunting and entertaining lodge at Mount Edgecombe. At Caerhays, descriptions of plasterwork, decoration and woodwork put in by the Trevanion family suggest that this was an astonishing building.

It is possible that around the middle of the 16thC, Trewinnard saw a similar modernisation. Although the Trewinnard family were on the decline, they retained lands, wealth and office, including time as stewards for the Duchy of Cornwall. The reason for supposing such a mid-century makeover at Trewinnard is the oriel window later built into the gable end of the Hawkins House. This is a special and delightful piece of stonework, typical of 1550, and may have been built into a parlour or family wing extension. It is thought to be a unique survival in Cornwall.

The re-used oriel window built in to the Hawkins House.

Trewinnard in the 17th Century

Trewinnard was, at the beginning of the 17thC, in the hands of the Mohun family. This became the home of the favourite son of Sir Reginald Mohun and his third, wealthy wife. The Mohuns were one of the greatest of families of the time in Cornwall. Despite his house and gardens at Hall, opposite Fowey and the great estate

The Mohun house would have had prestigious plasterwork like this example at Trewane, St Kew, which was fitted out for Brigett Mohun around 1632.

and house of Boconnoc, it was said he preferred to be at Trewinnard among the gardens there. Partly because we have evidence that Sir Reginald's other children had fine rebuilt and decorated houses, such as those at Trewane and Boconnoc, we assume that Trewinnard too would have been rather splendid, particularly as a favourite son with a wealthy mother from one of the richest and most powerful of families was likely to have followed the fashions of the wealthy.

Decorative window glazing, which included the arms of the Trewinnard Family was still present when Hals visited in the first quarter of the 18thC. Such glass and the collection of Trewinnard tapestries which, as explained in chapter 13, are thought to have been hung there, suggest that this was a very splendid courtyard house.

At the end of this chapter are two descriptions of house interiors in the 17thC. Although the two are of different status, they give an idea both of how such an early house worked and why changing times and standards caused older houses to be re-built, as were the two houses so described, and as was Trewinnard.

Decorative plasterwork was a 'must-have' status symbol of the early 17thC. This example from about 1630 was for a wealthy merchant in Penryn.

Plaster friezes were popular in the early 17thC. This pattern is found in more than one house in Cornwall.

Early first floor ceilings were barrel vaulted and common throught Cornwall. Pictured is one of few survivals in Cornwall at Harlyn House, St Merryn.

Left: There are several windows at Trewinnard which use pieces from older stone mullioned windows. Although now haphazardly re-assembled, they would have looked like this example from Trevadlock Manor, although Trewinnard's stonework had more roll work and were of higher status.

Surviving Elements.

The largest surviving piece of the medieval house, courtyards and operation is the cottage that stands today, downhill and to north west of the existing house, outside the kitchen door.

It is possible that this was the barton farm noted as within the farmhouse enclosure in 1820, and thought to have been on this site for some centuries before that. It is certainly the oldest surviving structure on the site. With thick walls, and a central chimney stack whose addition represents the earliest change from a central hearth to chimney, it also has a roof steeply pitched for thatch. Its position supports the plans suggested for the original mansion and the division of area between that mansion and the barton farm.

The walls of the existing mansion and outbuildings contain a considerable quantity of stone which appears in size and style to be from a pre-17thC building. Most of the window pieces appear to have been designed to accept the removable lead and glass frames of the time. Several mullions, cills, door and window sections were reused on the extension to the new Hawkins house. None are in their original build position, or fit together appropriately, but many of the mullioned window pieces show that they were from windows of high status work with double and hollow mouldings.

The oldest structure on the site is the cottage opposite the back door to Trewinnard Manor. The building is at right angles to the slope, with thick walls, and the roof is of a pitch to suggest it was designed for thatch. It has an early central stack.

A section of cill from a mullioned window, shows the hole that held the external protective bar and the slot for the lead cames of the glass window, lead-tied to the bar.

There are many surviving sections of mullioned windows, some showing work of high quality.

Part of a flattened four centred arch re used on the barn rebuilt in 1831.

A reassembled mullioned window to the cellar retains its bars.

Existing buildings have re-used stone from the earlier demolished house:
1. Massive quoins built into the north west extension.
2. Decorative pier heads survive in some eight places around the gardens.
3 The step to the front door, a fine piece of curved granite, may be a re-used hearth stone.

A second picture of the glorious mid-16thC oriel window built
into the Hawkins House during the 18thC.

Other survivals are few. Nothing of the chapel survives, save some pieces scattered to different houses in the neighbourhood. A collection of cut tracery that once stood on the front lawn has long vanished.

To the south west of the main house, at the bottom of steps to the southern cellar door, lies a curious entry between large stones. The construction appears on a different alignment and to be of earlier date than the Hawkins House. Inside is an opening into which a small man may crawl, cut within undisturbed rock. Tradition suggested, inevitably, that this was tunnel to the coast, a drain or a store. Its purpose remains unknown, but if it does *not* predate the early Trewinnard house, it may be some form of early store or cache.

Walls to the rear Tudor garden courtyard still stand and still form the boundary of the courtyard or farmyard to the immediate north of the site. Portions of this wall, although much repaired, may be of sufficient age to justify their being called medieval. In addition to the walled garden, there were garden areas below the house, including terraces for the long walk, garden and bowling green. The bowling green is now lost in trees, but its levelled plat can still be traced, the whole within the ringed ditch associated with the earliest Iron Age or early medieval farming settlement.

Finally, the outstanding 16thC survival is the splendid oriel window in the south east end of the manor.

House Descriptions from 1679 and 1698

Despite historic re-creation, museums and furnished rooms open to the public, it can be difficult to get an idea of layout and room use in a 17thC house.

Trewinnard belonged to a family of the highest status in Cornwall. Inventories exist for several buildings in Cornwall, and show the large number of small rooms which were needed for facilities when there were no shops around the corner. A good example is the description of the bishops large house at Cuddenbeak, outside St Germans. This house had a series of courts, of service rooms and ranges with many little rooms fitted in, above and around a main courtyard. It also had ranges with specific uses such as brewery or bakery and much of the buildings were for service use.

Two detailed accounts give some idea of how the mansion at Trewinnard might have been used. The first account below is for a priest's house in East Cornwall. Trewinnard would have been more splendid than this, but probably not so fine as the description of the Boscawen's house described in 1698.

Outside the southwest cellar door, at the bottom of the steps, is an opening just big enough for a man to enter, which leads to an underground chamber.

South west of the 1720 wing can be seen the corner of the west garden and then the spoil thrown over the site of the medieval house. Behind is the high bank built to provide privacy, with, on top, one of the water storage tanks.

North of the house is a cobbled courtyard, beneath which are drains, a cistern and perhaps the earliest well site. The 1820 study on stilts is in the centre.

Landulph Vicarage

The vicarage had a number of decorative plaster ceilings and stained glass. It was described in a terrier of 1679 as:

A Gate house, the walls of stone, with two chambers over, both planched and plaistored and covered with Shillin stone, and one ground room under which serves thereto for a celler.

The Gate house leads into a Court, on the north East Side of which lyeth this range of Houses,- a Stable, a Barne, a pound house with a Horse pound in it.

On the south side of the Court lyeth the Dwelling house, whereinto first the entrance is by an Entry, on the left hand of which as you enter the door there are two little Spences and three under rooms more for the keeping of Beer and other necessaryes. & . On the right side of this Entry there is another doore just against the other that leadeth into a room called the Hall, the floor of earth, and at the West end of it another doore, which leadeth into a grounde roome that serves now for a kitchen.

At the South End of the aforsayde Entry there is a door that leads into another court encompassed with a Dairy, an outer kitchen with a Dry over one side of it for malt, a malt house with a Chamber over it for wool or other things, and at the west side another little Court for poultry with a little house for the same in it.

For Chambers, there are five besides a Study and & little closet, one over the kitchen covered with Thatch and plaistered; another over the Hall, another over the Entry, another over the Butterye and another Over the Dairy all covered with Slatt stone ; the other roomes the South side of the little court covered with Thatch and the walls of the whole house made partly with stone and Partly with cob.

Tregothnan House

A grander house was Tregothnan, which belonged to the Boscawen Family, who were visited by Celia Fiennes in 1698.

Ye house is built all of white stone like the Rough Coarse Marble and Cover'd wth slate. They use much Lime in their Cement wch makes both walls and Cover Look very white.

There is a Court walled round wth open Iron gates and barrs.

The Entrance is up a few stone steps into a Large high hall and so to a passage that Leads foreright up a good stair Case. On ye Right side is a Large Common parlour for Constant Eating in, from whence goes a Little roome for smoking yt has a back way into the kitchin, and on the Left hand is a Great parlour and drawing roome-wanscoated all very well but plaine.

Ye Great Parlour is Cedar, out of yt is the Drawing-roome which is hung with pictures of the family, that goes into ye garden wch has Gravell walks round and across, but ye squares are full of goosebery and shrub-trees and Looks more Like a Kitchen garden as Lady Mary Boscawen told me, out of wch is another Garden and orchard which is something Like a Grove, Green walks wth rows of fruit trees.

Its Capable of being a fine place wth some Charge, the roomes above are new modell'd, 3 roomes wanscoated and hung as ye new way is, and ye beds made up well, one red damaske, another Green, another wrought some of ye Ladyes own work and well made up, wch is her own Roome wth a dressing roome by it. There is a dressing roome and a roome for a servant just by ye best Chamber.

There are two other good roomes unalter'd wth old hangings to ye bottom on wrought work of ye first Ladyes. Lady Margets work, yt was my Cos'n German, within that roome was a servants roome and back stairs, there was just such another apartment on ye other side.

Between all from the staires a broad passage Leads to a Balcony over the Entrance wch Look'd very pleasantly over the parke but in the Cupulo on ye Leads I Could see a vast way, at Least 20 mile round; ....

Chapter 10
The Ancient Chapel at Trewinnard

The first documentary mention of the chapel at Trewinnard was on 5 July 1372 when a licence was given by the Bishop of Exeter, Thomas Brantingham, to Henry Trewinnard and his wife. This license was to allow them to hold a divine service or allow it to be celebrated in their presence in their chapels of '*Trewennarde*' and at '*Trevyrvy*' (probably Trevorva, in Ludgvan). Since there is some evidence of an earlier unlicenced chapel, this was probably a licence that recognised an established building at Trewinnard.

The history of the parish in chapter 2 suggested that Trewinnard was once part of Lelant, and had an 'upland' chapel serving the high ground communities some distance from the ecclesiastical centre and church. Even today, one can trace the line of the old road from Trewinnard to Lelant. The parish boundary carefully follows the route of this deep cut old lane, disused for centuries, which once ran north east from Trewinnard. A relatively distant chapel could well have had a burial ground. However, the formation of the parish in the 12thC is likely to have removed that right, although its memory may have remained in legend. Such burial grounds were not common for manorial chapels.

The possibility of consecrated ground is sometimes deduced from the use of the word 'sanctuary' as a place or field name. On 5 July 1372 a '*Lower Sentuary*' was referred to at Trewinnard. The 1613 Terrier refers to a *sanctuary* between Trewynnard and Tredrey. Suggestions have also been made that the field south east of the Trewinnard chapel site had been called a burying place. However, it is not accepted that *sentuary* or *sanctuary* necessarily referred to a holy place but rather to land that belonged to a monastic or ecclesiastic establishment. None of the three sanctuary examples can be held as the site of consecrated or chapel ground.

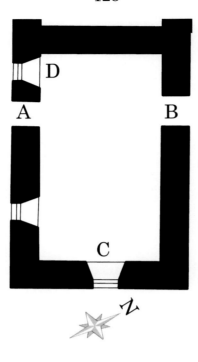

Conjectural plan of the chapel.
Dimensions: Approx 36ft x 18ft   A. Original Entrance. B. 'Hawkins' North Door.
C. East Window. D. Bowl said to have been built into wall in south-west corner .

Conjectural plan showing relationship of chapel to courtyard house.

The story that Deiphobus Trewinnard buried his murdered victim in the chapel might support the idea that burials were accepted at Trewinnard, were it not that it could also suggest that this victim was interred within the chapel because the burial ground had never been established.

Today, the tradition of a burial ground continues, since part of the field by the chapel has been made into a walled burial ground by the owners of Trewinnard for their family. A finely worked stone hedge surrounds a private cemetery at the south eastern end of what may have been the burial ground of the earliest chapel.

Where was the Chapel?

The identity of the site is based on a study of maps, on 'field walking', on documents, and on memories of the demolition.

The earliest surviving map of 1821, shows a long narrow building, which is thought to be the chapel site. Another building facing north east opposite the south door of the present house might have been considered were it not that the orientation of the map is inaccurate. The building would not have had a satisfactory east orientation, and was already demolished by the time of the tithe map in 1842, when it is said that the chapel still existed. The 1907 Ordnance Survey has a building with an orientation just south of east, built beside the track from the valley, at right angles to the slope of the hill, and not across the slope.

This site, on dry land near the top of the track

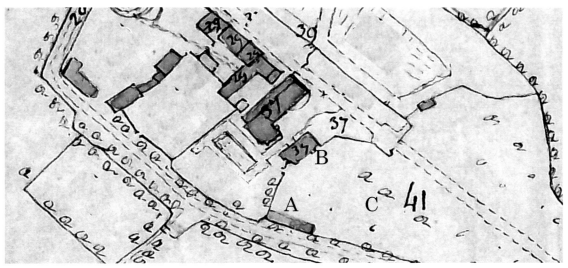

The 1821 map of Trewinnard shows the site of the chapel at A and a second building at B. C marks the so-called Cemetary field, which may have been an early iron age or medieval farmstead enclosure or a later *Lan,* the term used for a religious administrative centre.

from the old port and the river, on the way to a high downland cross roads, may have been on the site of an earlier iron age habitation. It is also thought to have been just outside the gate of the medieval courtyard mansion of Trewinnard.

The maps provide different scaled sizes for a chapel approximately 36ft long and about 18ft wide. Comparison with the chapel at Carminowe of similar date, and with other chapels, allows us to recreate a floor plan. It is likely to have had an east window, a single door straight into the lane and a lancet or two on the south side, but little else. It may have had a basin or piscina on the south wall. As at Carminowe, the windows could have been early narrow lancets, with early decorated gothic tracery to the east window. Charles Henderson, reported that some 14thC window tracery still survived and that around 1920, there were other bits lying in front of the main house.

It is unlikely that there was originally a north door facing the site of the present house. However, when the medieval house was demolished at the beginning of the 18thC, a path was required from the new house to the chapel, which required a door in the north elevation, a door which has survived on a house in St. Erth.

Part of a crocketed pinnacle was found in the lane 20 yards from the chapel. This could have been either on the chapel as on the east end gable at Duloe Chapel, or on a small tower as at Hall, Bodinnick, or on the Mohun mansion where it could have decorated a gable, as at Pengenna, St Kew (see inset).
It could also have been from internal chapel stonework.
Fragment is 10.5" high. Diameter tapers from 6" at broken base to 5" at smooth top.

Surviving Pieces of the Chapel

In 2011, Hamilton Hawkins told how he had helped demolish Trewinnard Chapel in 1946. He thinks the chapel was of similar dimensions to that shown on the O.S. maps and remembers an east window, fallen roof, some 'lovely blue' glass in a window and, in the south wall at the west end, the 'font' or piscina, which was with great difficulty loaded into the bulldozer. He recalls entering through doors on the north, thought to have been inserted by the Hawkins family.

The stone from the building vanished into a number of projects. Much was used in a new house at St Erth. This gained splendid granite floor slabs outside the entrance, two newel posts about six feet high for the stairs, some stained glass, much pine panelling and the doors to the porch. The glass has gone and the granite floor slabs removed or hidden by concrete bricks. Some panelling survives but would appear to be early 19thC wainscoting. The two stair newels of early 18thC design may have been the decorative woodwork for a canopy or internal porch.

The pair of fine early 18thC doors in the north wall were saved and used as the doors of the outer porch. Allowing for wear, the original size would have been 72",

An octagonal bowl of fine granite in a house at Hayle, was taken in 1946 from Trewinnard Chapel. The bowl is 35" long with an external width of 20.5". The chamfered sides are each 8" long. The internal bowl is 11" deep at one end and 3" deep at the other. The stone mass itself is approximately 13" deep at the thick end tapering to 7" at the other. One end has an inlet hole, the other an overflow spout. The basin's bottom outlet is modern.

top to bottom. They are of a design appropriate to the style of the shell porch at Trewinnard itself.

It seems likely that when Hawkins took over Trewinnard and rebuilt the house, a new north entrance was made in the chapel to allow easier access from the new house. Work in the chapel included wainscot panelling and additional decorative woodwork added in the style and fashion of the time.

The 'font' or stone basin taken from the south wall is now in a garden in Hayle. This proves to be unlike any other font. Although of good quality fine granite, with chamfered corners, it is oblong and with a cambered bottom which allows a deeper end at the small inlet hole and a shallow end by the lip. The drain in the bottom is apparently late 20thC. The stone work is of appropriate quality, but although it was built into the south wall, its original function is uncertain. Not only does it *not* look like a font, but manorial chapels did not usually have a font, the right of baptism being reserved to the parish church. There were exceptions, however, such as that chapel at Trembethow in St Erth which had a license for both chapel and font.

The final morsel that survives from the chapel is the part of a pinnacle found in the lane by the site.

Maybe time or excavation will turn up more pieces of this lost building.

Summary

It seems likely that Trewinnard started life as a chapel subsidiary to the monastic or church centre at Lelant, before becoming attached to the courtyard house at Trewinnard.

Following the departure of the Mohun family, the chapel probably decayed until refurbished by the Hawkins family at the beginning of the 18thC. The Hawkins family themselves ceased using the house as a principle residence when the dowager Mrs Hawkins died in 1780 and it seems likely therefore that through the 19thC, the chapel survived as a farm barn.

Although the east gable and the north and south walls were still standing in 1946, the roof had fallen in and the chapel was demolished. Carved stone was removed and lost. Until the cattle pound built on its site is removed it seems unlikely that further evidence will be found, although the landscape still respects the lines of the building.

A walk up the steep hill from the estuary can still allow us to to imagine the chapel on the right, just before the Trewinnard courtyard house.

Sun burst decorated doors to the porch of a house at St Erth, recorded as having been taken in 1946 from the north wall of Trewinnard Chapel.

One of two posts in 18thC style now in a house at St Erth, recorded as having been taken in 1946 from Trewinnard Chapel.

The two storey chapel
at St Erth Barton, Saltash.

The Interior of Tremaine church.

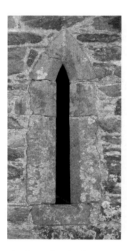

A chapel window re-
used at Carminow,
Helston.

A chancel and east window from the
chapel at St Erth Barton, Saltash.

Examples of similar chapels and windows suggest the appearance of Trewinnard chapel.

The Chapels of the Time

Developed from the early Celtic church, church and religion formed part of the controls developed first by the Saxons and then by the Normans. Bishops saw the church as a source of power and wealth. The population gained administrators and clerks, literacy and certainty. The development, donations and buildings of the church were boosted by the Black Death of 1349, which was followed by an upsurge in piety, and an increase in the number of chapels attached to gentry houses. The high point for the medieval church was reached about 1500, after which greater population, trade, centralisation and state courts, combined with envy of church wealth, meant conflict between state and church. This conflict resulted in the dissolution of Church enterprises and in particular of the network of chapels that underlay the monastic and episcopal system of the time.

Early Chapels

Many chapels originated as subsidiary cells to mother churches, but a chapel was also a place to stop and pray, or ask for safety on the next stage of a journey. They were erected at a 'holy' place or by a well, or served as healing centres. Some may have been erected to erase sites important to earlier belief or religion. Others were occupied by monastic anchorites, or were established in memory of a religious figure, or even of a dead ancestor. Inland chapels were designed to serve the more distant parts of an ecclesiastical area.

Chapels abounded in Cornwall. Piety may have had something to do with it, but so did the distance of hamlets and houses from the church, in a land of small steep sided valleys with boggy bottoms and difficult travel. By the 13thC, chapels had become matters not just of piety but also of social status. Gentry wished to show adherence to the complex rules that took hold during the 13thC and 14thC, when many believed you could pay your way into heaven. Obedience and support of the church came not just from belief, but also from political realism in a world where the church employed a third of the population and exercised considerable temporal as well as spiritual power. It was sensible not only to be seen as a good believer, but as one who could be relied on to support the interests of a worldly church, or who might contribute wealth to the church.

However, this was not just a matter of pragmatic politics, but also a question of the overpowering presence of religion and of the established church. Day to day life revolved around the saints that could help you through difficulties. This was a world dominated by religious images, buildings and priests which provided a culture that was almost the only colour, theatre and source of stories readily available. Religion pervaded all parts of normal life and yet had its own courts and rules separate from those of the state. It is comparable with life in those modern dictatorships where extreme rules and rulers pervade and regulate all aspects of life.

The plague and black death of 1349 gave urgency to those survivors who hoped that prayer would help them survive and so money was given to churches to secure a future life after death.

Two hundred years later, by 1570, the influence of Catholicism, of monastic centres, of imagery and church processions had died out with the outlawing of the catholic faith. Romantic stories of hidden priests and illegal services probably overstate the survival of catholicism and it was only a few families such as the Arundells at Lanherne who continued in their faith. In the meantime, in the void left in Cornwall by the disinterest of the Anglican Church, the population transferred some of their beliefs to places such as holy wells, and to witchcraft. The 1549 Prayer Book rebellion had been an expression of the Cornish dislike of being told how to worship, a local independence of spirit that continues today.

The independent spirit of Cornish local communities was by the early 18thC transferred to those Methodist and other chapels which formed a different brand of religion. By the 19thC, Cornwall could claim a multitude of Methodist-style chapels and quite small parishes could have four separate congregations with their own chapels, with many thousands being built around Cornwall.

Types of Medieval Chapel

In his 1957 book on the medieval chapels of Cornwall, Canon J H Adams claimed records for 700 medieval chapels. Among these are some 140 recorded by Dr Joanna Mattingly in the relatively small area west of Gwithian, with Helston and The Lizard.

The principle types of chapel can be summarised as follows:

1. Holy wells and the chapels of anchorites or holy men. Some small chapels perpetuate the site of an earlier Celtic cell or hermitage, such as that at St Cleer.
2. Chapels intended to demonstrate the triumph of Christianity over an older religion. One such chapel is that of Merthyr Uny, in Wendron, built in the middle of a much earlier sacred site. The building was 27 ft x 15ft with lancets some 3 ft high and 3 ft across both lights. The door was 3 ft wide and about 7ft to the top of the arch.
3. Chapels established as outliers of church centres. St Gothian's oratory was once one of four sites or chapels in the now sand-covered town of Connerton. When excavated it was 48'11" long by 12'2" wide internally, divided into two with a chancel about 17' 1" long.

4. Chapels designed as subsidiary places of worship in distant parts of a parish, some of which may have once had some burial rights. Menadarva on the Red River north west of Cambourne, was once a great Arundel house whose chapel predated the dwelling. It had started life as a monastic cell, then become a subsidiary parish chapel before becoming associated with the house of Menadarva. Its font survives at another church, although nothing else now survives except the site.
5. The wayfarer or travellers' chapel, designed to allow the traveller to give thanks for a journey or ask for blessings for the next phase of a journey. These included wayside prayer places, chapels at the gates of a town or castle, chapels on bridges and resting places along the many pilgrim routes that criss-crossed the country. St Michael's Mount was both a subsidiary to St Michaels in Northern France and also a place of pilgrimage. The little chapel at Chapel Rock, Marazion, demolished in 1645 was probably a chapel for prayer on the way or before crossing to the Mount. Similarly, the chapel at Hall, the old Mohun house above Bodinnick, which still survives, may have started as a place for prayer by passengers before taking the Bodinnick Ferry and only later became attached to the house at Hall.

It is possible that the church at St Erth may also have started life as a chapel, since the earliest chapels around St Erth were probably on the east bank of the ferry crossing, and on the hills to the west and east at Trewinnard and Lanuthnoe.
6. Chapels that provided private prayer rooms to a gentry house, for family and staff.

Baptism and Burial

Older pre-existing chapels with burial grounds and fonts did not usually require relicensing. Chapels for private prayer needed no approval, unless you wanted to have a mass (and bell) which needed a Bishop's license. This was because the rights of the Parish Church were jealously guarded, not just for theological reasons but for control of the population and the gaining of funds. No chapel services could be held on Sundays or on festivals. Baptisms, weddings, funerals and burials were not allowed. The parish church protected rights, services or celebrations which brought funds or donations.

One of the central tenets for the license of a chapel was that it should *not* have a graveyard. Not many chapels attached to great houses had burial rights- but examples are claimed for

Trewothack, St Agnes. The now demolished chapel was described by Henderson as forming the east wing of a quadrangle attached to a great house. It was said to have had a graveyard. The chapel had a piscina near the south end.

'Tynten', St Tudy. The chapel at this mansion had licenses recorded in 1330 and 1396. This too had a burial ground and was opposite a well. It has a square east window with three lights and a cusped cinquefoil head, an aumbry in the north wall. There was just a low pointed arched door and two small windows in the south wall and no other windows.

Trewinnard. It is possible that if the chapel was on the site of an earlier daughter or upland parish chapel, the tradition of burial rights may have survived. Its building could well have been similar to that described for Tynten or Carminowe.

Licensing

The early 14thC saw chapels become a status symbol, a must-have for any gentry house. A license from the bishop for your chapel may have been, rather like the often unimplemented 'license to crenellate', a sign of social arrival.

Chapels attached to private houses became more and more popular. In the early 16thC, Sir Thomas More claimed that there was: *'such a rabel [of priests] that everyman must have a priest in his house to wait upon his wife. No man al-*

most, lacketh now.' The right to a chapel or even a private oratory was bound up not just with faith but with social structure.

This may be why, despite often having use of a private chapel for mass, great families would support an aisle of the local parish church and pay for its upkeep. Examples of family aisles in Cornwall include Bosahan at Constantine, Pendarvis at St Gluvias, (Penryn), Coryton at St Mellion, Kestle at Manaccan, Mohun at Boconnoc, Michell/Peter at the 'new' church of St Merryn, and, of course, Trewinnard at St Erth.

The Manorial Chapel

Chapels were provided at great houses, castles and on the edge of townships, often sited right by the entrance. As at ferry crossings, so also at houses was prayer made for a safe journey or thanks given on safe arrival. In house after house, even in Cornwall, the site for the chapel is outside and to the left or right of the main entrance to the first courtyard, or over the gate at the entrance, as at Golden in Probus. Such chapels not only allowed prayer before or after travel, but also use by tenants or 'outsiders', without the need to allow them into the courtyards of the house. Examples in Cornwall include:

Bodrugan. The Bodrugans were for long one of the most powerful of families, until they chose the wrong side in 1483. Their 'castle' was demolished in 1786, but the chapel survived to be recorded. This was a long building outside the court with an outer area west of the chapel and a 14thC door of Pentewan stone. It had licenses granted in 1372 and 1424.

Bonallack, south of Constantine was a separate building outside the court.

Caerhays had a long narrow chapel with a central projecting stair and separated chancel. It opened from a door outside the outer gate.

Carminow, south west of Helston, was demolished in 1861. Surviving plans show a chapel just outside the porter's Lodge.

Pengersick had a chapel by the entrance to the outer court on the south west corner by the 'main' road. A license was recorded in 1391 and parts of the ruins can be seen in the famous Buck drawing of the site.

Penwarne in Budock had a detached chapel outside the court entrance.

Roscarrock: a detached chapel was once beside the road from the north west.

Rosteague, on the Roseland Peninsula, still has remnants of a chapel in a corner of the entrance court at the north end of the main building. Henderson recorded an arch of Pentewan stone. It was licensed in 1401 and again in 1433.

Shillingham: The ruined chapel south west of Saltash, still stands butting on to other buildings of the house and court-yard.

Trecarrell Chapel, newbuilt but abandoned in 1511 was outside the gate of the main court and hall. Replacing an earlier chapel recorded in 1405, the new design probably reflected the fashions of the time.

Trelissick, another manor to the north east of St Erth parish had a license granted to the owners in 1418.

Even when licenced, not all chapels would have had a full time resident priest. Instead the parish priest would have been persuaded to visit the house for a mass perhaps only a few times a year.

Some chapels were built with accommodation for a priest. In Cornwall they include:

Bosworgey in St Erth, which had a chapel with a resident priest for the family and was licensed in 1260, 1283, 1398 and 1420. This chapel existed (Henderson) before 1260, and was one where its proprietors had to pay a yearly tribute of one pound of wax to the altar of St Erth.

Caerhays appears to have had a first floor. It is assumed this was for a priest or perhaps to provide connection to the parlour or private wing.

Cotehele has a surviving chapel licensed in 1411. It is barrel vaulted with one entrance that was formerly just outside the gate and another entrance for the family. There is two storey priests accommodation alongside. There is a second 'votive' chapel in the wood.

Erth Barton, south west of Saltash, has a surviving two storey chapel. The undercroft seems to have been for storage. The early 14thC building has some surviving wall paintings, an external north stone stair to the first floor. It has one small north lancet window, one east window and two small lancets to the south. It is about 40ft x 20 ft wide.

Inceworth near Millbrook was a two storey chapel, probably that chapel for which 'Sir Richard de Campo Arnulph had a license in 1331.

Several chapels were recorded within the parish of St Erth. Henderson records licenses granted to Porthcullomb and Trevessa in 1043, Trewinnard in 1372, Treloweth in 1379, Gurlyn in 1406, and Trelissick in 1418. There was also a chapel at Treven. No doubt there were other chapels which came and went with the fortunes of their owners.

The story of the chapel at Trewinnard remains a good example for the history of such buildings.

Chapter 11
The Hawkins House

We suppose that the courtyard house of the Trewinnards had decayed during the latter half of the 16thC, since Martin Trewinnard either spent time elsewhere or was in prison and because his son had to sign away his inheritance. Management was in the hands of a steward or tenants.

When the Mohun family adopted the house, they would have extended and updated Trewinnard in a style which would have included mullioned windows, private chambers and extensive outbuildings. However, repair and maintenance probably came to an end with the death of Reginald Mohun in 1642 particularly as this was during the civil war, in which the Mohuns were on the losing royalist side and which was followed by the Cromwell protectorate. Between 1642, when the property passed to the three sisters of Reginald Mohun and 1685, when one third passed to the Hawkins family, the house can be supposed to have decayed when in multiple ownership and divided among different tenants.

Documents from Trewithen show that John Hawkins first took a lease of Trewinnard in 1650. Hearth tax records suggest that he and his wife Loveday shared the mansion of 12 hearths with his father-in-law George Trenhayle. We assume that John Hawkins made this his principal residence, but that like many a tenant, would not spend money repairing and improving someone else's house.

By the time of his death in 1676, John Hawkins appeared to be a man of some wealth and status, demonstrated by the two marriages to good families arranged for his son Thomas Hawkins. His first wife, Honor Praed, was from a Lelant family of landowners. His second marriage to Ann Belott was also to a family of standing and estate.

The family continued to live at Trewinnard as

A selection of houses built or renovated at about the same time as that at Trewinnard, helps place the house at Trewinnard in the pre-Georgian architectural fashion of the times. Examples shown include three seven-bay houses, similar to Trewinnard, and three five-bay designs from the same period.

Top Left. Croan, west of Bodmin, had a single room depth wing added in front of the earlier house by Edward Hoblyn, a lawyer around 1696.

Top Right. Trereife, Penzance, had a new single room depth wing built in front of the earlier house by John Nichols, a successful lawyer, around 1710.

Second Left. Rosemerryn, Budock, had a single room depth extension built onto the original house by the Mason family around 1720.

Third Left Tregassow was extended and rebuilt from 1692 by Thomas Coke, whose family had become rich on fraudulent tin dealing. Never finished, the owner died 'in a puddle of water', seeking more money to satisfy a demanding wife.

Bottom Left. One of the most curious but beautiful of houses is Great Treverran, near Tywardreath. A small two room and stair hall extension was added to the earlier house by John Thomas in 1704, combining late 17thC design with eccentricity.

Bottom Right. Glebe House, Philleigh: A new wing was added on an old site around 1730.

Trewinnard Manor as it might have appeared *as first built in the 1690s*. It has a chimney at each end, and a regular pattern of windows, before the lower (north) end was re-ordered. The hall chimney may not be part of the earliest phase. The design is similar to the houses shown on the opposite page.

tenants until the purchase of a one third interest in 1685 made the Hawkins family part owners. It was ripe for the addition of a modern extension and Thomas Hawkins appears to have been wealthy enough to consider 'making a statement' as the owner of a new built house. The interest he now owned in the freehold gave him an incentive to improve the mansion, rather than lay out money purchasing another property elsewhere.

We assume that the old buildings were in poor condition. Courtyard houses were typically a collection of narrow ranges with no corridors, a lot of outside walls, scantle roofs with no lead, and a design that looked a hundred years out of date.

A description of Glebe House Philleigh in 1727, shortly before it was completely rebuilt, describes a *'house partly stone, partly mud, covered with thatch; a hall floored with boards and ceiled, a parlour, not ceiled, floored with lime, a small chamber above and a dairy adjoining; a little buttery adjoining the hall; a kitchen floored with stone, a chamber over the entry and three chambers over cellars and woodhouses, all ceiled'*.

Although the Trewinnard mansion would have been finer than this, the description gives some idea of how an up-and-coming lawyer would have considered the old house, when it was compared with the designs and building plans of his gentry friends and clients.

Designing a New House

It is a mistake to consider the buildings of Cornwall as isolated from fashions prevailing in the rest of the country. Fashions flow by imitation 'downward'

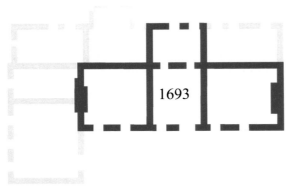

1. The first 1693 building is marked in red, with one room each side of a hall, and a stair tower with two doors to the hall.

Five schematic plans illustrate the progression of the main building phases.

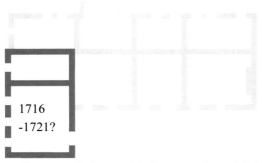

2. The second phase added a new wing with its own stair, west of the first block, and included altering the windows and levels of the lower end.

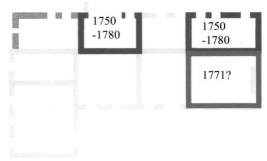

3. The rear was extended, and cellars provided, including excavation under part of phase 1. The area dotted green at top left, was probably added at a later stage, and then further altered.

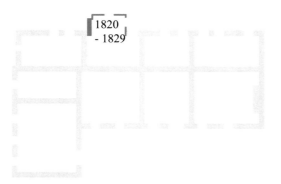

4. A 'study' was built on stone piers behind the house. Although matched to, or reusing early materials, it is thought to have been added between 1820 and 1829.

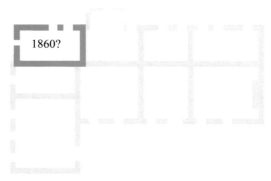

5. An additional storey was added over the underground water storage cistern. Later alterations were made to the first and attic floors of this part.

from the centre of power and wealth. The Restoration of 1660 had meant many country gentry, particularly former royalists, had perforce to visit London. The disproportionate number of Members of Parliament for Cornwall also assured London connexions. Solicitors and businessmen found fortune and work in London and it was in London that the upper gentry could make contacts, seek office, or learn of new fashions in dutch or french architecture.

The house built by Thomas Hawkins was at the forefront of new designs in Cornwall, with only Tregassow appearing to have been started as early.

Tregassow was unusual in being modern in outlook, but retaining features such as the large smokehood chimneys more appropriate for the style and practices of a 100 years earlier. It too had gardens formed when the ground level was raised around an old house to provide prospects and a garden entrance to the main or first floor.

A number of houses of similar design were built in Cornwall about the turn of the 18thC, many of them such as Tregassow, Trereife, or Croan, by lawyers like Thomas Hawkins. Although since altered by extensions, recreation of the original design for Trewinnard shows that it was very similar in design to other houses of the period. This pre-Georgian period of English Baroque continued not only in the middle gentry but among the wealthiest of owners, and examples could include Harlyn from 1690, Menabilly between 1710 and 1715, Antony in the 1720s and Boconnoc and Port Eliot from the 1720s all of which started before the arrival of a more mannered 'Georgian' style.

Other styles were popular.
Top: Pentillie Castle, in a design of 1692, shows an early baroque french palace.
Centre: Rosteague is a typical gentry house, with a new facade built onto the old building.
Below: Lancarff is another house where earlier buildings were merely given a new facade.

A New House

The previous courtyard house at Trewinnard occupied the top half of the domestic part of the house and farm enclosure. A new building needed to look away from the farm, with a high status façade which could be reached and viewed on arrival. It is possible that the existence of the old chapel restricted building against that end of the old Trewinnard, and it is apparent that the only available building land was that directly below the mansion. Rather than backing on to the early house, it is thought that, unlike almost all other extensions of the time, the new house was built in line with the earlier Hall, but further down the slope, on the other side of a stable court, which continued in use. The new house turned its back to the farmhouse, its yard and mud.

Details of the front door, window, shell hood and bracket, stairs, doors and panelling
in the early phase of the house

The First Phase of Building

The plan shows how small was this building, and how occupiers would have needed to retain the earlier buildings for service rooms, dairy, outer kitchens, wood stores and so on. The new villa was only three rooms wide. A front door led into a hall which had one room on each side, reached by a curved-top doorway with heavy mouldings. Under the room to the right was a low kitchen, made possible by the fall in the underlying ground level. To the rear of the hall, two doors led to a stair tower, jutting out from the building. The stair tower had access to a back door to the yard and to the lower ground level, down hill. Upstairs, the stair gave access to only three rooms, each opening directly off the stairs without use of a corridor. The door mouldings to the eastern bedroom are still in place.

In this house there were no service or staff facilities and, save for the service room below the lower end, no proper kitchen since all these facilities were provided by the old buildings. The former farmhouse, across the yard from the back door of the new building, cannot have been a kitchen if it was indeed the farmhouse for the Barton farm.

As has often been noted, part of the charm of this building is the completeness with which original features have been retained. These features are restoration baroque rather than Queen Anne, although simplified for a conservative and money aware lawyer. The design included 18 pane hornless sash windows, (9 panes per sash) in the latest small pane style. The windows have the wide glazing bars and internal ovolo mouldings of those early windows. Their lintels seem to be single pieces of granite cut to appear as soldier arches, a cheap method of so obtaining this effect. Outside, the tall narrow windows were regularly placed and the main entrance has a delightful shell hood on decorated brackets, over double doors each with a curved top with circular mouldings in the spandrels. The shell hood stands over a half rounded monolithic stone. This cannot be a millstone but may be a hearthstone taken from the original mansion.

Inside, much late 17thC panelling survives, complete with deep mouldings and restoration door cases. It is possible that the staircase and banisters are of that early 1690 date as is the panelling around the hall and elsewhere, much of which is thought to have survived from that time. The corner cupboard in the existing entrance hall has a double hinged door covering moulded shelves and a shell moulding.

The chimneys are thought to have been built in

A corner fireplace in the central first floor bedroom.

brick from the first, rather than as brick which replaced earlier stonework. A fireplace across the corner of the hall is matched by a similar fireplace in the bedroom above, which could be a later insertion, or date from the original build. This third flue runs diagonally across a first floor partition wall to a centrally placed chimney. The roof has steep edge-purlin main frames designed to take broad rafters which carried slates without intermediate batons. This was a roof typical of 1690 and similar to dendro-dated roofs at Harlyn House. Some of the timber, particularly that towards the west, where the original hip end can still be traced in the roof work, is of lighter timber, some with carpenter's marks, which had been reused from an earlier building,

Shell joinery around the opening to the deep window seat recess of the oriel window.

A Second Phase and Extension

It seems that the building was soon considered too small. It may be that the cost of maintaining the old manor was thought not worth the trouble, or that the son did not wish to live with his mother, the widowed Mrs Hawkins (the former Ann Belott), who wanted a fine modern house or to spend her recovered dowry. In any event an extension was built uphill of the existing house.

In 1716, Christopher Hawkins inherited the house when his father died. It is possible that this motivated the second phase extension or that it followed his marriage to his cousin, Mary Hawkins, in 1721. Despite surviving account books, there is no record of it being built, save that it appears to have been finished before the coach house, a later development, was built in 1735. I suspect that the new wing, with its own front door and stair, was built between 1716 and 1721, as accommodation for his mother, allowing he and his wife to move into the earlier wing, before they moved up to London.

This wing was built against the end wall of the earlier phase, and ruined the symmetry of that first build. It is curious that there seems to have been little attempt to work to a scheme of improvement, or to plan for 'wings' or further architectural elements in the new style, as was being planned at this time by Hawkins cousins at Pennans, Grampound.

Because of the sloping site, the new extension had to be dug into the ground and almost as far up the hill as the earlier mansion. Excavation allowed the first floor to be on the same level as the existing house, and to provide a cellar for much (though not all) of the sub ground floor. The decision to build this extension around

The entrance front to the new wing, with door and case.

1720 also implied the demolition of the old courtyard house, since the basement windows of this addition are made with mismatched early 17thC mullions, cills and heads. The spoil from excavation was cast uphill of the house ensuring that the uphill garden was at the main floor level of the whole house with further spoil heaped in a great bank over the ruins of the early house. It is now difficult to work out the original ground levels of that courtyard house, because so much earth has been moved uphill in preparing the building platform for the present house, the levelled lower garden may represent the original ground level of the hill at that point.

A walk up the lane from the estuary pool to the lane above the house shows that in addition to raising the ground levels over the old house, a very considerable walled bank, now carrying water tanks on top of it, was built to give privacy from the lane and farm traffic.

The new building was independent in space and facilities, with its own front door, separate staircase and separate storerooms below. The wing has a particularly fine door with panelled pilasters and a formal pediment. It is of nine panels with, above, a six paned over-light and first floor window above that. However, there are no windows or fireplaces in the gable end, (possibly to allow display of the recovered tapestries) and no window beside the front door. The rear elevation is a completely regular and plain four bay unit, the north west bay being given over to a stair hall. These windows look over what would have been a garden that was separate and private from those living in the first new house. Inside the panelling and joinery appear original. They are in a late 17thC style with deep cornice mouldings, high wide baroque skirtings, restoration door cases, and shutters with fine h-hinges. It is possible that the stair is of 18thC date.

The impression the exterior makes is of inexpensive 'owner design' utilising available space and needs, rather than one intended as a status improvement. It had been suggested that this was an extension influenced by the work of Thomas Edwards at Trewithen. However Thomas Edwards was only ten in 1720 and his first work in Cornwall appears to have been in 1735, a date too late for him to be involved at Trewinnard. Nothing that Thomas Edwards drew was quite as plain as the extension at Trewinnard, whose door case, in any event, looks back to an earlier style and does not seem typical of his work.

When Philip Hawkins of Trewithen died in 1738 only three years after Thomas Edwards had started at Trewithen, his death meant that the Hawkins family of

The blank gable end of the 1720 extension, with to the left an entrance to its cellar and before it, the entrance to the puzzling granite covered store.

The garden front of the new wing.

A fireplace in the new wing shows a later frame over an early 18thC moulded grate opening.

Trewinnard would inherit Trewithen. The Trewinnard Hawkins family therefore had no incentive to further develop Trewinnard.

The Stable Block

The next phase of building appears to have been the new coach house, built around 1738.

The stable yard of the earlier mansion had remained in use, but was directly before the front door of the house. It was also unlikely to have been able to accommodate wheeled vehicles of any size.

The Hawkins accounts record payments to the mason *for works about ye New Stable* between 25 July and 16 September 1738. The bill divides work between that finer masonry work presumed needed for the front elevation and that to the back wall, which cost only half as much. This year's accounts also included a bill for 'healing' or slating the roof and for some of the paving of the stable, but the bills amount to some £15.00 only, so it is suspected that other entries are missing.

The stable has a central two bay coach house with horse stables to the right or north, which had good access from the rear. It is thought the left wing was for the coachman's accommodation. An ashlar plinth ran along the front although this appears altered where old openings have been blocked. In the middle, the coach house bays break forward from the line of the building below a pediment which is of the most rudimentary and simplistic, cut price design without any decoration. The carriage doors are set in blind arches with projecting keystones. The existence of crested ridge tiles on the stable block until around 1990 would have been re-used from a building of much earlier date, implying in turn that the old mansion at Trewinnard must have been largely demolished by 1735.

The coach house of 1738.

Stable yard and gate pier.

The cobbled stable yard and stable block.

Yard gate piers and joinery.

The coach house seen from the garden terraces.

The stable block today is a fine survival, set off by the large area of cobbling in the yard before it. This cobbling and the surrounding stable yard walls, the piers with re-used earlier stone caps and the timber fencing on the low walls at the end make a coherent and pleasant whole, the cobbling, in particular, being set off by the decorative use of white lumps of quartz, presumably from clay works.

The north east elevation shows the insertion of the oriel window.

Adding to the Rear of the House.

Demolition of the old mansion also provided materials for filling in the areas beside the stair tower, under a single monopitch from the main roof. These alterations appear of later date, with pieced soldier arches typical of the mid 18thC. Although the phase of works necessarily included the removal of the reception room to the east of the hall, the raising of the ceiling to make a high kitchen and the insertion in the east first floor bedroom of the oriel window, it is not certain that they directly followed the 1620 extension. There are bills for work on the kitchen, cellars and 'chamber' in 1755, shortly after Christopher and Mary Hawkins moved to Trewinnard in 1750. Their move to Trewinnard as their main home meant that they required a better kitchen with more space. This phase of works to the rear of the building included digging out the foundations of the rear wall of the main house to make a cellar, while supporting that house on piers and timber joists and fitting out the cellars for bottle and bulk wine store. This cellar also re-used mullions, cills and lintels from the demolished mansion.

The work included adding a small set of steps down into the new bedroom at the lower end, now fitted with its oriel window, whose insertion could only be done when floor levels were changed. This could always have been the 'best' bedroom. It is possible too, that the alterations were driven by the need for a larger kitchen and for accommodation for junior members of the fam-

Top: A view of the rear from the north shows the oriel window and rear extensions built around the stair tower.
Below: The back door with cut soldier arch lintels.

ily or servants in the attic, to which a small stair was now provided. The alteration required the repositioning of windows to meet the new floor levels, a considerable change to the look of the front elevation, and one that suggests pure practicality, without interest in appearance, perhaps motivated by the view that Trewithen was now the house of family importance.

The Hawkins Accounts Ledgers

Accounts of household income and expenditure as kept by Christopher Hawkins and his steward can still be seen in the Royal Institution of Cornwall. They provide much interesting detail on household expenditure and have been well analysed and described by Cedric Appleby.

Although no works of great size are noted in the ledger between 1750 and 1764, a few items are worth mentioning since they may provide a clue to the different building phases.

1727	A cellar is referred to.
1729	'Purchased marble for the best parlour, together with a picture to go over it'.
1730	'Insurance of my house, one guinea'
1732	300 bricks to finish chimney in September.
1734	Payments were made for labour and material 'for making ye New Lane Hedge'.
1734	Payments were made for opening up and clearing the conduits in the Brewhouse, [perhaps a part of the old mansion not yet demolished].
1755	Considerable work and decoration in kitchen, chamber and cellars. This may have included fitting of bells.
1759	Paid £2.13s for painting the hall in December.
1761	100 bricks purchased from Copper house, (for a chimney to the house).
1761	Paid nearly £30.00 for an 'iron oven, grates etc...' (presumably for the improved kitchen) together with payment for repairs to 'the chamber clock', upstairs.

In 1766, the year before his death, Christopher Hawkins paid for fire insurance, therebye gaining the mark still attached to the house.

In 1965, The Royal Exchange Assurance wrote to confirm that *'the mark in question was issued by us to an insured during the year 1766, but due to the fire which consumed our offices in 1838, I regret to say that we have no details of the property or contents covered by this policy. You may be interested to know that we started issuing fire marks in 1720 and continued until about the middle of the 19thC. During this period it was our custom to*

Fire insurance mark of 1766, set above the west wing entrance.

affix one to every building which we insured as a visible sign of protection, and this was of course helpful to the private fire brigades which we used to maintain. The mark itself usually had the policy number stamped on it as is the case of [this] mark. It was said that firemen would watch a house burn, if it did not carry the mark of the insurers for whom they worked.

It was probably also around 1760 that, the separation of the two wings and their two stairs no longer being necessary, a corridor was built on the first floor, so reducing the size of the earliest two bedrooms. These works must have been completed by the time that Boswell visited, since he appears to refer to these little stairs and different levels.

A date of 1771 scratched in one pane of the kitchen may be the date for other works, since that is a date during the widowhood of Mary Hawkins, when it seems less likely that major building works would be undertaken.

A pane in the kitchen has been signed and dated 1771. Signatures include Henry Dover, James T, JH and what may be the 'marks' of others. This may record completion of work to the kitchen.

18thC Descriptions of Trewinnard

In 1757, James Heywood, whose daughter Anne, had married Thomas, the son of Christopher Hawkins, visited Trewinnard and noted that the house:

'is a very pretty neat house, five rooms on a floor, stands in the centre of a garden pleasantly situated and kept in great order. It is built with stone with sash windows. The gardens are well shaded with trees, the gravel walks well roll'd and preserv'd clear from weeds. There is a very pleasant prospect from the house as well as gardens, the sea flowing every tide within a quarter of a mile of the house. The stables are large and built of stone'.

Forty years later, in 1792, the diarist James Boswell was staying with his friend the Reverend Temple at the vicarage of St. Gluvias in Penryn, and visited Trewinnard and several other gentry houses. He wrote of Trewinnard that the house was *'in a better part of the country...there is an air of antiquity and cultivation about it. The house is indeed a collection of strange rooms huddled together with a number of inconvenient passages and narrow staircases'.*

Another comment of the time recalled that the house *'had an astonishing number of small corridors up and down with various rooms'.*

An Extension on Stone Piers

Based on changes recorded in plans of the house, this study extension appears to have been added between 1820 and 1840 and probably before Sir Christo-

The rear hipped extension on stone piers.

pher Hawkins' death in 1829.

It was built out from the rear of the house on stone piers, decorated with a modillioned cornice outside and fitted with reused panelling and fittings inside. The windows are of 18thC pattern and similar to others of the house, so are perhaps those that were in the rear wall *before* the extension was added.

The structure is of light timber which has been given, early in the 20thC, a pebble dash coating, with displayed imitation quoins to the corners. Inside only half the room is built on the stone piers, the remainder being in an earlier rear extension. The fittings and joinery design match the panelling and details of the rest of the house. There is a fine 6 panel door of 1810 style with a brass lock box of the same date. Lattice work cupboards imitate other work in the house. The room also has a disused oil light fitting projecting from the wall.

The interior of the extension on piers.

Changes of the 19th and 20th Centuries

Perhaps because after 1738 Christopher Hawkins knew that his son Thomas would inherit the splendid and much larger house at Trewithen, it would seem there was little incentive for either he or his grandson, Sir Christopher, to spend money on alterations to a house to which they did not have the whole freehold. The house at Trewinnard remained a secondary or gentry home for Christopher Hawkins through to his death in 1832. In 1832 there was still a separate farmhouse but on his death the mansion house itself became a single tenancy with the farm. For 100 years, tenants occupied the house, so that little money was spent on the house itself. Alterations were restricted to the farm yards, or small matters such as the addition of an outside privy.

19thC alterations to the rear of the house.

Inside, it is possible that the alterations made to the kitchen were done in the 19thC. These included the removal of the stone wall to the rear of the kitchen and the insertion of a narrow servant's stair with 19thC panelling. This could lead, via an extra small bedroom, to the attic. The internal kitchen door, split into two halves and with a serving shelf, is an example of that division between outside and inside labour which was typical of the late 19thC.

The earlier kitchen fireplace was also enlarged to take a cast iron range. Space was taken from a lobby for the storing of furze on the left and, to the right, from a bread oven and to the right of that again, a copper. The remnants of both are now hidden behind a finely joinered early corner cupboard.

In the north west corner, beyond the parlour, a further room was added over a large water cistern or

The fine two panel outer door to the rear, complete with knocker.

tank. On top of this water tank was built a small service room and on top of that again, bedrooms with upper windows, whose remains can only now just be seen beneath the roof. The roof pitch was altered to go over this rear extension as it was over the rest of the rear extensions.

Water must always have been a problem on this site. The courtyard to the rear of Trewinnard has been shown to have a brick lined well or water storage chamber buried under the yard. Its purpose isn't clear, since it is not certain that it was ever part of a foul drainage system, and is more likely to have been for water storage. It may once have had a function as a well but this is not certain.

After the Second World War, bathrooms and partitions were installed to make a bed and breakfast business, but these seems to have been removed so carefully in recent years that they are no longer apparent

In the 1950s the demolition of the old chapel took place with subsequent landscaping of land immediately outside the front door.

The Cottage in the Yard.

Across the yard from the back door of the present house is a building thought to have been the early farmhouse. The thick walls and a central chimney stack of late 16thC design suggest that it is the oldest surviving structure on the site. The roof pitch remains at approximately 55 degrees suggesting that this was a roof designed for thatch.

Although much altered, it is likely that this is a 17thC structure which incorporates earlier elements. It is thought this was the farmhouse for the Barton farm and always 'faced the other way' towards the stables. As a farmhouse, it cannot have been used for service and kitchen to the early 18thC manor house.

Trewinnard Court

The Hawkins affection for Trewinnard Manor was emphasised in 1912, when the new choir school in Truro, funded by the widow of C.R.T. Hawkins and named Trewinnard Court, was designed with Trewinnard in mind.

The design is a rather heavy Edwardian interpretation of the building at Trewinnard. Two side wings project from a central façade which has sash windows and heavy granite quoins. The roof has a tall roof lantern. Over the front door is a shell porch which imitates that at Trewinnard, but achieves none of Trewinnard's grace.

The south east elevation of the early farmhouse, now a cottage, and the cobbled yard between it and the rear of the main house.

The early farmhouse, now a cottage, with the rear of the stable block to the left, viewed from the north west.

The cobbled yard to the rear of the house, with, to the left, part of the rear extension raised on pillars.

The shell hood over the front door of Trewinnard Court, Truro.

Two different views of the entrance hall.

Two different views of the dining room and of two tapestries.

Left: The parlour to one side of the hall.

Right: The four poster bedroom.

The main stair in the early stair tower.

The rear, tapestry hung
stairs of the first extension.

An 18thC corner cupboard masks the old bread oven in the kitchen.

Two views of the 'farmhouse' kitchen.

The servants stair, inserted within the thickness of the wall in the old kitchen.

Above: Photographs of the kitchen.

Misleading History

As with many old houses, misleading stories of its history persist in local memory. One such was the newspaper report of 1913 that praised Mrs Hawkins for her work on the church of St Erth, but commented that since the death of Sir Christopher Hawkins in 1829, the family home at Trewinnard '*has been reduced in size to suit the requirements of what is now a farmhouse*'. There is no evidence of such a demolition or reduction in size, save for the removal of the courtyard mansion 180 years earlier.

Another report suggested that '*The house contains two ballrooms and a dungeon, but the house has been drastically modernized*'.

In 1956, an advertisement about Trewinnard Manor reported many unusual 'facts', including the smugglers' tunnel that ran under the ground from Trewinnard to St Michael's Mount, some five miles distant.

Such a tunnel seems even less likely than the inevitable stories of the headless Trewinnard coachman or the strange figures in the drive, stories which seem to be common to many places around the country.

Trewinnard Today

By 1780, therefore, the house looked much as it does at present. The last remnants of the courtyard mansion had long been demolished and the grounds it occupied landscaped. The interior of the house, despite 20thC alterations, remains 18thC in appearance and feel. The main façade of Trewinnard continues to have great charm. The house and its surroundings are a particularly felicitous blend of historic interest, and family home. Features such as the shell door hood, the panelling, the original sash windows and the outstanding masonry of the early Oriel window, combine to make Trewinnard unusual.

Trewinnard: the entrance front.

Four plans from 1821 to 1863, trace changes in the house, gardens and farm.
These plans should also be referred to for the chapter on gardens.

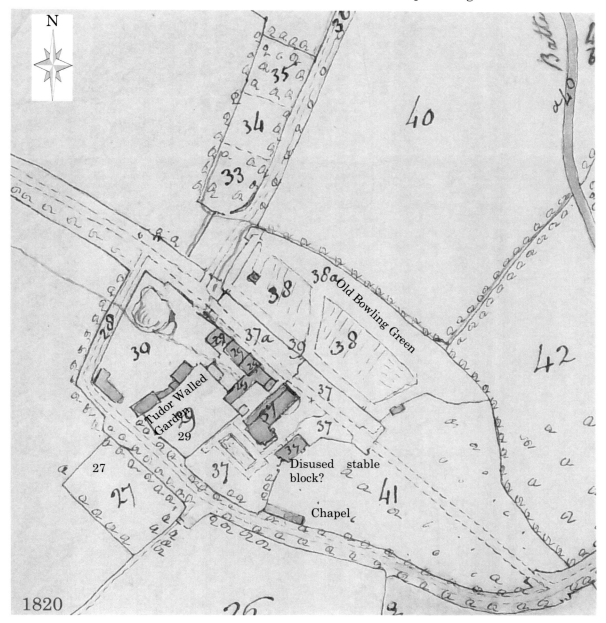

Trewinnard, drawn by Mr Proud and copied for Sir Christopher Hawkins between 1821-30.
The key has been lost, but it is thought that it would be similar to that for the Tithe map of 1842.
1. Note the leat for the water supplies, the diagonal walk to the old Bowling Green, and the formal garden south west of the house. There is no parlour on stilts north west of the house.
2. Area number 29. This walled area is thought to be the site of the Tudor walled garden.
3. The supposed chapel building is shown as longer than on later plans.
4. To the south east of the mansion is a building thought to be a stable block. It had been demolished by the time of the tithe map.
5. Area number 27. This is thought to have been added as a walled garden during the 17thC.

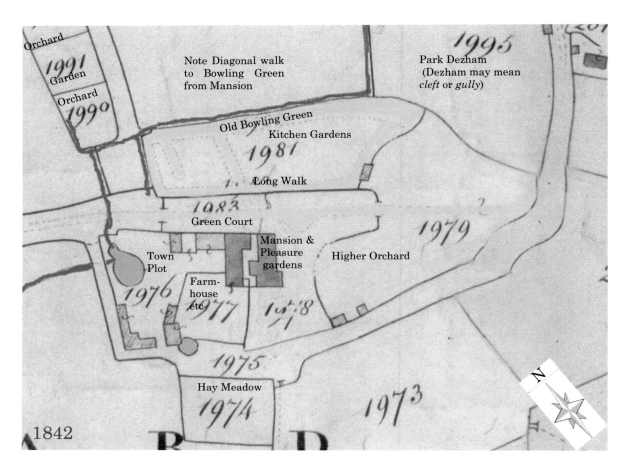

A plan of Trewinnard, prepared for the tithe map of 1842.

1. The pillared study has been added to the rear of the mansion.
2. The farm buildings appear to have been altered and a horse pond added to the south west.
3. The garden at 1974 is now clearly used for hay.
4. The name of the old bowling green survives.
5. The so called cemetary field, no. 1979, survives as orchard and gardens rather than pasture.
6. The building outside the front entrance has been demolished as has, it would appear, the extension to the former chapel.
7. The yellow colouring for walkways has been added to the original.

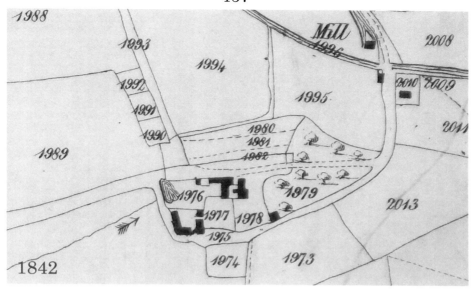

Plan of Trewinnard, by R Symons, surveyor, based on the tithe map of 1842.
The details and coding appear the same as that of the plan on the previous page.

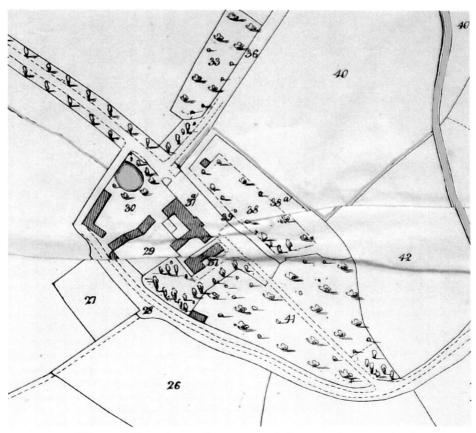

1863 Plan of Trewinnard, prepared for auction particulars.
This copy retains a crease across the centre of the original which alters the mansion plan.
The house appears to be based on 1820 draft since the northern study on pillars is not shown.

A drawing of Trewinnard dated 1835, is thought to be by Mary Esther Hawkins (1778-1861), mother of both John Heywood Hawkins and CHT Hawkins. It shows the 18thC box hedges and formal garden layout, before later alterations.

Four plans from 1821 to 1863 trace changes in the gardens.
These are on the pages immediately preceeding this chapter.

Chapter 12
The Gardens of Trewinnard

Although Trewinnard was mentioned in *The Parks and Gardens of Cornwall* by Douglas Ellory Pett, new research suggests the gardens deserve greater attention. They remain splendid tudor and georgian gardens with much from five hundred years of gardening.

The 16th and 17thC Garden

The 16thC saw an increased interest in the design and layout of pleasure gardens, although such gardens were designed not so much for the growing of plants but for walking and leisure activities such as bowling. A Jacobean garden would normally have one small enclosed area which would be used by the family and a second larger area, still based around a formal layout, which was intended for visitors.

The earliest garden at Trewinnard would have been a private, enclosed area close to the medieval mansion. It is thought that these private family gardens lay immediately north of the courtyard house, and that the walls to that garden can still be traced on the 1821 plan (area 29 in the plan on page 155) and in surviving sections today. The more 'public' gardens of walks and bowling green were below the central road, below the earliest stable block and downhill of the present house (37 and 38 in the plans on page 155).

Although it seems unlikely that the 17thC gardens ever extended beyond the ditched and banked enclosure of the earliest farming hamlet, these gardens were said to be the favourite gardens of the Mohun family, father and son, in the first half of the 17thC. At this time, the Mohuns were one of the leading families of Cornwall. They were proud of their gardens and great walks at Hall, their original house opposite Fowey, where Carew wrote that the Mohuns had had one of the longest and most splendid 'long walks' that he had ever

seen. Their chief residence was Boconnoc, where there were large formal gardens, and a deer park.

A garden of this time had small formal areas intermixed with promenades, terraces and a bowling green. The earliest plans on pages 155-157 show three long terraces below a green courtyard. These gardens were noted as a long walk, kitchen garden and bowling green, although the area recorded as the kitchen garden was probably shrubs and hedges in the 17thC. It is amazing to consider that the 17thC garden layout has survived so long and that even the levelled bowling green can still be traced below the present gardens close to the bank and ditch of the boundary.

The garden at Trewinnard retains stonework and pillar cappings which appear to date from the early 17thC, when they are thought to have been used in the formal gardens of the time.

18thC Influences and Garden Design

From 1700 there was a general change in the design of gardens. By 1750 gardens had become important in the social status of owners. Rather than small inward looking gardens for retreat or terraces for walking and sport, gardens were opened up for vistas, promenades and larger areas of scene painting. One of the most telling examples of the new 'garden' is a guidebook of 1749 for the great gardens of Stowe. This publication, intended for the gentry, lists 77 monuments for the visitor to admire. However, it does not mention a single shrub, tree or flower. Whilst this may be an extreme example, it suggests that gardens were intended to offer vistas, views and opportunities for walking rather than for botanical study or amusement.

In Cornwall there are several examples of the changed approach to gardens. Although a small patterned garden within a walled enclosure was designed for Rosteague by John Kemp around 1700, these 'dutch' influenced designs soon became included within landscape schemes over a larger area, which by the middle of the 18thC had become very different.

This change is demonstrated by the designs for

Two drawings (c.1730) of Prideaux Place, Padstow by Edmund Prideaux, show the formal 17thC garden still retained. It is possible that the Mohun garden could have had similar features.

a new house at Pentillie Castle, commenced in 1698, which had courtyard gardens laid out with corner and intermediate viewing towers in an old fashioned style, but with long rides set out beyond the enclosed space. At Antony, rebuilt around 1722, a formal garden with decorative corner towers was surrounded by further landscaped areas beyond. At Bake, a Prideaux drawing shows the formal garden by the earlier house, to which was attached a new wing, façade and garden. At house after house, a new facade was built to face away from the working side of an earlier house, and the 'new' side then provided with a new style garden.

At Pencarrow new facades, gardens and approach roads were built facing away from the earlier house. At Menabilly, a prestigious façade was added together with a formal walled garden, complete with mounded lookout point. Walks or rides were laid out in the areas beyond the walls. Menabilly is also an example of raising a garden level around a house so that you could enter directly from the garden to the original first floor, leaving service areas below ground. At Boconnoc House, the medieval house was clad with a new mannered facade, the garden was landscaped with walks, vistas and miles of drives and, by the third quarter of the 18thC, larger gardens replaced the smaller formal gardens of an earlier age. At Prideaux Place similar changes in layout can still be traced. Even a less wealthy gentry house such as that at Harlyn was altered by Gregory Peter from 1690 with a new wing, façade and formal gardens with the obligatory exhedra and viewing point. The Pendarves family built a new house, Pendarves, outside Camborne with an open area in front of the house. This was bounded by what was perhaps the earliest ha-ha in Cornwall with, at its centre, an exhedra decorated with statues of classical figures. This early 18thC garden was evidence of changing taste and a wish to show an interest and knowledge of 'classical' culture.

Around 1720, another walled garden was added at Caerhays some way from the earlier Tudor enclosure with its terraces, walks, bowling green and ponds. The new walled garden was designed with water features, terraces, an octagonal banqueting house, viewing mounds and two turrets from which to admire the scenery. Beyond the walled gardens perhaps a further 50 acres or so was laid out with walks and in particular tree plantations. This area was described in an inventory of 1753 as including *'the flower garden, spalier hedge garden and kitchen garden, the new wilderness, malt house grove and John Eddy's orchards, nursery near John Eddy's orchards, cherry garden, garden top*

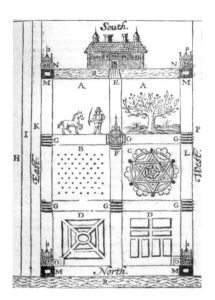

A Garden plan by Gervase Markham of 1638.

Rosteague, St Mawes
A garden by John Kemp c1700.

The restoration house of Stowe, Kilkhampton, North Cornwall, *Drawn by Prideaux c 1717.*

the orchard meadow, garden above the ash hill in the Grove, the orchard beyond the ash hill neat Lower White Stiles, the new orchard including the nursery, the nursery near the White Style stable, the Nursery in the Helland stable, Gidle Orchard, Park Grove as far as the gate into Churchtown field, the present park Lawns..'. John Trevanion of Caerhays spent much more money on his garden than most, but was not alone in changing not only the façade and appearance of his house, but also the gardens and grounds that went with it.

Bake, c 1716
drawn by Edmund Prideaux.

The Hawkins Garden at Trewinnard

Arriving from London in 1750, Thomas Hawkins must have been influenced by changing fashion and by the example of his cousin Philip, who had built a new house at Trewithen with large gardens in the new style. A different approach to garden design also reflected a change in the social interaction of house and garden. For centuries the house had been seen as integral to, and part of the stables, kitchens, farm and service operation. Horses were stabled in wings before the door, and staff entered through the main entry. Now a different concept required separation of service and staff functions with two sides to every mansion, one for visitors and family, the other for service and staff. At Trewinnard this was presumably the reason for the demolition of the earlier stables which stood in front of the present front door and which were replaced by the building of a new stable and coach house at the rear or north of the house.

Menabilly, showing new facades, raised formal gardens and viewing point, c.1740.

The Hawkins family were businessmen and managers who became very wealthy during the 18thC. They maintained a town house at Helston during the first half of the century, but their business interests and clients introduced them to all the changes in fashionable garden design. It seems likely that they wished to show that they too were of similar status and interests. When James Heywood visited Trewinnard in 1767, Christopher Hawkins arranged for him to see Mr. Bassets new house at Tehidy. James Heywood noted that Tehidy *also has fine gardens well laid out and a long canal well stocked with fish.* He also visited Trelowarren and commented on the enormous sums being spent on that house and the considerable garden alterations. The Hawkins family would have wanted to ensure that they too made improvements to the garden.

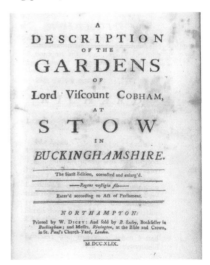

The Garden guide to Stow, Buckinghamshire, printed 1749. It lists 77 monuments but no trees, plants or flowers.

By the time of James Heywood's visit, the Hawkins garden scheme appears to have been complete. The enlarged garden added four new walled areas to the tudor plan. One of these was on the top of the hill

The Ha-ha & Exhedra, Pendarves, Cambourne.
Illustrated in Borlase 1758.

and three other enclosures for orchards were towards the river. Demolition of the earlier house and stables and the building of a new stable allowed the area before the front door of the Hawkins house to be landscaped. Landscaping also hid the foundations and site of the old house, where was also placed a formal garden of walks and hedges. A new wall was built along the top of the site against the road from the mill to provide privacy.

The Hawkins account books for this and earlier periods show the sums spent on walls, on gardens, on daily maintenance and garden labour. The Hawkins may also have improved the leat which brought water from Trencrom Hill some two miles away. This came to a large new reservoir or pond by the house and then travelled around the gardens before going towards the mill below the house, which last may have been one of the incentives for the investment in the water supply.

James Heywood described the gardens of Trewinnard as *"the gardens are well shaded with trees. The gravel walks well rolled and preserved clear from weeds. There is a very pleasant prospect from the house as well as [from the] gardens. The sea flowing every tide within a quarter of a mile from the house."* Walks, orchards, views and prospects were all important in the gardens of the time.

Once Christopher Hawkins' widow died in 1780, and the families of Trewinnard combined with the Hawkins family of Trewithen, all incentive for improvement and garden alteration at Trewinnard was lost. Sir Christopher Hawkins continued to use Trewinnard as his base, but lived primarily at Trewithen, and was famous for a certain meanness in spending money on house and garden.

The Garden since 1840

After the death of Sir Christopher Hawkins in 1829, the leats and water supplies to the various parts of the garden are likely to have fallen into disuse. The division between mansion and farmhouse became blurred by tenancies. It is thought that the Hawkins family paid little attention to house or gardens between 1829 and their eventual sale of the property in 1930. Lake suggested that by 1860 *"Trewinnard House has been so much altered latterly as scarcely to leave a trace of what it had been in former times [when] the gardens showed pleasing specimens of cut yew, trim box and trained thorn hedges."* One of the implications of this lament is that it implies that the yew, box and thorn had probably survived from the early 17thC garden.

The gates and stone piers dividing the gardens from the stable yard.

Stone piers survive from the early 16thC gardens.

The hedges of 'the long walk', first laid out 400 years ago.

During the tenancies of the nineteenth century many of the farm buildings were rebuilt in the Victorian manner and parts of the garden given over to agricultural use. With the exception of those areas taken into the farm, the gardens continued to be used by the farming families, although, as disinterested tenants, the gardens around the house became overgrown rather than altered. Some gardening must have continued. In the mid 20thC, when the farmhouse operated as a guesthouse, it advertised pleasant surroundings and gardens.

After the Second World War, there were further alterations for farm use and in addition to the demolition of the old chapel building, other works changed the layout of the garden. These included, around 1955, further landscaping to the immediate east of the house (opposite the front door). Here spoil was moved and landscaped to make a new ha-ha wall. To the south east of this area new rockeries were built which may incorporate some of the stone from demolished early buildings.

Over the last forty years, the gardens have been re-vitalised and maintained. Walls have been repaired and a new enclosed area for a swimming pool and pool house built at the north east end of the southern gardens. The gardens now include a formal area immediately uphill of the present house, built on part of the building platform of the original mansion. Although now part of the farmyard, the medieval walled garden can still be traced. South east of the front door are good privet hedges and below the house the original terraces can be seen. The original bowling walk can be walked, although it is now somewhat overgrown at the bottom of the garden.

The 18thC boundary walls around the courtyards, stables and along the garden are still in place and some decorative stonework appears to have survived from the earliest buildings.

The area of the garden now known as the cemetery has become a field, as have the orchards outside the line of the original Iron Age boundary ditch. At the top of the hill, the mid-18thC walls from an enclosed orchard can still be found, although this walled garden has long since been given over to modern farm buildings and barns.

The modern gardens of Trewinnard remain based on the layout of the tudor gardens as altered by the Hawkins family in the mid 18thC. They remain of particular interest as retaining much of the earliest in garden design and in demonstrating the development of the gentry garden over a period of five hundred years.

The mid 20thC Haha, south east of the house

The Haha was added around 1955 to extend the garden to the south east and improve the outlook from the house.

The Nott family assist in endless maintenance.

A swimming pool and carefully designed bath house were added by the Nott family, below the stables.

The rockeries and walks to the front of the house.

Tudor terraces and walks still survive.

The upper garden, where the bank covers the Mohun house.

The lower garden.

Sir John and Lady Nott, and their family at the blessing of the Burial Ground.
Left to right: Sir John Nott, Miloska Nott, Esther Langrish, The Very Revd. Michael Langrish (The Lord Bishop of Exeter), William Nott (eldest grandson), Sasha, Rosa, Raffaella, Hugo, Julian, Abigail, William.

The Dedication of a Burial Ground

To the east of the gardens, a family cemetery has been built near what may once have been a burial ground to the early chapel.

In March 2012, the new enclosed burial ground was blessed by the Bishop of Exeter during a service which included the words :

Heavenly Father, whose son Jesus Christ was laid in a tomb: Bless, we pray, this land as the place where the bodies of your servants may rest in peace. Through your Son, who is the resurrection and the life: who dies and is alive and reigns with you, now and for ever.

Sir John Nott and the Bishop of Exeter plant a tree given by his children to commemorate Sir John's 80th birthday.

Stonework to the burial ground.

Below: Plantings of poppies and wild flowers.

Life at Trewinnard

Details of tapestries: Top left: No 8;   Top Right: No 5;   Centre left and bottom: No 2;   Centre right: No 9.

Chapter 13
The Trewinnard Tapestries

One of the glories of Trewinnard is the tapestry collection. Tapestries were heavy decorative hangings intended to give dignity, decoration and draft-proof warmth to the halls and rooms of the medieval house.

They were also evidence of status and had earlier been seen as symbols of authority. They were of course portable and the rich would have taken their tapestries with them as they travelled. Such tapestries became elaborate illustrations of stories, myths and legends as well as showing the hunting scenes which many of the owners may have preferred. Many were intended to illustrate a moral or contained a mass of symbols then well understood, but now to us unfamiliar.

Although first used in halls, they became particularly popular as houses were divided with private apartments. They were common in most gentry houses from the mid-16thC onward, when Flanders took over from France as the chief manufacturing centre. Flanders continued to dominate the market through the 17thC.

Tapestries continued to be hung in English houses until their use was overtaken by the preference for framed paintings at the end of the 17thC. Even in the mid 18thC tapestries were still being commissioned and hung on the walls of great houses.

Cornwall has few recorded tapestry collections. A tapestry hung at Godolphin until recently and there are, no doubt, single examples elsewhere in the county. Mount Edgecumbe has two newly restored tapestries, once part of the family collection at Cotehele.

The best known collection in Cornwall is that at Cotehele. Around the time of the Restoration it was said that there were some seventy different tapestries there, although many tapestries are now thought to have been moved to Cotehele by the Edgcumbes in the 18thC.

The tapestries survived at Cotehele, despite

their fading, because they were seen as 'oldeworld' by the Edgecumbes. Over the years, they have become reduced, chopped up, and rearranged. The collection now has two complete tapestries and around fifty-five incomplete tapestries or fragments, most of which are of Flemish origin. The surviving items date mainly from around 1660 and so are generally of a later style and date than those of the Trewinnard collection.

The earlier tapestry collection from Trewinnard, is thought to have been hung in the Tudor and Jacobean building at Trewinnard some time before 1642, the date for the death of Reginald Mohun. After some 370 years, they are dulled by time and the fabric, although much repaired through the years, has become brown. It is difficult to imagine now how bright and clear these tapestries would have looked with greens, bright blues, gold, silver and bright reds. Although dull and worn, there is still an astonishing amount of detail to be made out.

The Trewinnard tapestries are little known in Cornwall and this fine collection is a considerable achievement in acquisition and conservation.

The Hangings at Trewinnard

The tapestries are probably of Flemish origin and date from between 1580 and 1640. Compared with the dated pieces at Cotehele, the tapestries at Trewinnard all seem to be in an earlier manner in subject, design and border. The inclusion of ladies with ruffs suggest that two could be of late 16thC date. They are largely of wool with some additional silk threading, and restored, conserved and relined in recent years, are now in sound condition for their age.

They appear to have 'turned up' in the Hawkins house at Trewinnard during the 18thC. Although it is possible that a Hawkins of the time purchased them as a job lot, they are not the sort of covering that would have appealed to the modernising Hawkins family for the smart late 17thC house they were building. This new house was one that eschewed old fashioned wall hangings and was fitted with wooden panelling. From the restoration of 1660 onwards, tapestries, although still available, were being dropped in favour of other styles and materials for internal decoration. Tapestries had become, save for a few choice specimens, decidedly 'old fashioned'. It is clear that these tapestries were not well respected, or seen as expensive purchases, since it is recorded that they had to be cut about to fit the new house, one even having a hole cut out for a fireplace.

The unlikelihood of their having been purchased

for the new Hawkins Trewinnard house suggests they were already on site, hanging in the older house, which is thought to have been demolished in the first quarter of the 18thC.

Until 1642, Trewinnard was lived in by Reginald Mohun, second son of the Mohuns of Boconnoc, one of the greatest families in Cornwall. Reginald Mohun described himself as 'of Trewinnard' and the tradition endured that Trewinnard was the 'favourite Mohun residence' of this Reginald and of his father, Sir Reginald Mohun who lived from 1564 to 1639 and whose aunt Isabella had married Martin Trewinnard. At this time, Trewinnard, although old fashioned, remained one of the great courtyard and hall houses of west Cornwall and a house where such hangings would have been typical. The Mohuns were also rich enough to have tapestries filled with figures, which were more expensive than simpler pieces.

It therefore seems likely that these tapestries were hanging in the old house at Trewinnard. However, despite an uncertain verbal tradition, there is no evidence of the tapestries at Trewinnard before the 18thC.

A 1964 letter from a Mr Hawkins to Mr Pascoe, then the owner of Trewinnard, refers to a *tapestry found behind the plaster, and now framed on the wall of the stairs* [at Trewinnard]. This siting suggests that the tapestries had been hung in Trewinnard during the 18thC. It is unlikely that the old tapestries would have been hung over the 'new' and fashionable wainscoting or panelling. It is possible that the old house tapestries were therefore re-hung only on the first floor of the west extension to the Hawkins house. This extension was built with the stone from the earlier house then being demolished. The design of this 'extra' north west wing is eccentric in having neither fireplaces nor windows in the gable end, and no window to the south or entrance side of the four poster room on the first floor. This design may therefore have not been eccentric, but intended to provide large wall spaces for the wall hangings taken from the old mansion then being demolished.

Left at Trewinnard after the death of the widow Mary Hawkins in 1780, the tapestries remained there. In the 1860's, Polsue noted that *in one of the chambers of the [Trewinnard] mansion was tapestry representing the victory of Constantine, with his celebrated vision of the cross.* Around 40 years later, Bishop Stubbs visited Trewinnard and was *charmed by the tapestry hanging in the principal rooms,* although it was noted that much of the tapestry was apparently mutilated; one had had a large piece cut out of the middle so that the tapestry

could fit round the fireplace.

In 1912, the Hawkins family of Trewithen contributed £3000.00 towards the repair of the church and the Trewinnard aisle at St Erth. Mrs. Hawkins, having first sent the tapestries to the South Kensington School of Needlework for repairs and for missing parts to be made good, gave eight of the tapestries to the Bishop's home at Lis Escop near Truro. These tapestries later moved around diocesan properties, including Copeland Court, where, until 1983, they were hung in a ground floor room and in the chapel. Another two tapestries were given by Mrs Hawkins to the Truro Museum.

Six other border frieze pieces with a foliage pattern were mounted in the panelling of the southern Trewinnard aisle of the church, where they remain.

Of the Hawkins tapestry gift, eight are now back at Trewinnard and one is in store at the house of the Bishop of Truro. Two have been found at the Royal Institute of Cornwall in Truro, together with others alleged to be from Trewinnard. Since there now seem to be more tapestries and fragments than originally listed, the current list may include tapestries not then considered worth restoring beyond the ten noted by Mrs Hawkins.

By 1983, the Textile Conservation Centre at Hampton Court Palace suggested that the tapestries held by the Bishop needed urgent conservation. Partly from the need for expensive conservation and through a lack of hanging space, the diocese offered eight tapestries for sale. The owners of Trewinnard, Sir John and Lady Nott agreed to restore them and then return them to hang at Trewinnard, where they remain.

The Scenes shown on the Hangings.

The stories illustrated are from biblical or classical texts. Such allusions not only flattered the culture and knowledge of both owner and visitor, but also reflected their general familiarity with mythology, the stories of the bible, the classical world and their myths.

A very different modern education makes it unlikely that we are familiar with the stories so illustrated.

Section of frieze to tapestry number 9.

The Tapestries:
Description and Identifying Record

Each surviving piece of tapestry has been numbered, and these numbers used as codes for the illustrations. Photographing the large and detailed hangings in restricted space and furnished rooms proved difficult. Colour balance is at best a compromise and the brilliance and varied colours of the tapestries are not well reproduced. The small illustrations can not show the details in each tapestry, but can give an impression of the picture. Measurements are approximate.

Detail from The Judgement of Solomon, tapestry number 3.

1.	*'The Continence of Scipio'.*
	(103.75"x 142.5" : 2.70m x 3.67m). East wall of the dining room
	Scipio was a roman general fighting in Spain around 200BC. A popular story told how, in return for gold and gifts, he returned a woman hostage to her young man. This tapestry is based on designs by Giulio Romano, although simplifed and woven in reverse to other surviving examples. It has the same figure of the bride and the three figures in attendance on the throne returning the future bride to her betrothed, in return for a ransom of golden vessels. A soldier with laurel leaf crown on the left hand side is seated on a canopied throne and gestures to a woman in the foreground. To the left of the seated figure a woman in a skirt with shoulder attachments stands beside him. Behind the throne are two helmeted guards with halberds, chatting to each other. Three figures, older men, bring gifts. There are two other figures in the background, which has a landscape that includes a multi-churched town and formalised greenery. The clothing style suggests a date very early in the 17thC. The border to this tapestry is complete to the top and the sides, is about 40cm wide and shows floral sprays and cartouches. The border to this and to number 2 are similar, suggesting they were part of a series.

2. *Constantine and the Vision of the True Cross before the Battle of Milvian Bridge.*
(101.5" x 172.5" : 2.60m x 4.42m) Hanging in the four poster bedroom upstairs.

A vision appeared to Constantine before his final battle against Maxentius at the Milvian bridge in AD312. An almost life size soldier, with laurel crown and cloak stands on flowered grass on the left with behind him a soldier with shield and an attendant or woman(?). In the foreground, a page holds further armour which includes a blazened shield. Constantine looks across a valley landscape with a bridge and above that a turreted and walled town. The 'sky' landscape has two further towns and hills and a banner which flies the words *In Hoc Syno Vences* (by this sign shalt thou conquer).The motto leads the eye to a flag emblazoned with the older Christian *Chi-Ro* symbol, (a logo of the two Greek letters that begin the word Christos). To the right of the tapestry, other figures balance the composition. A young boy holds a magnificent horse and, behind, a soldier holds an SPQR standard topped with laurels, with further figures behind.

The borders to the top and sides are complete; the lower border is missing. The top border is of flower sprays. The side borders have a heavier vertical spray and long central ornaments. The border to this is similar to that of tapestry number 1. This tapestry has been attributed to Enghien.

Details from tapestry 3.

3.   *The Judgement of Solomon.*
     (0.67m x 4.11m) In store with the Bishop of Truro. (February 2012)
     This frieze tapestry in wool and silk has three scenes separated from each other by a satyr standing like a pillar. The first scene (1.22m long) shows a throned king with the name *Sipioen* above him. He gestures to a kneeling woman and two men. The second scene (4.11m long) shows a woman kneeling before a throned king.
A baby lies in a bundle on the floor, and a baby is also held up by the ankles by the soldier to the left of the king. The third final scene (1.11m long) shows a man and woman walking together. The woman appears to be holding a baby.

Details from tapestry 3. King Solomon with the disputed baby lying at his feet.

4.   *The Sacrifice of Manoah and the Foretelling of Samson's Birth.*
(97" x 100" : 2.50m x 2.56m) Oudenarde(?) 17thC. Hung in the first floor passage.

An angel with wings stretched to heaven rises from flames and a fire over a lamb set before an altar. A bearded man holds his arms out to an angel and a woman cowers beside him. There is a pot in the foreground. The background is of stylised clouds. The side borders have been removed. Top and bottom 28cm borders have floral sprays.

The story is from Judges 13:19-20. The wife of Manoah was barren. Manoah offered to make a sacrifice for the promise made by the angel of the lord that his wife would conceive. *'So Manoah took a kid with a meat of offering and offered it upon a rock unto the Lord; and the angel did wondrously; and Manoah and his wife looked on. For it came to pass, when the flame went up toward heaven from off the altar, that the angel of the Lord ascended in the flame of the altar. And Manoah and his wife looked on it and fell on their faces to the ground'.* The son was called Samson.

5.   *The Escape of St Paul.*
        (92" x 77" : 2.36m x 1.95m) West side south stair case.
        St Paul steps from a basket lowered from the city wall of Damascus with, in the background, a bridge and distant town.
        Then the disciples took him by night and let him down by the wall in a basket.
There are no other figures. The floral border is still attached on all four sides and is about 10" wide although it may have been reduced in height. The tapestry appears of different and later style to others. This would seem to be from the second half of the 17thC since it was probably made in Oudenarde after Raphael's Acts of the Apostles or perhaps after designs of Abraham van Diepenbeeck (1596 - 1675).

6.　　　*The Continence of Scipio.*

(96" x 126" : 2.46m x 3.20m). Dining room, west end.

This tapestry repeats the story of tapestry number 1. The kneeling figures are the same, but woven in reverse with two soldiers behind them. The figures, reading from the left have one guard with halberd, short sword, breaches, helmet; in the middle an old man with long moustaches bends with behind him a woman also bending. In front of them another man with beard, moustaches and decorated hair appears to be kneeling. Another man stands guard in the background. The kneeling figures may be offering gifts. The whole is in a landscape setting. The border to each side has a twisted pillar *(salmonic)* into which is carved cherubim.

The top border is of flowers. This is probably the left hand side of a much wider tapestry which has been reduced in width.

7.   *Ahasuerus, King of Persia, receiving Esther.*
  (100" x 57" : 2.56m x 1.46m) Hung on west wall of first floor landing to south stair.
  A bearded man with a crown, cloak and sceptre with pantaloons and breeches, and two attendants to his right, greets a woman with a ruff and cloak, who is attended by two ladies, one of whom also has a ruff. In the background is a building with pillars, throne and in the centre a (priestly?) figure, a second onlooker on the central castle and two seated onlookers to the right-back, before a small town or building.
  Many of the details are most unusually picked out with white paint. The tapestry is missing the left hand border and this may in fact be the right hand section of a long cartoon design. The border has, half way down the right, a grotesque figure with arms in the air holding an urn(?). The top frieze has, to the right, a woman with a halberd and in the centre two women(?) kneeling each side of a prayer desk.
  The tapestry has been reduced in height and the bottom border cut and joined.

8.   *Unknown subject.*
(98" x 98" : 2.55m x 2.50m) (Enghien C1575?). East wall of the South staircase.

A king with crown and neck chains of office is in the centre on a throne with two attendants. The throne is canopied and has two 'renaissance' pillars. He holds one sceptre. Two(?) further men on his right offer him a crown and orb; a woman to his left, who wears a ruff, offers him a sceptre. Behind her another man offers a model town or fort.The background includes two figures, one with a spear behind a balcony to the left and two figures behind a balcony to the right back. The tapestry is square and is probably at its original size, save that the bottom border, of which a central ornamental medallion can be seen, has been removed. The side borders include conventional musical instruments. Both the top and side borders have figures and the two top corners have crossed leg seated figures. It has been suggested that the subject is either Esther and Ahasuerus or David and Bathsheba.

9.   *Solomon and Sheba?*
      (100" x 50": 2.50m x 1.28m) (Enghien 1575?). North wall of the south first floor landing.
      This piece is missing both side borders, and was probably the centre section of a wider cartoon story. A king on a throne greets a crowned queen bearing a flower in each hand.   The king has a crown, holds a sceptre and his throne is canopied and carries a cloth of state. He has four attendants, one with halberd. Two further figures are in the middle distance with a castle and another building behind. The kneeling queen has an attendant and there is a beehive(?) on the ground between the main figures. Behind a pillar near the throne is the castle or town and landscape with towers and furniture. The top frieze, which includes a man playing a lute, is of wider and different pattern to the simple frieze to the bottom. Similarities suggest that another part of the same tapestry could be hanging at Westwood Manor, a National Trust Property.

10.   *Subject uncertain.*
        (3ftwide x 5 ft : 0.92m high x 1.54m wide) Sited on the main staircase at Trewinnard. This panel of worn and frayed tapestry is now framed and under glass. Surviving letters say that it was found during renovations at Trewinnard 'behind some plaster'. It is presumed that it was found hanging behind a section of lathe and plaster walling over stone. Bishop Mumford of Truro said that the hanging obviously showed the story of Jesus and the adulteress:
        He that is without sin among you, let him first cast a stone at her. (John 8 v7).

St Erth Church:
Fragments mounted on the wall of south aisle

Six pieces of border are displayed in the Trewinnard chapel. The carved inscriptions to the panelling in the Trewinnard aisle include:

This Chancel has been restored by Jane Ellen Hawkins, widow of Christopher Henry Hawkins of Trewinnard..... This tapestry is from Trewinnard. Eight pieces adorn the walls of the residence of the see at Truro and two pieces are in Truro Museum.

It is not clear whether these pieces were once at the top, the bottom, or the side of a tapestry. They are shown in the order of position from the east end. Tapestry measurements are masked by the cloth and timber mounting and are only approximate.

11. St Erth: Dimensions 0.660m x 0.330m.

12. St Erth   Dimensions 0.290m wide x 2.300m long.

13. St Erth   Dimensions 0.390m wide x 1.680m wide.
Mounted above a doorway. Certain similarities with missing border of no 12.

14. St Erth   Dimensions 0.450m wide x 1.100m wide.
Items 21 and 22 may have been joined as the side border of a tapestry.

15. St Erth   Dimensions 0.460m wide x 1.100m long.
Once mounted above no 21.

16. St Erth   Dimensions 0.320m high x 0.280m wide.
A fragment mounted on its side.

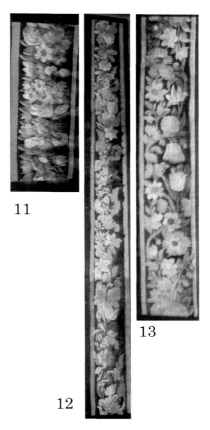

11

13

12

Three pieces are set round a doorway in the north wall.

14   15

16

17.   *St Peter and St John at the Temple (?)*
        (2.26m high x 2.24m wide)
        Royal Institute of Cornwall
        This tapestry was one of those from Trewinnard which
was given by Mrs Hawkins to the Royal Institute of Cornwall,
where it remains in store. The style of the tapestry is similar
to that of tapestry number 5. The border is complete on all
four sides and is similar to the border of tapestry number 5.
The subject of this panel of Flemish tapestry may have been
taken from the centre portion of Raphael's cartoon 'St Peter
and St John at the Beautiful Gate of the Temple', or may illustrate the story of Lazurus.

18   *The Feeding of the Five Thousand (?)*
        1.630m wide x 2.310m high
        Royal Institute of Cornwall
        This tapestry was one of those from Trewinnard which
was given by Mrs Hawkins to the Royal Institute of Cornwall,
where it remains in store. The style of the tapestry is similar
to that of tapestry number 5. The border is similar to that of
tapestry 5, but is incomplete on the left hand side. This may
be another copy from Raphael's Cartoons. The subject is not
certain.

19, 20, 21, 22, 23.   *Items not yet identified.*
        Royal Institute of Cornwall
        These numbered items are included for the sake of
record, but may refer to pieces or remnants that no longer exist. In addition to the two Trewinnard tapestries at the Royal
Institution of Cornwall (items 17 and 18), four other pieces of
tapestry from Trewinnard, (items 19 to 22) and a small fragment (item 23) are said to be noted on inventories at the Royal
Institution of Cornwall.
        No further information on these items was available.

Chapter 14
Highways and the Trewinnard Coach

In recent years Trewinnard has been notable as the home of Sir John Nott, and for its association with the Trewinnard Coach. This magnificent vehicle, now in the Royal Institute of Cornwall is so called because it was to Trewinnard that Thomas Hawkins brought the coach when he moved from London around 1750. It stayed there until restored by Mrs Hawkins in 1909/10 before being given to the Royal Institute of Cornwall, in Truro, where it remains at the centre of their Museum.

Thomas Hawkins and his family appear to have used the coach only to go to church. Such a coach was sufficiently rare for it to be considered special in the 18thC, particularly so in Cornwall.

The bringing of the coach to Cornwall was probably a statement of status rather than for use as practical or useful transport, since the roads were unsuitable for the coach.

Early Roads

Travel around Cornwall had long been difficult. The first tracks tended to run along the ridgeways where the ground was firmer. Transport of goods and people had always been easier by boats which could float up estuaries and small rivers to provide access to much of the county. Although some trackways continued in use, most hamlets or villages were linked by paths, now known as 'church paths', rather than roads. For farms and those unable to use the sea, transport of all goods including farm produce was always by small ponies. Part of the reason for this road poverty was probably that heavy items could go round the coast and that there was no great need for an area of small population with little passing trade to create roads for carts.

There had been no earlier road system in Cornwall which could have been maintained or adapted.

Although the romans have long been thought to have made little ingress into Cornwall and although it is often stated that paved roads stopped at Exeter, this is not true. There were a number of roman roads around Cornwall, most of them at the edges of the county and designed to connect ports, signal stations or the forts or fortlets above them. However, since these roads were not paved, the tracks soon wore out and most fell early out of use. Some roman roads can still be traced. There are two good long straight roads each side of the valley at St. Erth. The trackway to the west may have been a ridgeway linking a number of Iron Age sites and that to the east of the Hayle estuary was a roman road linking a series of small forts.

Trewinnard was a port on the Hayle estuary and on the easiest route through to the sea at St Michael's bay. As a port, Trewinnard was central to the most common method of transport which was by boat. As a transhipment base, the tracks around the site, the ridgeway and the ways across the watershed may have meant Trewinnard was better served by roads than many places and, therefore, unlike other farm sites where the only track available was likely to have been a deep, muddy, single-file, stony water-worn way.

Where old trackways have been by-passed but remain, it is possible to see that they can never have been used by wheeled traffic. For instance, an important track at Tucoys, east of the Helford River, ran down past a mill and onto the coast via a number of clapper stone bridges. It was useable by ponies but can never have been wide enough or able to take wheeled traffic. Celia Fiennes records in 1698 that even farmers cleared their hay, straw, furze or gorse and oil from their lands not on small carts but on strings of ponies.

Other early transport methods included litters whose poles were carried by men or ponies, but these were only for the most important and wealthy of people, or for the sick, for women, or for clergy. Another forgotten method of transport was the single horse drawn litter with a sloping litter resting on poles dragged along the ground. These were in use for goods and the desperate; most other travel was by foot or by pony. A visit to any 16thC house in Cornwall shows that houses have a mounting block. This not only makes mounting a horse easier for a man but is absolutely essential for a woman riding side saddle. The mounting block at Trewinnard reminds us that it was not just men but also women who had of necessity to ride a horse.

Celia Fiennes made a journey around Cornwall in1694. This wonderfully adventurous woman travelled

The mounting block in the stable yard at Trewinnard.

A view of the ferry at Lelant, drawn by T. Raffles Davison

alone, accompanied by only one or two staff and staying with relatives and acquaintances. As she makes clear these were journeys where horseback was the only practical option. Her diary emphasises that bridges were few and that any stream must be crossed by a ford or ferry.

Fords, Ferries and Bridges

The advent of bridges transformed road travel. Finance for bridge repair was always a problem because the wear and tear was caused by through traffic, whereas maintenance was the responsibility of the local parish. Nevertheless, the first great advance for roads in Cornwall was probably the building of bridges. Examples include that bridge at Constantine for passage between Penryn and Gweek built at a cost of £6.13s.4d in 1572. The building of the 1468 bridge at Wadebridge replaced the dangerous long ford of the Camel, which had had a chapel at each end. The bridge at St. Erth, thought to have been built before 1340, was therefore the most important early change in the landscape around Trewinnard. The previous width of the waterway and the need for the old ferry crossing below the bridge, is shown by the length of the causeway necessary each side of the bridge. Save for fords, the Hayle estuary had, until then, presented a difficult barrier all the way from its mouth up to the hamlet of Relubbus, whose name suggests it was the lowest and first practical ford over the river.

Lower down the Hayle there were ferries across the estuary to Lelant but these must have been terrifying journeys which justifed a prayer in a bankside chapel before embarking. The use of fords was common, but those around the Hayle were treacherous. It is said that during one of his preaching tours, John Wesley's carriage left sound ground when crossing the Hayle, and so

The centre arches of the bridge at St Erth,
and the narrow canalised stream of modern times.

fell into deep water and treacherous sands.

The dangers of the Hayle estuary lived on in tales recorded to the mid-19thC when it was reported that *wayfarers [were] often lost through a lack of strength of horse or rider in the sands'* and that *'horseman and horse would go round and round like the tin in a jigger, when once in the eddying sand, [then would] quickly sink from sight and were lost for ever.*

Ferries continued to operate across the Hayle using a small boat known as a *praham* until the end of the 19thC, but were not considered safe or reliable.

Road Improvements.

During the 16thC and 17thC there were some improvements in the roads by local owners. One key to the age of a road is whether there are stone facings on the banks that line what was often a steep water-worn cut, such stone edgings being a sign that a road is a later or improved road. However, roads were a right of passage and their floor continued to be owned by the adjoining landowners rather than by a communal authority. The landowners would resist any imposition of communal need and tracks were easily ruined by heavy loads, animals, dragged goods and so on, with no redress to the owner and so no incentive for him to maintain a route.

After an Act of 1555, parishes were required to maintain tracks using 'statute labour' and larger landowners were also required to provide men and materials. However it was clear that this system never worked well. Two hundred years later, writer after writer suggested that roads had become impassable and had not been maintained at all. Increasing traffic merely made the situation worse and the cutting up of tracks by the iron shod wheels of carriers and carts was a country wide problem.

In west Cornwall, where wheeled traffic was difficult, horses appear to have been the norm for almost all travel and transport right up to 1760 although this too had its problems. Many writers comment on the problems of bad weather, others on the problems of horses on trackless land, of danger of bogs and holes, of losing the way, or of being assailed by the vagrants and robbers who frequented the moors and wastes between farms.

Travel was therefore usually by foot or by pony. As late as 1792, the date of James Boswell's visit to Cornwall as a 52 year old, he notes walking many miles in his visits and, after a drunken evening at Killiow, making a night-time return ride of about eight miles, apparently with his daughters also on horseback. He wrote: *'it was not agreeable riding home at night'.*

Coaches and Wheels

There is little record of early wheeled or coach traffic in Cornwall, whose existence necessarily followed the existence of roads capable of carrying them. It is reported that King Charles I brought a coach with him, when he visited Cornwall during the Civil War, but by and large there were just no tracks or roads which could take wheeled traffic. The earliest roads sank slowly into the ground and became "V" shaped with the bottom cut up by hooves and water. They became water runs unable to take wheeled traffic. In 1716, when the Assizes were first held at Bodmin, a road had to be improved from Launceston to Bodmin just to allow the judge's coach to arrive, suggesting that wheeled traffic elsewhere in the county must have been worse than difficult.

Some coaches may have been used around 1700 in the far east of Cornwall. Sir James Tillie, at Pentillie, a man of great self importance, left to his wife in his will of 1704 his *coach chariot calash and set of six horses with choice of two other horses and cows..,* all of which were almost certainly kept at Pentillie. His neighbour, William Coryton of Newton Ferrers left his wife, in a will of 1711, the *best chariot, harness, coach horses, gelding or mares, with the grey gelding she usually rides on.* William Glynn from Glynn east of Bodmin also left a coach and horses to his wife in 1727. However, all these instances are from the east of Cornwall; references for coaches further west are few. The earliest seem to be that for a chaise used in Truro in 1760 by William Lemon of Carclew, five years after the first turnpikes

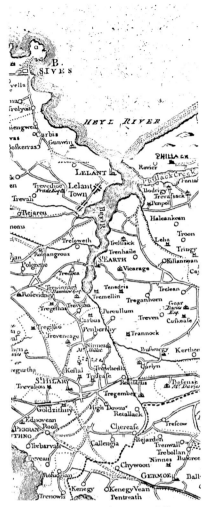

Thomas Martyn's map of Cornwall, 1748, was the first to give some detail of local roads. This excerpt shows the Hayle Estuary which is shown as wide all the way to Trewinnard.

Courtesy Royal Institute of Cornwall

had opened immediately around that city. There is also a reference in Christopher Hawkins' accounts for the rent of a chaise in Truro in May 1763. The ownership of a carriage was a matter of status, and further east, where roads improved rather earlier, more gentry families were likely to have wheeled carriages as a form of showing off.

There had long been a tradition that the Trewinnard Coach was the first and only coach in the west of Cornwall in the mid 18thC. Wheeled transport was sufficiently rare, even as late as 1750 to be remarked on. This tradition is supported by John Davy's recollection in 1836 that his mother, talking of a time around 1760, said that any wheeled vehicle was rare and that when a coach did appear in Penzance, it had caused a sensation. Pamela Dodds, in her analysis of 18thC building accounts, noted that waterborne carriage was used so far as possible for delivery of building materials, but on land, that there was some evidence for the use of a 'plough'. The word suggests dragging, but may have come to be applied to 'a team of draught beasts harnessed to a wagon', although it is possible that the wagon was not always included. There is reference to a wheeled wagon in west Cornwall in 1737, and another in 1762 of a driver cutting across the sand outside Penzance when *the driver of a plough laden with tin for Penzance coinage found himself and the plough of a sudden surrounded by the sea.* A rented *plough* was used for dragging stones at Trewinnard in 1763. However, both two wheeled and four wheeled carts or wagons are not thought to have arrived in east Cornwall until the end of the 18thC and in the west rather later.

At the time, the details of travel and transport were of course commonplace, so that such details were all too seldom noted. In 1757, Christopher Hawkins' son's father-in-law, James Heywood, visited his daughter's family and places such as Trewithen, Tehidy, Trewinnard, St Michael's Mount and Penzance. Part of the journey to Penzance was by *post chariot... over the sands near the seashore for about two miles..*, presumably because landside roads were not realistically passable. James Heywood noted that of the roads throughout Cornwall it could be said that *I never saw a cart or wagon loaded in this county... but what were drawn by Oxen and horses together...the roads at present are bad for Wheel carriages in many places, but there is a turnpike road about Truro which many are employed in mending, which when finished will be as good as many about London.*

T. Raffles Davison drew this picture of the coach, a visitor attraction at Trewinnard, in the 1880s.

The Trewinnard Coach

The Trewinnard Coach, admirably researched by Cedric Appleby, appears to have been built for the Spanish Ambassador between 1680 and 1700, although designed in a french or spanish style typical of styles earlier that century. The design of the coach closely resembles a carriage in the Portuguese Royal Collection at Lisbon and is built on a heavy farm-style undercarriage. The present wheels, whose iron rims are not continuous, are said to be of relatively light construction with unusual spacing of spokes. For both coachman and owner the vehicle must have been an uncomfortable and difficult ride on almost any road of the time. Described at the time as of commodious size, the body seems rather small and cramped to us.

Hawkins family tradition suggests that the coach was purchased when an unpaid bill for making the coach was settled by Thomas Hawkins. He then lent it to the Sheriff of London before keeping it for his own use in London. With the exception of 'The Speaker's Coach', built in 1698 in similar style, the Trewinnard coach may be the oldest surviving coach in Britain.

The coach was brought to Trewinnard when Thomas Hawkins moved from London, but was little used save for journeys to church. The widow, Mary Hawkins, continued these journeys after the death of her son in 1766 and her husband in 1767. She was reputed to have had the horses put to the carriage so that she could be taken about a mile to church twice on Sundays.

On her death in 1780, the chassis of the coach was used to carry her coffin to the church, pulled by her four matching black horses. After that, in accordance with her will, the horses were turned into the fields and

Two pictures of the Trewinnard Coach, at Trewinnard, show it before restoration, around 1900. Because Mary and her husband were Hawkins by both birth and marriage, the coat of arms on Thomas and Mary's coach shows the doubled arms of the Hawkins family, representing the two sides of the same family.

The Trewinnard Coach, in the The Royal Institute of Cornwall
Photo Charles Woolf; Courtesy Royal Institute of Cornwall

like the coach, never used again.

Stored in the stables, the coach remained at Trewinnard as an object of interest and curiosity, although newspapers reported that it was being stripped by souvenir hunters. In 1848, Davies Gilbert mentioned the coach in his Parochial History of Cornwall as one of the wonders of the area. Tourist interest, anecdotes and visitors continued to keep the story of the Trewinnard coach alive. Postcards of it were to be had at the end of the 19thC.

Covered with graffiti and stripped of pins, mouldings, and leather and suffering from 129 years of neglect, the coach was by 1909 in a poor state. Mrs Hawkins then had the coach taken to Bristol to be restored by J. Fuller, a restoration that cost £215 3s 6d, including the transport from Truro to Bristol and back to the Royal Institute of Cornwall, where it remains today.

This great carriage may not always have been drawn by horses. Unshod oxen were still used in the fields by farmers, but the Hawkins accounts record two bills for the iron shoeing of four oxen during 1756. This suggests they were being used on hard or stony surfaces and fits with the tradition that the coach used by Mary Hawkins would, on occasion, have to be hauled through the muddy roads by oxen rather than by horses.

In 1909, the coach was dismantled at Trewinnard for repair in Bristol. This picture shows the two workmen posing in the detached body. *Courtesy Royal Institute of Cornwall*

The Costs of Horse and Coach.

The Hawkins account books, also summarised by Mr. Cedric Appleby, show the enormous amount of money spent by the Hawkins family on their stables, horses, coachman, staff, and liveries. Not only did the stable block have to be built, but then maintained. Judg-

The new stable block built by Christopher Hawkins in 1738 for his coach, carriages and horses.

ing from the shoeing bills for 1756, they probably contained some 10 or so animals. The bills for repairs to the great coach, and lesser vehicles were considerable. Even the annual tax on the coach was £4.00, a sum equivalent at the time to half a year's salary for a qualified man. The accounts list repairs to wheels, leather, paintwork, training, purchase and dealing in horses, uniforms and wages. The coachman's wage rose in five years or so from five to eight guineas a year, which was more than was received by the farm manager or the schoolmaster. The cost of maintaining horses, carriages and coachman may have represented some 15% of all household expenses at Trewinnard for each of the years from 1753 to 1757. Although an enormous sum for the time, such costs should be compared with the £23 spent by Christopher Hawkins for a return journey on horseback to London in April 1756, and a return trip to Bath in November 1762, costing £25.4s.6d including accommodation and food.

The coachhouse below a simple undecorated pediment.

It is of course difficult to assess the real value of money against spending power, but it is probably not unfair to say that the operation of the coach, stables and horses was a material element in the household budget. It might be compared with a man of today who runs three of four cars, each changed every two or three years, whose maintenance is not only a chauffeur but also the bills from a luxury garage.

The Hawkins accounts record the costs not just of the coach but also of a chaise, purchased in 1759, and a cart or trap. A prestigious Landau was bought in 1755, but is likely to have been of little practical use for local tracks; it appears to have been sold around 1760.

Despite the sums which the accounts show that

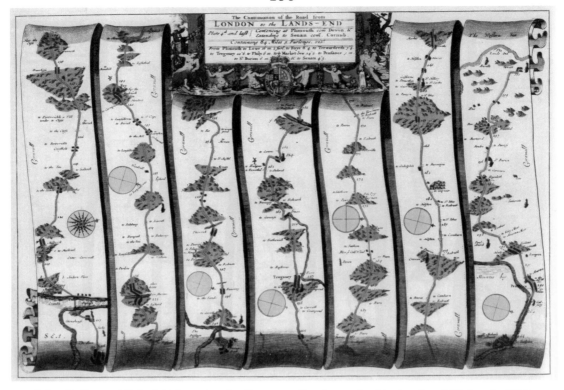

John Ogilby published *Britannia*, the first travellers' map for England and Wales, in 1675.
It had 100 ribbon maps and sheet 28 shows the last section of the road from London to Land's End.

the family spent not only on their carriages but also on the roads, the Hawkins wheeled vehicles were little used. Judging from the bills for necessary repairs to the coach and, in particular, to its wheels and springs, such carriages suffered badly on the tracks of the area.

Road Improvements and Turnpikes

The Hawkins family continuously contributed to improving the roads around St. Erth, partly for their own benefit and partly for the public. Their own trade and transport of goods would have gained from the improvements of the bridge, but around 1755, they appear to have paid for the new road which ran from Trewinnard, past Trewinnard mill and along the east side of the estuary to the church. They also funded improvements to the west road through Tredrea to St. Erth bridge. Communications were so important to the business interests of Christopher Hawkins, that it was this that probably ensured his funding and overseeing of the repair of roads and the improvements to the bridge and causeways at St Erth in 1750. The Hawkins accounts record regular payments to 'Bethuel Bastard' for works on the highways.

The first useable road map for Cornwall was that

printed by Martyn, a map which Christopher Hawkins purchased in 1749. With few direct through roads, the map has a network of interconnecting tracks with remnants of the earlier ridgeways. These lanes were really only suitable for travel on horseback. Some of the roads on the map are shown by dotted lines where they wander, unmarked, over moor or unenclosed land.

Improvements west of Truro only started in the mid-18thC, when the quarries of Cornwall began to produce more stone. The mines were the leaders in the development, not only of the tramways for shipment of minerals or slate to the coast for production elsewhere, but of wider roads, since quarried stone required heavier wagons for transport to the nearest port. Despite such small improvements, complaints continued about the uneven and stony nature of the roads, which were a problem for the hooves of horses as well as providing a very unsettled ride.

The Turnpike Roads

The road system of England had been in decline for many years and responsibility for upkeep continued to be a problem. It was only the introduction of turnpikes, which were private fee-paying roads, that made any difference. The earliest turnpike trusts in England started in 1707, but in Cornwall the early trusts only appeared within town boundaries from about 1754. Some improvements were made to roads without turnpike status and in 1765 Richard Gough noted that two roads from Land's End to Penzance had been widened and 'lately made fit for carriages'. Population growth, trade, changing commerce and wealthier gentry were requiring better roads and the Falmouth-Helston-Marazion turnpike was authorised by Act of Parliament in 1761. This route to Penzance from Truro went towards Falmouth then through Stithians and Helston, such early turnpikes showing a very different road pattern to that to which we are now accustomed.

Cornwall remained behind the rest of the country in such roads. It was notable that Christopher Hawkins recorded his first encounter with a toll on the turnpike at Exeter in 1776. Even around 1800, F. Trevithick, in his Life of Richard Trevithick, wrote that only one post chaise was for hire in the whole area west of Truro. This was kept for the use of the higher gentry by a Mr Harvey in Cambourne. This much envied post chaise was said to be the only comfortable carriage available and was used by mine owners and engineers for inspecting workings.

After 1761, Parliament authorised no toll roads west of Redruth until the Redruth-Hayle road of 1839

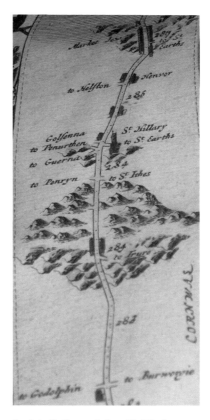

A detail from John Ogilby's map of 1675 shows St Hillary, with the turnoff to St Erth.

and a short extension from Penzance to St Just of 1863.

Coach travel was still rare until the 1790s when the first stage coach ran on alternate days between Exeter and Falmouth. Such public wheeled transport lasted only for fifty years or so before the railway train took over as the principal method of transport in England.

Until the the end of the 18thC, the horse remained the only sensible, viable method of travel. Difficulties in travel defined the lives of most Cornish, who were said to seldom travel beyond their parish boundaries. It is really very difficult for us to imagine how restricted were the geographic limits of a man living in St. Erth or on a farm near Trewinnard, and how much this would change with the arrival of the train.

Travels around Cornwall in 1698.

Celia Fiennes (1662-1741) was an enthusiastic and unusual woman who journeyed round England between 1684 and 1703. In 1698, when about 36, she visited Cornwall, travelling with only a couple of servants as company, although she was able to rely on a network of gentry relatives and connections for stopping places.

She kept a diary of her travels, and the following extracts give some idea of the difficulty of travel at that time.

'From Plymouth I went 1 mile to Cribly Ferry wch is a very hazardous passage by reason of 3 tydes meeting. Had I known ye Danger before, I should not have been very willing to have gone it, not but this is ye Constant way all people goe, and saved severall miles rideings, I was at Least an hour going over, it was about a mile but Indeed in some places notwithstanding there was 5 men Row'd and I sett my own men to Row alsoe I do believe we made not a step of way for almost a quarter of an hour, but blessed be God I Came safely over; but those fferry boates are soe wet and then the sea and wind is allwayes Cold to be upon, that I never faile to Catch Cold in a fferry boate as I did this day haveing 2 more fferrys to Cross tho' none soe bad or halfe soe Long as this. ......

Here I entred into Cornwall and soe passed over many very steep stony hills, tho' here I had some 2 or 3 miles of Exceeding good way on the downs, and then I Came to ye steep precipices-Great Rocky hills -ever and anon I Came down to the sea and Rode by its side on the sand, then mounted up againe on ye hills wch Carried me along Mostly in sight of ye Southsea. ....and soe had more Lanes and a Deeper Clay Road wch by the raine ye night before had made it very Dirty and full of water in many places, in the Road there are many holes and sloughs where Ever there is Clay Ground, and when by raines they are filled with water its difficult to shun Danger; here my horse was quite down in one of these holes full of water but by ye good hand of God's providence wch has allwayes been wth me Even a present help in tyme of need, for giving him a good strap he fflounc'd up againe tho' he had gotten quite down his head and all, yet did retrieve his ffeete and gott Cleer off ye place wth me on his Back. ..... I fferryed over againe Cross an arme of ye sea, here it was not broad but Exceeding deep....

This Hoile is a narrow stony town, ye streetes very Close, and as I descended a Great steep into ye town, soe I ascended one up a stony Long hill farre worse and full of shelves and Rocks .... Well, to pass on, I went over some Little heath Ground but mostly Lanes, and those stony and Dirty, 3 mile and halfe to Parr; here I fferry'd over againe, not but when the tyde is out you may ford it.

I crossed ye water on a Long stone bridge and so through dirty stony Lanes 3 mile and then I Came into a broad Coach Rode which I have not seen since I Left Exeter, so I went 3 mile more to Mr Boscawens-Trygothy-a Relation of mine.

...... and soe went for ye Lands End by Redruth 18 miles, mostly over heath and Downs wch ....because since ye warre they Could not Double ye poynt at ye Lands End, being so neer Ffrance ye pirats or Privateers met them. Indeed at St Ives ...... they Carry all their things on horses backs soe that of a market day wch was Fryday you see a great number of horses Little of size wch they Call Cornish Canelys. They are well made and strong and will trip along as Light on the stony road without injury to themselves, where as my horses went so heavy that they wore their shoes immediately thinn and off, but here I met with a very good smith that shooed ye horses as well as they do in London, and that is not Common in the Country, but here I found it soe, and at a place in Westmoreland by ye ffells a smith made good shoes and set them on very well. ....

So I went up pretty high hills and over some heath or Common, on wch a Great storme of haile and raine met me and drove fiercely on me but ye wind soone dry'd my Dust Coate. ...

The people here are very ill Guides and know but Little from home, only to some market town they frequent, but will be very solicitous to know where you goe and how farre and from whence you Came and where is ye abode.... Could not roast me anything, but they have a Little wood for such occasions but its scarce and dear wch is a strange thing yt ye shipps should not supply them. They told me it must all be brought round the Lands End and since ye warre they Could not have it. ......

Ye Lands End is 10 mile ffarther, pretty steep and narrow Lanes, but its not shelter'd wth trees or hedg Rows this .... The houses are but poor Cottages Like Barns to Look on, much Like those in Scotland, but to doe my own Country its right ye Inside of their Little Cottages are Clean and plaister'd and such as you might Comfortably Eate and drink in,

and for Curiosity sake I dranck there and met wth very good bottled ale. .... Then I continued my returne from Pensands to Hailing and now ye tyde was down and so much Land appeared wch lay under water before, and I might have forded quite a crosse, many yt know ye country do, but I tooke ye safer way round by ye bridge. ...... to Redruth.

These places as in some other parts, indeed all over Cornwall and Devonshire, they have their carryages on horses backes, this being ye time of harvest, tho' later in ye yeare than usuall being ye middle of september, but I had ye advantage of seeing their harvest bringing in, wch is on a horse's backe wth sort of crookes of wood like yokes on either side-two or three on a side stands up in wch they stow ye corne and so tie it wth cords, but they cannot so equally poise it but ye going of ye horse is like to cast it down sometimes on ye one side and sometimes on ye other, for they load them from ye neck to ye taile and pretty high and are forced to support it wth their hands, so to a horse they have two people, and the women leads and supports them as well as ye men and goe through thick and thinnsometymes I have met with half a score horses thus Loaded-they are Indeed but Little horses their Canelles as they Call them, and soe may not be able to draw a Cart, otherwise I am sure 3 or 4 horses might draw 3 tymes as much as 4 horses does Carry and where it is open Ground and roads broad, wch in some places here it was, I wondred at their Labour in this kind, for the men and the women themselves toiled Like their horses, but the Common observation of Custom being as a second nature people are very hardly Convinc'd or brought off from, tho' never soe inconvenient.

..... and so was forced to stay where I Could hear but one Sermon at ye Church, but by it saw ye fashion of ye Country being obliged to go a mile to ye parish Church over some Grounds wch are divided by such stiles and bridges uncommon, and I never saw any such before; they are severall stones fixed aCross and so are Like a Grate or Large Steps over a Ditch that is full of mudd or water, and over this just in the middle is a Great stone fixed side wayes wch is the style to be Clambered over. These I find are the ffences and Guards of their Grounds one from another, and Indeed they are very troublesome and dangerous for strangers and Children.....

...these parts not abounding wth much accomodation for horses, theirs being a hard sort of Cattle and Live much on Grass or ffurses of wch they have ye most, and it will make them very ffatt being Little hardy horses, and as they jest on themselves do not Love the taste of oates and hay, because they never permit them to know the taste of it. But my horses Could not Live so, Especially on journeys, of wch I had given them a pretty exercise, and their new oates and hay suited not their stomach. I Could get noe Beanes for them till I Came back to St Columbe againe ...., these 12 mile from Cambleford was not Little ones and what with the wet and Dirty Lanes in many places I made it a tedious journey. .....'

Celia Fiennes,
Through England on a Side Saddle
in the Time of William and Mary.
London: Field and Tuer, The Leadenhall Press, 1888

A Visit to Mr Nott's Coaching Inn in Wales, 1801

A century after the journeys of Celia Fiennes, Charles Nott, an ancestor of Sir John Nott was visited at his coaching inn in Wales by a traveller, 'Mr M', who recorded his visit to Carmarthen with his wife and son at the time of the Napoleonic Wars.

"Monday 7 September 1801

We drove to the Ivy-bush Inn, a very ancient built house, with oak stairs and floors to the rooms rubbed brown, but good accommodation and civil people; indeed Mr Nott, the master, appears to be far above the common rank of Inn-holders in Wales. He possesses a very large farm about a mile from the town, and undoubtedly has the best Chaises and Horses in the country.

While dinner was preparing we surveyed the town, which is considered as the principal one of South Wales. It is well supplied with everything, the shops are good and well furnished, and plenty seems to abound. The streets were full of soldiers, the Cardigan Militia were quartered here and the Carmarthen Fencibles. The 'Bush' alone had 35 privates and 5 Officers quartered there.

After agreeing with Mr Nott for a chaise for a few days to be ready in the morning, we retired to rest. Our berths were not first-rate, but we slept well, having long since got the better of being over nice...

Monday 14 September 1801

A fine grey morning, we were ready to set off at 7 o'clock. Mr Nott was already risen, and had prepared tea with us, which he refused to charge for, indeed the attention and polite behaviour of this gentleman and his family, the superiority of his horses and carriages, the skilfulness and civility of his drivers entitle him to that preference which he so eminently receives.

In a stout, well-built chaise, and four fine horses, we set off for Aberystwyth, a journey of 50 miles, to be performed in one day, and with the same poor animals – we dreaded the very idea, but Mr Nott assured us the horses would go through it with ease......"

Private collection

Chapter 15
Railways and Aeroplanes

The Coming of the Railway

Railway speculation and railway mania had affected much of the country during the mid-19thC. Mineral tramways transported mining products, and there were a number of such lines serving the mineral mines of Cornwall. However, Cornwall was rather behind in providing passenger services. It was not until May 1859 that Prince Albert opened the viaduct which carried the Cornish Railway across the Tamar from Devon to Cornwall. Visitors could then come to Cornwall by rail.

In 1837, an early railway opened in west Cornwall to serve the Hayle foundry and the Redruth copper mines. In 1843 they added a very limited passenger service and in 1852 the line was extended with a station to serve St Ives, at St Erth.

Many proposals were made for financing new lines, although some of these proposals seemed harebrained. In 1877 the Mayor of St Ives, Thomas Cogar, wrote that 'during the last forty years and upwards, numerous railway schemes for connecting St Ives with other parts of the county and with the Metropolis have been promulgated,... some of which have been altogether abortive [or] never exercised with effect'.

Changes in ownership, gauge and route, meant that replacing the Truro to Penzance line was delayed until 1877, the Act of Parliament for the line from St Erth to St Ives not being passed until 1873. By this time both mines and fisheries were in decline and it was apparently only the possibility of holiday resort visitors that persuaded the investors to go ahead. The St Ives line was the last built to Brunel's broad gauge, and was converted to the narrower gauge used through the rest of the country in 1892.

West Cornwall looked forward to the arrival of railways with great excitement. We may now find such excitement difficult to understand, but the railway was seen as a panacea for trade, for allowing greater movement and astonishingly swift travel, a life and society change which would improve the world. The railway not only brought immediate wealth to landowners, but suggested opportunities for making wealth, for moving, for trade and, of course, made a dramatic change to the outlook and activities possible for the population.

This photograph shows one of the Duke class of engines designed to serve the hilly routes of Devon and Cornwall. Each engine was given a local name. St Erth, a Duke class engine, was built in 1897 and worked for 40 years before being withdrawn in 1936.

We are accustomed not only to railways and to the much stranger idea of airplane travel, but complain about noise, pollution and inconvenience rather than being excited by what they offer us. It may therefore be difficult to imagine the enthusiasm with which the first noisy, smoky, dirty and often uncomfortable carriages were greeted. The excitement in the new line that ran past St Erth station, rebuilt in granite in 1877, is apparent in newspaper articles of the time. One such report runs to about 10,000 words of 'purple prose' in describing the new line that ran from Redruth past St Erth, and Lelant to St Ives and then on to Penzance.

After a description of the countryside and delightful seascape, the route of the railway, the method of work and continuing work was described in detail, together with apologies where it was felt the scenery did not live up to the wonder of the railway line itself. Each feature along the route was noted, including the station master's house and the waiting rooms. These were thought to be inadequate for the number of passengers likely, although it was reported with approval that 'as in all the stations, it is pleasant to note that females, whether the bearers of 1st or 3rd class tickets, are cared for by separate accommodation'.

The journalist even included favourable comment on the contrast between the 'luxurious carriage which has brought us from Penzance at the rate of 30 miles an hour' and the 'old coach at Trewinnard .....with its lumbering wheels and its roomy body suspended by large leather bands'. This long report demonstrates the enthusiasm and admiration for the arrival of the new method of travel and the changes in travel conditions, frequency and trade that then became possible.

The railways allowed the development of a new tourism business for Cornwall and also transported the flowers, bulbs and vegetables which grew in and benefited from the early spring of Cornwall. Miloska Nott used to deliver her boxes of Trewinnard daffodils to St Erth Station each day, for delivery all over the country. The Cornish trade in early varieties continues today.

Air Travel around St Erth

It was also hoped that air transport would develop in Cornwall and that, like the coming of the railways, the airplane would bring new life to the far west. There was particular excitement about the possibility of air flights during the 1920s and 1930s and a number of airfields were proposed around Cornwall. Planes could land on long grass strips, which meant that a number of landing 'fields' were possible. Such fields carried their own penalties, such as the field near Constantine Bay which advertised to pilots a warning that the ground was marred by rabbit holes.

A landing field at Trewinnard was considered as an airport which would be near Penzance. The site, known as Rosevidney, was on high ground at the end of a ridgeway, on the site of the Iron Age fort immediately outside the present entrance to Trewinnard on what is now Trewinnard farmland.

Flying was promoted by Sir Alan Cobham's circus, officially called *National Aviation Day Displays*, which visited Cornwall several times to publicise aeroplanes. He visited seven different fields with a dozen aircraft. His visits included the fields at Rosevidney (Trewinnard) and the one at Hayle. In December 1932, sporadic hopes for flying in the area included unsuccessful plans to site a flying club and school at Trewinnard as part of a glamorous country club which would provide shooting, tennis and other activities as well as flying.

In February 1934 Trewinnard was bought by A. E. Ellis, a councillor of Penzance Town. Mr Ellis then offered part of Trewinnard to the council as an airport, without profit to himself. A newspaper reported: *Airport for Penzance: We understand that Trewinnard Manor has been purchased by a Penzance resident. ...Some time ago there was an attempt to form a flying club in the district and Trewinnard Manor House to be the club house...it is hoped that this beautiful old building will not be demolished to provide foundations for a roadway...*

An early attempt to encourage passenger flight started in October 1933 under the name Provincial Airways Limited. It seems to have had occasional flights into Hayle and Newquay and on 1 March 1935 the service was extended to Penzance, where they are thought to have landed on the Rosevidney/Trewinnard field. The service didn't last long because the company went bankrupt towards the end of 1935.

The first flight from Penzance to London was detailed by the Cornishman and the Cornish Telegraph with great excitement. A minute by minute account of the flight fills two complete columns, describes the flight procedures and what could be seen and includes subti-

A De Havilland DH.84 Dragon, which entered commercial service in 1933 and is known to have been used in SW Cornwall. It could carry six passengers each with 45lbs of luggage. *Photo by Ruthas.*
Licensed under Creative Commons Attrib.3.0

tles such as 'Flying In The Rain', 'The Engine's Lullaby', 'Advantages Of Air Travel' and so on.

Between 1932 and 1936 the field at Rosevidney/ Trewinnard appears to have been used fairly often as a landing field but all such displays ended with the Second World War.

Reading the literature of flights and flight arrangements for the 1920s and 1930s reminds us how different flying was then. For instance, a book called *The AA Register of Landing Grounds* provided a short guide and map. The entry for Hayle recorded a small landing field, the owner's name, the landing fee of one shilling per seat, local hotels, fuel and local transport. It also warned of the state of the field.

'*Warning. Half the ground slopes down to the south east corner. There are two mounds and some small depressions to be avoided. These are marked on the plan. Cattle or sheep may be pastured.*' This suggests that air travel of the time was not only different but to the modern experience, almost casual.

During the second World War, the landing field at Trewinnard seems to have had some work, remembered by Hamilton Hawkins in 2011 as diggers extending and re-levelling the field so that larger planes could land. However, the Rosevidney/Trewinnard field seems only to have been listed as an emergency landing strip for disabled aircraft and does not appear to have been used during the Second World War. The only record of flying activity over Trewinnard seems to have been the accident when two spitfires collided over Tregethas Farm, St. Erth, in March 1942.

The rumours of the use of a landing field persisted. Late in the 20thC, Sir John Nott considered reopening the field to private flying, since there was sufficient length of runway and wind for a small plane. Nothing came of this; the field continues in agricultural use and as the site of what may have been one of the more important Iron Age centres in the area.

After eighty years of discussion, air travel still seems barely viable in Cornwall, particularly as Ministry of Defence fields fall out of use. Plymouth airport has closed and the future of Newquay airport seems uncertain. There is continuing debate about the viability of the helicopter and fixed wing flights which provide so important a connection for the Isles of Scilly.

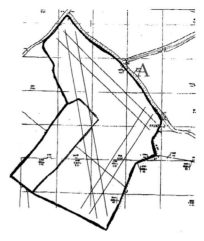

A map of the Rosevidney fields, now part of Trewinnard, as proposed for a diversion airfield during the second world war. Three landing strips for different wind directions are shown. Since one runway encroaches on a field boundary still in position, it seems that not all this work was carried out. An Iron Age encampment is thought to have been sited in the centre of this plan.
A marks the entrance to the drive to Trewinnard.

Chapter 15
Mills, Mines and Cellars

The defining feature of the landscape around Trewinnard is, of course, the Hayle estuary which has changed much over the last seven hundred years. The river became clogged when around 1340 the bridge and a long causeway was built. The estuary was further filled with sediment and waste from the mines along its banks and from that most important of early mining areas, Godolphin Hill.

The sediment from tin streaming and mining was so great a problem that a 1531 Havens and Ports Act for Cornwall and Devon was enacted to control the silting of ports, harbours and mills. Maintenance had long been a financial drain on the funds of waterside landowners.

Two pictures of the streams of the Hayle river.

The accounts of Christopher Hawkins show considerable sums spent in regulating the leats, streams and flows of the estuary. His costs record a new bridge and causeway below Trewinnard leading to a new road on the east side. A selection from his account books gives some idea of the regular expenditure.

1750   Payment on ye river [presumably on banking and leats]
1752   Payment of Copper dues, Tin dues, and Tin streaming dues (that is in the river).
1755   Charges for making a bridge across the river by the mill and making the new road between Tremelling stamps and St Erth Churchtown [on the other side of the river].
        Payments were also made for 'turning the river'.
1755   Quarry work
1756   Many payments for the 'long bridge' and the new road
1756   Payments for men and tools at the quarry
1756   Payments to Bethuel Bastard for repairs to the Parish roads.
1757   A payment for 'stopping in the river'.
1760 - 1763   Payments on the roads to the parish in every year
1764   Payments for 'making a new cut in great river'.
1764   Payment for the 'liberty of a road over Tredrea moor'.

Flooding was a problem not only for the estuary but into St. Erth itself whose parish council appeared constantly concerned with flooding. Reduction in the flood plain continued with the reclaiming of land at Tremelling moors, just north of Trewinnard, for a Council refuse dump. It was then covered with power station ash and has only recently returned to farm use.

It was not until the National Rivers Authority acquired such overall control that the problems of dealing with many landowners, each responsible for their own length of bank, meant that better control of the water flow and defence against flooding could take place.

In the 1950s alterations were made to canalise the river. Whilst John Nott was MP for St Ives, there were endless requests for his help in seeking to control the flooding of land and homes along the upper reaches of the Hayle. This flooding has now been reduced by the flood barrier built to control the tidewater at the mouth of the river. Canalisation, pump stations and embankments have changed the appearance of the estuary and reduced the risk of flooding. The road to the water at Porthcullum now ends at an embanked canal rather than running down to a deep pool surrounded by a wide estuary of streams and reed.

Water Mills: an introduction

Milling was necessary to change grain to a consumable food. Early grinding was done by rolling grain back and forth on a hollowed stone called a *saddlestone*. This was in time replaced by a quern where grinding was done round and round. Polished hollowed corn grinding stones from the late stone age were found in 1867 at Mounts Bay and an example of the later saddle

Below and left: St Erth Bridge.

stone can be seen at the Wayside Museum, Zennor.

The tedious business of grinding was transformed when sufficient power could be found to grind
corn between two horizontal grinding stones. Although
animals were used to turn the stones, water or wind was
a 'free' power which eased and speeded the process.

Cornwall is unusual in having no known examples of windmills, and the Domesday book for Cornwall
lists only six watermills which, even if understated, is
accepted as an indication that they were few in number.
The water provided the motive power to grind corn so
that it could be used as a food. In practice this meant
oats, or more usually barley, known as *grist*. The most
common mill was a grist mill. The mill machinery and
miller's skill could do far better than a householder
working a small stone for the couple of hours needed to
provide enough for the day.

As water mills spread after the 12thC and, because they were financed by the manors, use of the mill
required a charge taken of anyone's grain. The manor
either rented out the rights or employed a miller who
took a cut, not only for his own fees but also for the man-
or. By the 16thC, Cornwall had been subdivided into
smaller manorial districts, each of which had a mill, so
that a typical parish had several different mills. Milling
was controlled by *Soke Law* and under accepted custom
a tenant was obliged to grind his grain at the manorial mill, the manor court enforcing fines for those who
disobeyed. To ensure all grain went to a mill, there were
times when domestic grinding stones were smashed if
found.

A mill was central to the economy of the middle
ages. Important to both landlord and neighbourhood,
they were valued investments in the medieval era. Mills
often headed the list of a manor's or family's assets and
a mill rent could be similar to that of a good-sized farm.

The different ways to power the wheel with water reflected an improving technology. The earliest mills
used a horizontal paddle in a stream, which was inef-
ficient and reliant on an uncertain water flow, particularly in summer. Water power was then improved by using a vertical undershot wheel turned by water running
beneath it. Embanked leats, (canals), races and mill-
ponds gave better control and supply as did improvements in the cogs and transmission of the water effort.
These earthworks and embankments allowed the use of
the breastshot wheel, where water hit the wheel at mid-
height. Finally the more efficient overshot or pitchback
wheel, popularised in John Smeaton's book of 1752-3,
supplied water right to the top of the wheel.

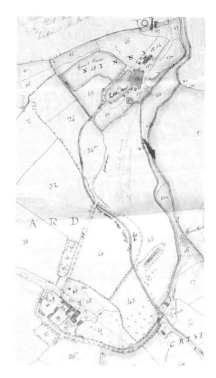

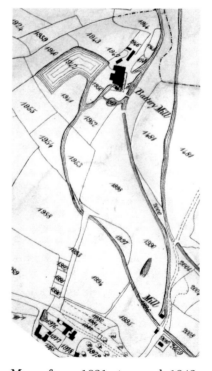

Maps from 1821, top and 1842,
below, give some ideas of the engi-
neering and landscaping required
for water courses, leats and water
management at Trewinnard.

In many cornish valleys, the changing technology can be tracked as mills moved down stream to improve the water flow to the wheel. The effort and labour in making the leats, ponds and canals of a mill system must have been considerable. Valleys as short as that at Penberth, near Land's End, had several mills competing for water. There, Boscean, the mill nearest the sea, received water not from the stream but from the hill behind. A leat turned a small undershot wheel, later converted by embanked leats to take a breast shot wheel.

In Cornwall, mills were used not only to grind corn but, from the 15thC, to prepare cloth in fulling mills (locally known as 'tucking' mills), and to operate 'stamps' where vertical wooden beams shod with iron fell to crush the ore below. Mills were used for papermaking (Penryn and Constantine), bone crushing (Penryn), gunpowder, (Trago Mills, Liskeard) and even for snuff. Elsewhere, mills became the powerhouse of the Industrial Revolution, operating a variety of machinery, whose buildings, whatever their use or purpose, became known through their use of water power as *mills*.

Millers were notoriously dishonest. Not only did they take advantage of their customers' inability to read and write, but they also used false weight, that is weights either made heavier so that it appeared the miller was giving good measure, or lighter by holes scraped in weights and then disguised. Millers also issued their own tokens as a form of coinage, another source of contention.

The miller was therefore likely to spend much time in argument and legal wrangle. Disputes arose not only about measure, but also about the rights of mills, the right to use or avoid a mill, about rates, about use of water, the building of weirs, competition for water with miners and about rights to water or the taking of water from further upstream. For centuries the courts were full of disputes.

Water mills continued to operate in the 19thC, but they had been in decline since the decline of Soke law practice, which caused much dispute until the 1769 Mills Act attempted to provide some order and control of unscrupulous millers. A greater change was achieved by use of more detailed leases, charges, and legal agreements. Decline was accentuated by the availability of water turbines from the 1820s and by the repeal of the Corn Laws in 1846, which allowed the import of milled grain. Some mills continued to operate into the 20thC, but most traditional mills had gone by the end of the 19thC.

Trewinnard Grist Mill

The ground levels suggest the wheel was on the up-hill side, fed by a leat. An inscribed stone appeared to read *'Petters 1824',* possibly the date of a renovation. This building was demolished in the 1980s to make way for a horse exercising area.

Trewinnard Mill, the Grist Mill

This mill is mentioned in 16thC documents and was always noted as a separate tenancy in the documents of Trewinnard Manor. Like most mills, the miller had a farmhouse, the mill, and a small holding, which, as elsewhere in Cornwall, was about 15 acres. Situated north of the pool at Trewinnard, it was served by leats.

Documents referring to the mill are few, save one or two records of repair. In 1759 James Wearne was paid for work on the Mill which included the *'healing'* or slating of a new roof. By 1782, the mill was in poor shape and referred to as that *'toft or pair of old walls formerly a grist mill, but now in ruins, called Trewinnard mill, [premises being late in occ. of Michael Williams of Gwennap, decd.] with premises belonging, being three small dwelling-houses, orchard, garden and three small meadows'.* The lease of the mill was parcelled with that of neighboring Battery Mill in 1782. A dated stone on the mill suggests another renovation was carried out in 1824 for a Mr Petter. By the 1851 census, it seems that the occupation of the head of the household was no longer that of miller so the mill may have ceased to operate. At the end of the 19thC, a farm labourer was employed at Trewinnard Mill, presumably on the small holding. By the start of the 20thC, the mill was known as 'Vincent's Tenement', and in 1930 it was noted that the tenants were the 'Misses Vincent'. Although the last mill building was demolished in the 1980s, the miller's own farmhouse still stands on a rise, south of the track up to Trewinnard, and by the site of Trewinnard Pool.

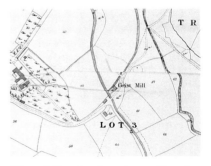

The 1863 sale plan shows Trewinnard mill, its leats and races, clearly marked as a grist mill.

The Battery Mills

In 1782 a 99 year lease was signed to allow John Williams to build a dwelling-house and stamping mill [for tin from Tolgullow]. The lease included an empty cottage and the mill at Trewinnard and a *small piece of Mungumpus downs… to make stamping floors, and for building or burning house*. Another agreement of 1782, given by Christopher Hawkins allowed the leasee to *erect a mill or mill head, ponds, houses and other erections and [from] Trewinnard grist mills, with liberty to convey water thence to new mills and so to the river flowing under St. Erth bridge*

The Battery Mills had been set up in 1781 by the Cornish Copper Company of Hayle to smelt and roll copper. They required two long leats to bring water to the mill, where were also excavated large holding ponds. Water power was used to operate the hammers and blow the fire hearths. Examples of surviving hammer mills are said to be rare in Britain.

By 1806, the mill needed further water management and the company sought to improve the outflow of water by adding another arch to the *west end of St. Erth bridge, being a public county bridge, hitherto repaired at charge of county and to maintain arch in good repair and scour levels of river.*

However, since it was said that each ton of ore required three tons of coal to work it, Cornwall could not compete with the smelting works of Wales, where coal was cheap and plentiful, so the mill closed in 1821 and appears to have become an 'iron manufacturary', before reopening in 1856 as a shovel and tool manufacturer.

In 1839, when the tithe apportionment was prepared, James Gilbert paid rent for both Battery and Trewinnard mills, the first having some 25 acres and the second just over 12 acres.

By 1851, when the census return was prepared for the mills, the residents seem to have been divided into two groups. William Gilbert, an 'iron manufacturer' was the head of the household and lived with his brother of 51, a male servant of 20 and a girl servant of 16. James Gilbert was the head of the other dwelling and employed 35 persons in iron manufacturing and 2 labourers for the Mill farm. He lived with his wife, a son of 25, two unmarried daughters of 24 and 20 and a female servant.

Today, there are few signs of the old buildings, which were demolished during the 20thC. The site now some dwellings, small businesses and a dog hydrotherapy centre.

	TREWINNARD.			
1940	The Slip,	1	0	14
1941	The Island,	1	0	38
1942	Great Pond,	2	0	30
1943	Garden Field,	2	0	3
1944	Miners Hole,		3	11
1945	Meadow,		1	26
1946	Garden,		1	12
1947	Two Dwelling Houses, Out-houses, and Mowhay,			34
1948	Waste,	1	1	28
1949	Batter and Rolling Mills,		1	20
1950	Little Pond and Part of River,		3	31
1951	Banks and Pool,			37
1952	Garden,		2	37
1953	The Grove,	1	2	16
1954	Part of do.	1	2	0
1955	Do.	1	3	38
1956	Garden,			27
1957	Chipmans Moor,	1	3	28
1958	Do.	1	1	9
1959	Lower Century,	2	2	26
1960	Higher do.	2	1	9
		25	1	34

	TREWINNARD GRIST MILL.			
2001	Grist Mill and Common,	1	1	17
2003	Waste adjoining River,			30
2004	Mill Moor,	1	1	21
	Waste in do.			34
2005	Mill Moor,	1	1	22
2006	Waste adjoining River,			25
2007	Mill Moor,	1	3	29
2008	Do.	1	1	31
2009	Stable, Lane, &c.			35
2010	House and Garden,			27
2011	Park Foge,	2	2	20
2012	Waste,			36
2013	Higher Park Foge,	3	0	5
		14	1	12

TREWINNARD.

The two separate mill sites at Trewinnard were in the hands of Gilbert Jones at the time of the 1839 Tithe apportionment.

Details of the two mills prepared for the auction of a freehold interest in 1863.

Copper House Mill

In the mid 18thC a tide mill was built at Copper-house, Hayle and used to grind meal for the horses that were used in the factories, local foundries and mining businesses. It had two undershot wheels, 20ft in diameter and 8ft wide.

Carbis Mill

Carbis Mill was upstream of Trewinnard, and was both an ancient mill grinding site and later provided stamps for the near by mines. It is said to have been one among several mills in the upper reaches of the Hayle river and continued in operation into the 20thC. The last miller was Richard Berryman's widow who continued grinding for seven years after his death in 1941.

The stamps at Carbis Mill had a separate water wheel. Stamps had iron bars which water power drove up and down to pound rock into a dust, so that any ore could then be extracted. They ran day and night and could be heard for miles.

Carbis Mill was upriver of Trewinnard Pool.
These two photographs show the leat supplying water to two independant broad overshot wheels which drove two pairs of stones and other machinery. The wheels can be seen at the gable end. The picture also gives an idea of the width of the river before it was canalised.

Water Supplies and Leats

Mills could not operate without water. A famous leat to Trewinnard brought water all the way from Balnoon on the side of Trencrom hill via an aqueduct along banked and trenched leats, with a branch to the former clay works by St Erth station, before heading to the pond at Trewinnard, from where there were supplies to the garden. Long thought of as built to supply sweet untainted water to Trewinnard Manor, it is possible that the leat was in fact much older and intended to improve the water to the mill. A deed of 1556 mentions that Martin Trewinnard had rights over a watercourse that travelled over a neighbour's land. An earlier 18thC deposition to Thomas Hawkins, (noted in the RIC Henderson papers) claimed that around 1612 *'Pashow Donne did take upon a rack rent the barton of Trewinnard from Sir Reynold Mohun'* and claimed rights over the water. The long leat was marked on plans of 1821 and 1839, and in the sale particular of 1863, but it is not certain when it fell out of use.

Water and Reed Beds

The estuary was long used to supply reeds for thatching of buildings, for withies, and for managed fish ponds. There was a square reed bed in the estuary above Carbis Bay, from which commercial harvesting took place, but few such waterside activities now survive, save for some fish ponds.

Mining

The earliest mining of the estuary was tin streaming. Trewinnard Manor itself is not marked by the remains of old mines and most of the working mines in the parish seem to have been east of the river, at Tremelling, owned by the Trewinnard family, or south and west of Trewinnard. There were attempts to establish mines around Trewinnard, but experimental diggings came to little. One field, no 1944 on the tithe map, is known as Miner's hole. Another small mine whose position is now lost was somewhere on the north east of Trewinnard land. Wheal Elizabeth, known charmingly as *Wheal Skull*, was probably a 17thC mine in the low lying ground between Trewinnard and Trewinnard Bal. Any work ceased there in 1838.

The Trewinnard family owned one of the richest mine groups of 16thC Cornwall, at Tolgullow, now better known as St. Day, which remained at the heart of the early 19thC mining boom. The Hawkins family, and particularly Sir Christopher Hawkins, also invested in mines. Dealing in tin was an essential part of any business life. In 1767 James Heywood commented that *'the tin trade seems to be the principle scene of business, blocks of tin lying in great quantities about the streets [of Truro].*

During the 19thC, some 32 mines were listed as operating in the parish, and further mines were bunched around the river further south of Trewinnard.

Silt Dredging

Dredging of the mud and silt that had accumulated downstream of earlier mine workings, produced a profitable amount of tin and mineral. This dredging has itself changed the run of the river and pattern of the estuary, included the former great pool at Trewinnard, now filled and separated from the rest of the river.

View of the dredger which operated around the 'stamps'.
Photograph in Tredinnick's History of the Parish of St Erth, 1936

From c.1873 to 1913, Ralph Andrewartha was tin streaming at the bottom of Tremelling Moors by Wheal Squire, opposite Trewinnard. Drifting by dredgers for alluvial tin took place in the silt from Trewinnard, past Portcollum and Godolphin to Tregonning Hill. Around 1929, the River Tin Dredging Company started operations in front of Trewinnard Mill. During the Second World War, the Ministry of Supply took over the employment of men to mine or stream the St Erth valley for tin. The river was diverted away from Trewinnard in order to pump for tin and the river pool at Trewinnard dredged down. It is said that this pool, in which was found the boat mentioned in chapter 1, was very deep and that it was some 60 to 80 feet to the bedrock.

Cellars

The word *cellars* was used not to describe an underground store, but rather a warehouse, often close by a port. They were the big shops of the 18thC and a mix of trading depot, B&Q and Tesco and had a wide variety of goods. Both the Trewinnards and the Hawkins invested in trade and in particular in cellars. Christopher Hawkins was noted as a partner in a cellar in Gweek in 1760 and in the mid 18thC appears to have made a good profit from another cellar which he operated at St. Erth/Hayle.

Not only did he trade through the cellar, but

also used it for his own supplies, obtaining a variety of objects such as coals, iron nails, hellingstones (slates), lime, laths, British salt, window glass, glass bottles, gunpowder, candles, whetstones, brooms, box irons, turpentine, scythes and on one occasion, two cheeses.

Clay Pits and Quarrying

North east of the village, St. Erth had clay pits, which provided white clay to the foundries of Hayle.

At Trewinnard there were some 18thC quarry pits by the turning from the main road from St Erth to Rosevidney, and a field recorded in 1839 as Great Quarry Croft lay north of the section of drive nearest the road. No other quarries are known.

Stories and Legends

All interesting sites acquire the usual stories of underground tunnels from the manor, of mine shafts, smuggling trails and water drains. At Trewinnard, all can, I think, be discounted. No evidence of any has been found.

Today

The Hayle estuary has been described by conservation assessors as a steep sided valley in an area of historic landscape, adjacent to a nature conservation site. Long term planning suggests it should remain a "wetland" site. This should ensure that there will be little change in the splendour of its present landscape.

Chapter 17
Cooking and Recipes

Until the end of the 18thC, not many recipes were written down. Methods of cooking were held either to be obvious, or part of the 'secret' trade or skill of the cook and of no interest to the literate gentry; those who could read and write tended not to work in the trade of cook. Few records survive, therefore, for what was eaten in the ordinary, as opposed to grand, households.

Such recipes as we do have will either be those of magnificence, or those held as unusual. Sadly, no recipes seem to have survived from the days of the Trewinnard family, and there are no known housekeeper's notes from the early days of the Hawkins family.

It is probable that the Hawkins family may have used one of the early 'receipt' books. Such books included recipes not just for cooking, but also for household care, and for anything from medicines to furniture or household repairs. Even the word recipe was not originally restricted to food, but described a method of achieving some result.

The first so called cook books were therefore really manuals for a housekeeper, and it was in this tradition that Mrs Beeton published her book, a book allegedly lifted from earlier books on housewifery.

The Recipes of the 17thC Cook, John Nott

One of the earliest of these manuals was that written by a namesake of the Nott family of Trewinnard. John Nott, who, so far as is known, was no forebear or relation of the present family, collected his 'receipts' and those of other cooks and household advisors into an individual and original dictionary form, published in 1723.

John Nott, then in old age, claimed to have cooked for great noble families, for magnates and for other exalted types. His heyday was probably from 1650 to 1715, a period that included that period of social change which

The picture shows the sort of Restoration Banquet at which John Nott excelled. Painting by Filippo Zaniberti of a banquet for the Doge in Venice, c 1630

followed the Restoration. This was a period with complex multi-coursed dinners and banquets where showmanship was as important as the food. To have succeeded as the master chef, John Nott must have been not only a great cook but a competent organiser of the considerable staff needed to prepare, cook, decorate and serve.

John Nott's book is a fascinating record of the recipes for such long or complex meals and in particular for the numerous 'dessert' or sweet courses. His book shows how different were the resources of the Stuart table; fish was important, as were preserves and sweet dishes. Even this book, designed for the rich, reminds us how little of any animal or food went to waste, and how nearly anything could be made into an acceptable, though perhaps to us, somewhat unusual, food.

It is said that an early sausage recipe by John Nott can be tried in the restaurants of the Houses of Parliament. It seems appropriate, therefore, to include one of those 17thC recipes which are from the same date as the first new house at Trewinnard.

John Nott provides eight alternative recipes for sausage. The first of these combines boiled pork bones with salt, pepper, onion, shallots, minced meat, cloves and mace, sage and spinage (with the suggestion, if the sausages are for 'prompt' eating, that oysters could be added).

Other recipes use different ingredients, or different methods; several allow for a quantity of veal to be added. All appear to require you to *fill the guts with these ingredients, and prick them often to let out the wind and to make them fill better. When the sausages are filled, smooth them with your hand, tye them in lengths according to your mind and broil them on a gridiron over a slack fire. .'.*

These practical sausage recipes include *Oxford Skates* (a fairly spicy sausage with much egg,) another for a sausage including meat with no skin, for *Bolonia sausages*, or for *Royal Sausages*. These last were a particularly complex meal that included partridges, gammon bacon, veal and decorative beef steaks. They remain a reminder of how different preparation and cooking once were.

Once prepared, sausages would be *'hung up in the chimney to dry'* or were *'dried...in a tin stove over a fire made of sawdust for three or four days'*. Often, the length of time a cooked meal could be stored was stated, storage periods that are unlikely to be followed today.

Printed below is therefore a copy of one of John Nott's 17thC sausage recipes. For modern times, it seemed simpler to make up the mixture and then use a modern sausage machine to fill the skins. Once filled, the sausages were fried and served. However, unless you add some oil, they may not have had enough fat in the mixture to allow grilling. No oysters were added.

To Make Sausages.

Having provided sheeps guts that are well clean'd, take good pork, either leg or loin, break the bones small, boil them in just water enough to cover them;

let it be well scumm'd, and season the liquor with salt, pepper, whole mace, onion and shallot;

When they have boiled till all the goodness is out of them, strain the liquor, and set it by to cool;

then mince your meat very small, season it with salt, pepper, cloves and mace, all beaten;

shred a little spinage to make it look green, and a handful of sage and savoury;

add also the yolks of eggs, and make all the minced meat and herbs pretty moist with the liquor the bones were boiled in;

then roll up some of your minced meat in flour, and fry it, to try if it be season'd to your liking, and when it is so, fill your guts with the meat.

If they are for present spending, you may mince a few oysters with your meat.

Green John Nott sausages, ready to cook.

From the Cook to the Housewife

Early recipe books or household manuals were seen as '*necessary for mistresses of families, higher and lower women servants and confined to things useful, substantial and splendid and calculated for the preservation of health and upon the measures of frugality...*' Such books were commonplace among the gentry houses of the 18thC in Cornwall and are delightful, since they move from a recipe for soup, to a method of re-powdering a wig; from a linament to cures for those bitten by a mad dog; from methods of making scents to methods of curing ham.

These *receipts* introduce us to a world of forgotten food products, when foods and spices which we now recognise were only then becoming practical. Sadly, there are no records of meals at Trewinnard, or of late 18thC recipes used by a Hawkins cook.

In the next generation, Trewinnard would have been home to the typical farm cooking common to the 19thC and 20thC, which was centred on farm available ingredients, and a need for calories.

A *Cornish Farmers Diary* records milk, dairy products, oat and occasional barley flours and breads, a few vegetables such as potatoes, eggs, the occasional chicken, much offal and, of course, the products of the house pig, central to the economy of every farmhouse. Journals also record rabbits, fruits and produce from the small herb or fancy garden kept by the farmer's wife.

Throughout this time the 'gentry' were unlikely to cook for themselves, although the lady of the house might keep speciality recipes for guests or to record a family favourite. Since cooking was regarded as a specialist activity, it was the management of the cook that was seen as of importance. One has only to read the memoirs and records of the gentry to realise how much of a mystery the work of the kitchen remained until after the Second World War.

A Recipe from Modern Times

Lady Nott, whose early life was spent on a farm in Slovenia, has always cooked for her family. This recipe is one of their favourite standbys. She maintains that 'it doesn't amount to much'. Her family say they have to eat it all the time.

Game soup with a touch of egg is filling, easy and means that just one course will often satisfy the guest. It is original and tasty.

Miloska's Pheasant Soup
Serves 6-8

Ingredients

       Four or five good sized carrots, or in number as you may wish

       Three Leeks, or as you may wish

       Two good sized Onions chopped small

       One Pheasant plucked and drawn

            (Usually, the remains of 3 or 4 cooked pheasant are easier)

       Fresh Parsley

       Salt

       Whole Peppercorns

Method

- Chop carrots, leak and onions and place into a large saucepan.
- Add plenty of fresh parsley.
- Season with salt and whole pepper corns.
- Place either a whole raw pheasant on top of the vegetables, or,
  In the absence of a whole pheasant, substitute 3 or 4 pre-cooked pheasant remains
- Completely cover the pheasant with water.
- Simmer slowly for 2 hours with saucepan lid on.
- Remove pheasant and vegetables after 2 hours.
- Strain the combined liquid through sieve.
- Bring liquid to the boil.
- Then beat in one whole egg with a fork.
- Take off the heat as soon as egg has been added.
- Serve immediately.

Principal Sources, References & Further Reading

Adam, Canon JH   Medieval Chapels of Cornwall   RIC journal 1957

Appleby, Cedric   1. Christopher Hawkins and Trewinnard, 1750-1767   Dissertation edited for
     'Homes and Households in West Cornwall' 1550-1950 Penwith Local History Group 2010
     2. The Trewinnard Coach   Article written for Royal Institution of Cornwall. 2011
     3. Guide to Parish Church of St Erth

Benney, DE.   An Introduction to Cornish Watermills, Bradford Barton, Truro. 1972

S.Baring-Gould   Cornish Characters and Strange Events Two Volumes 1908
     Includes a chapter on Sir Christopher Hawkins

Blight J T   Ancient Crosses and Other Antiquities in the West of Cornwall. London Penzance 1856

Blight J T   Churches of West Cornwall Parker & Co 1885 Republished from Gentleman's Magazine 1862-64

Baskott, Michael   Roman Military Signalling between Forts in East Cornwall: March 2010

Richard Carew of Antonie, esq   The Survey of Cornwall 1602
     1. Edited by F E Halliday Augustus M Kelley New York 1969
     2. Edited Paul White Tamar Books 2000

Coulthard, H R   The Story of an Ancient Parish: Breage with Germoe   1913

Cornwall County Council, 1996. Cornwall Landscape Assessment 1994
     Countryside Commission and Cornwall County Council:

Dodds, Pamela   1. Thomas Edwards of Greenwich
     Country House Architect to the Gentry of Cornwall from 1736-1760; Dissertation 2000
     2. Building Country Houses on Cornish Estates   CHN Conference Paper 2002

Dunkin, Edwin Hanlow Wise   Monumental Brasses of Cornwall 1882 Brass of Elizabeth Trewinnard.

Fiennes, Celia   Through England on a Side Saddle in the Time of William and Mary Leadenhall Press 1888

Gilbert, C.S.   An Historical Survey of Cornwall, Ackerman, London. 2 vols. 1817 & 1820

Gilbert, D   The Parochial History of Cornwall (4 volumes) Nicholls, London.1838
     Includes historical notes by Hals and Tonkin

Green, Daniel   Research notes provided to Sir John Nott.

Hawkins, Hamilton   Recollections of Trewinnard house and Chapel in 1946 taken down in 2011

Hefford, Wendy   The Tapestries: Chapter 5 of National Trust book on Cotehele, 1991

Henderson, Charles 1. Royal Institution of Cornwall: Henderson Papers
     2. Cornish Church Guide   D Bradford BartonLtd Truro 1925 & 1965
     3. Essays in Cornish History, Clarendon, Oxford. 1935

4. The 109 Ancient Parishes of the Four Western Hundreds of Cornwall, 1955
JRIC, II.3, 1-104.   Medieval church and chapel material.

5. A report on the early history of the Trewinnard Family 1918
Described by Henderson as 'the first paid work he had ever undertaken'

6. 109 Parishes in Penwith, Kerrier, Powdar & Pydar
Compiled 1910-24 Written 1923-24 RIC journal 1955,56,58 & 60

Heywood, James   Diary of my Journey into the West of England. 1757.   Private Collection

Hitchins, F and Drew, S.   The History of Cornwall (2 volumes), Penaluna, Helston.1824

Hoskins, W G   The Making of the English Landscape   Hodder and Stoughton 1955

The History of Parliament: Vols 1509-1558, 1558-1603, 1604-1629 ed. various inc S.T. Bindoff, 1982

Irving, John H.B.   The Hawkins of Trewithen   (Trewithen Guide) Castle Cary Press, undated

Jaggard, Edwin   James Boswell's Journey through Cornwall, Aug-Sept 1792: RIC Journal 2004

Jago, Fred.WP   English-Cornish Dictionary London & Plymouth, 1887

Kowaleski, Maryanne   The Haveners' Accounts of the Earldom & Duchy of Cornwall 1287-1356

Lake's Parochial History of Cornwall by Joseph Polsue   4 Volumes c 1865-1872
This includes: William Hals (1655-1737) Parochial Histories unpublished 1737
Thomas Tonkin, (1680-1742) unpublished 1742

Langdon, Andrew   Stone Crosses in West Cornwall   Federation of Old Cornwall Societies 1999

D & S Lyson's   Parochial History Cornwall (Volume 111 for Cornwall)   1814

Maclean, Sir John, Parochial and Family History of the Deanery of Trigg Minor 1879 (British Library reprint)

Mattingly, Dr Joanna Cornwall and the Coast Mousehole and Newlyn Victoria County History Phillimore 2009

Maxwell, I.S.   The Domesday Settlements of Cornwall   1986

Moule, Thomas   The English Counties Delineated: or, A Topographical Description of England, 1838

Nicholson, Chris   The Trewinnard Coach, Article in Carriage Driving Magazine 1989

Nott, Sir John   1. Here Today, Gone Tomorrow   Autobiography Politico's Publishing 2002
2. Mr Wonderful Takes a Cruise   Ebury Press(Random House) 2004
3. Family and research papers;   correspondence

Nott, John (Fl 1700)   Cooks and Confectioners Dictionnary   1726
Introduction and Glossary by Elizabeth David   Reissued Lawrence Rivington 1980

Orme, Nicholas   Nicholas Roscarrock's Lives of the Saints: Cornwall and Devon
Devon & Cornwall Record Society 1992

Padel, O.J.   Cornish Place-Name Elements, English Place-Name Society, Vol 56/57, Nottingham 1985

Payton, Philip   Cornwall, A History   Cornwall Editions Ltd Fowey 2004

Penhallurick, R.   Tin in Antiquity, The Institute of Metals, London   1986

Penaluna, William   The Circle or Historical Survey of 60 Parishes and Towns in Cornwall   Helston 1819

Pett, Douglas Ellory   The Parks and Gardens of Cornwall, Alison Hodge, Penzance 1998

Price, William   Archaeologia Cornu-Britannica, or an essay to preserve the Ancient Cornish
Language,..with..grammar..and..vocabulary   Redruth 1790

Prideaux Edmund (1693-1745) Topographical Drawings: Reproduced by permission of Mr & Mrs P Prideaux-Brune

Pugsley, Steven   Landed Society & the Emergence of the Country House in Tudor & Stuart Devon,Exeter 1992.

Rowe, John   Changing Times and Fortunes A Cornish Farmers Life 1828-1904 Cornish Hillside Publications 1996

Rowse, A.L   Tudor Cornwall   Jonathan Cape 1941

Sothebys: Tapestry assessment: Private memorandum. June 5, 1996:

Stevens, James   Cornish Farmer's Diary   Edited & Published PAS Pool 1977

Stoate, TL,   1. Hearth Tax Returns for Cornwall
2. The Cornwall Military Survey 1522 with the Loan Books and a Tinners Muster Roll
c1535, Stoate, Bristol.1987

Syson, Leslie   The Watermills of Britain   David and Charles 1980

Tamarside Archaeology Geophysical survey: Les Dodd & Peter Nicholls: 2012
Taylor, Patrick   The Toll-houses of Cornwall Federation of Old Cornwall Societies 2001
Textile Conservation Centre, Hampton Court Palace: Report by Caroline Clark, Sandra Barnard and Karen Finch. 1983
Thorn, C & Thorn, F.   Domesday Book, Cornwall, (Translation Oliver Padel)   Phillimore, 1979
Tredinnick, H. Reginald   History of the Parish of St Erth. 1936 Typescript: Cornwall Studies Centre, Redruth
Trewithen Estate, Trustees   Permission for use of Hawkins family portrait reproductions.
Turner, Sam   Making a Christian Landscape
                         The Countryside in early medieval Cornwall, Devon and Wessex University of Exeter Press 2006
Victoria History of Cornwall
SCSTyrrell   Personal papers, records and photographs
                         Research and papers on Roman Cornwall

Books and studies of the domestic architecture of Cornwall are not included in the list above.

General:

The Cornwall and Scilly Historic Environment Record (HER, held and maintained by Cornwall Council) and Listed Building records (held by English Heritage) were consulted to obtain a baseline for archaeological remains. Further field work has been undertaken by Peter Herring and Stephen Tyrrell.

The Cornwall Record Office (Cornwall Council) and the Courtney Library of the Royal Institution of Cornwall (Truro) and other archives were visited to study historic maps and documents.

The recipes were used by Mrs Kate Tyrrell and the results eaten by family and volunteers.

Maps consulted include:

1. British Museum   Cotton Augustus I I, f 35,36,38,39   South Cornwall Defence map c 1539/40
2. Early county maps: Christopher Saxton (1579), John Norden (c1597), John Spede (c 1610), Joel Gascoyne (1699) (Reprinted by Devon and Cornwall Record Soc, 1991)
3. Thomas Martyn   *A New and Accurate Map of the County of Cornwall from an Actual Survey,* 1748 Copy at Royal Cornwall Museum, Truro.
4. Larger-scale 19thC and 20thC maps (Ordnance Survey 1813, 1876 and 1906)
5. A survey of Trewinnard manor carried out in 1821: Copy in Cornwall Record Office
6. The 1841 parish Tithe Apportionment Map (with schedules of land use, ownership, occupancy and value).
7. Maps and plans in Auction Particulars for Trewinnard and others. 1863. Cornwall Record Office.

Illustration credits:

We have tried to trace the origin and owners of all photographs used, crediting the owner where possible. Some pictures have been provided from sources said to be available for copyright free use. We apologise for omissions or inaccuracies. Where requested, the origin of a particular picture has been noted alongside the illustration.

Some illustrations made available by the Nott family are used with their permission.

Most photographs were taken and provided by S C S Tyrrell.